Letts study aids

Revise Biology

A complete revision course for O level and CSE

Julian Ford-Robertson   MA(Oxon)

Head of Biology Department, Haileybury College, Hertford

Charles Letts & Co Ltd.
London, Edinburgh & New York

First published 1979
by Charles Letts & Co Ltd
Diary House, Borough Road, London SE1 1DW

Revised 1981, 1983
Reprinted 1986

Design: Ben Sands
Illustrations: Stan Martin and Tek-Art

ISBN 0 85097 593 X

Printed and bound by
Charles Letts (Scotland) Ltd

Preface

The principal aim of this book, which first appeared in 1979, is to provide a concise body of biological facts and ideas in such a form that they can easily be revised. The information is carefully chosen to fit all the GCE 'O' level, SCE and CSE syllabuses in Biology. A unique feature of the book is a table of analysis of all these syllabuses, topic by topic, so that pupils may select for revision only those sections that are necessary for their own particular Examination Board.

The other aims of this book are both to help pupils understand *how to learn* effectively and *how to use their knowledge* effectively in the examination room. Lack of ability in either of these fields is a common cause of failure by otherwise able examination candidates. To help prevent such avoidable failure, there is advice on learning techniques and also on question analysis (using questions set by various Examination Boards).

To assist in the learning process each chapter has a test-yourself section by means of which the pupil can test his or her progress. Answers are provided and are keyed back into the relevant text sections.

While this book has been written principally for pupils to use on their own, its use does not end there. Teachers should find that the concise yet clear format and the large word-saving diagrams provide a sound framework upon which to base their teaching. The book has the advantage, as a text, of allowing teachers who favour an experimental course to spend less time on note-giving, and the questions provided can be used to monitor progress.

The 1981 edition of *Revise Biology* includes a number of important changes. The table of analysis has been brought up-to-date and expanded to take in the Scottish Certificate of Education syllabus. This has involved the inclusion of some new material. Elsewhere the text and diagrams have been improved and in some places more recent developments have been included such as those relating to mammalian digestion and osmoregulation.

A section on past examination questions (and how to tackle them) and a comprehensive index have also been added.

I have been greatly encouraged by the way both pupils and teachers have received the first edition of *Revise Biology*. It has not been regarded as a mere 'crammer' and I hope that this new edition will continue to serve, as intended, as an effective basis for learning and revision both in the classroom and at home. Finally, whether the existing GCE, SCE and CSE examination system is replaced by a single nation-wide 16+ examination or not, this book will provide adequate coverage of Biology at this level for many years to come.

In the preparation of this book I have been greatly assisted by helpful criticism and advice from C G Gayford, BSc, MEd (Science Education), PhD, Postgrad. Cert. Ed., Lecturer in Education at the University of Reading; K R C Neal, MA (Cantab), FIBiol, Head of Biology at Manchester Grammar School and my colleague at Haileybury, P A Chamberlain, BSc and from pupils. Without the artistic expertise of Stan Martin and the patience and understanding of the staff at Charles Letts & Co Limited this examination aid would have had limited value. I am also most grateful to Mr B Arnold of the Scottish Education Department for his advice on SCE material and all the Examination Boards who have given permission to reproduce their questions.

To my wife Anne, and to Ian, Justin and Angus I owe a special debt for their patience, assistance and encouragement.

The 1983 Revision takes account of a number of amalgamations of examination Boards and of changes in syllabus content. The table of Analysis also now includes the Northern Ireland GCE syllabus.

The text shows some improvements and additions to meet syllabus needs, e.g. the mosquito and malaria control, the structure of ommatidia and venereal diseases.

Julian Ford-Robertson 1983

Contents

17 A variety of life

Section I

Introduction and guide to using this book

Revise Biology is written especially for those who need help in preparing for their GCE 'O' level, SCE or CSE examinations. The book contains the following:

—advice on **what your syllabus requires:** a table of syllabus analysis (pages 2–7).
—advice on **how to learn:** learning made easier (pages 9–14).
—**what to learn** in readily revisable form: information, lavishly illustrated (pages 15–157).
—means of **assessing your progress:** short self-test questions with answers (pages 158–192).
—advice on how to **show the examiner** that you know what he is asking for: an outline of good examination technique, using past examination questions (pages 193–198).
—practice in answering examination questions (pages 199–218).

If you follow this sequence in the use of this book, you will have a good chance of success.

Section I: Using the table of analysis of GCE, SCE and CSE syllabuses (pages 2–7). First select from the top of the page your own Examination Board. The key to the initials for the Boards may be found on page 8. Below the name of the Board are details of:

(*a*) the number of theory papers and their length;
(*b*) whether there is a practical part to the examination or whether your teacher does this assessment:
(*c*) the percentage of marks allocated to compulsory and free-choice parts of the theory papers;
(*d*) the content of the course, topic by topic. This core material has been divided into numbered units, not all of which need be studied for your own syllabus.

Select carefully the units you require by referring to the symbols:
● unit required for a syllabus
(●) unit required, but with reservations. These reservations may include such things as 'less emphasis than that in the text' or 'this organism suffices for a part of the syllabus, but is not specifically named'.
o optional
Ⓑ option B
Blank: unit not required.

The table of analysis must be regarded only as a helpful guide. If you send for your Board's syllabus and for copies of past examination papers (use the addresses on page 8) you will be able to judge more easily what the special features of your syllabus are. Your teacher will also give you advice, particularly on units marked (●).

Before using the core material, first take care to understand *how* you should revise (pages 9–14). Do not exceed your 'concentration time' (page 12).

Section II: Using the core material. Work through each unit referring only to the parts you need. Use every memory aid you can, including your own pattern-diagrams.

Section III: Testing yourself: Once you have worked through a unit turn to the back of the book for the appropriate self-test unit. Enter the answers in the spaces provided. When you have completed this, turn to the answers (pages 187–192). Each answer is keyed back to units in Section II. If you have not answered most questions correctly, then turn back to Section II to revise more thoroughly the units that you have not mastered.

Section IV: Examination technique for biology examinations. The advice given ranges from tips on organising what to take into the examination room to how to use your time well.

Section V: Practice in answering questions. Build up your confidence by trying to answer these examination questions.

Table of analysis of examination syllabuses

		SEB	AEB	Cambridge	JMB	London	NIEC	Oxford	O and C	SUJB	WJEC	O and C 'Combined Science'	
	Level	O	O	O	O	O	O	O	O	O	O & CSE	⅔ O	
	Number of theory papers	2	2	2	1	2	2	2	2	1	2	2	
	Number of hours for each theory paper	1 / 1½	1½ / 2½	2 / ½	2½	1½ / 2	1½ / 2½	1 / 2	2 / 2	2½	1½ / 1½	⅔ / 1½	
	Practical – paper or assessment (Ass.) or optional (Opt.) (% of total marks)	No	Photo Qs	1 hr (27%)	Opt.	No	No	No	1 Q (10%)	No	No	No	
	Teacher assessment (Prac.=practical)	No	No	No	No	No	No	No	No	No	No	No	
	Theory – % mark, compulsory questions	75	38	72	50	40	45	44	40	40	36	33	
	Theory – % mark, free choice questions	25	62	28	50	60	55	56	60	60	64	67	
	Life												
2.1	Characteristics of organisms; cells	●	●	●	●	●	●		●	●	●	●	2.1
2.2	Organelles – detail		●	(●)	(●)	(●)	(●)	●	(●)	(●)	(●)	●	2.2
2.3	How the nucleus controls the cell		●					(●)				●	2.3
2.4	Enzymes	●	●	●	●	●	●	●	●	●	●	●	2.4
2.5	Units of life beyond the cell		●		●	●	●			●	●		2.5
	Classification												
3.1	Linnaeus & his classification system	●					●	●			●	●	3.1
3.2	Keys	●									●		3.2
3.3	Plant kingdom	●					(●)	(●)			●	●	3.3
3.4	Animal kingdom	●					(●)	(●)			●	●	3.4
	Foods & feeding												
4.1	Food	●	●	●	●	●	●	●	●	●	●	●	4.1
4.2	Holophytic, holozoic & saprophytic nutrition	●	●	●	●	●	●	●	●	●	●	●	4.2
4.3	Mineral salts for mammals & angiosperms	●	●	●	(●)	(●)	●	●	●	●	●	●	4.3
4.4	Carbohydrates, fats & proteins	●	●	●	●	●	●	●	●	●	●	●	4.4
4.5	Vitamins	●	●	●	●	●	●	●	●	●	●	●	4.5
4.6	Photosynthesis	●	●	●	●	●	●	●	●	●	●	●	4.6
4.7	Limiting factors	●	●		(●)	●	●					●	4.7
4.8	Leaf structure & photosynthesis	●	●	●	●	●	●	●	●		●	●	4.8
4.9	Amino acid synthesis		●	●	●	●	●	●	●	●	●	●	4.9
4.10	Mineral salt uptake by roots		●	●	●	●	(●)	●	●	●	●	●	4.10
4.11	Feeding methods of animals	●	●		●		(●)			(●)			4.11
4.12	Digestion & its consequences	●	●	●	●	●	●	●	●	●	●	●	4.12
4.13	Experiments with digestive enzymes	●	●	●	●	●	●	●	●	●	●	●	4.13
4.14	Mammal teeth & dental care	●	●	●	●	●	●	●	●	●	●	●	4.14
4.15	Mammal alimentary canal	●	●	●	●	●	●	●	●	●	●	●	4.15
4.16	Herbivores & carnivores – teeth & jaws	●	●		●		●		●	●	●		4.16
4.17	Herbivores & carnivores – gut	●	●		●		●		●				4.17
4.18	Absorption of food at villi	(●)	●	●	●	●	●	●	●	●	●	●	4.18
4.19	Storage of food	●	●	●	●	●	●	●	●	●	●	●	4.19
4.20	The liver	●		●			●	●	●	●	●	●	4.20
4.21	Diet	●		●		●			●	●		●	4.21
4.22	Saprophytes	●	●	●	●	●	●	●	●	●	●	●	4.22
	Water & transport systems												
5.1	Importance of water	●		●		●	●	●				●	5.1
5.2	Diffusion, active transport & osmosis	●	●	●	●	●	●	●	●	●	●	●	5.2
5.3	Water uptake & loss in angiosperms	●	●	●	●	●	●	●	●	●	●	●	5.3
5.4	Transpiration	●	●	●	●	●	●	●	●	●	●	●	5.4
5.5	Transport of organic food	(●)	●	●	●	●	●	●	●	●	●	●	5.5
5.6	Water uptake & loss in animals	●	●		●	●	(●)	●				●	5.6
5.7	Blood systems	●	●	●	●	●	●	●	●	●	●	●	5.7
5.8	Mammal blood & other body fluids	●	●	●	●	●	●	●	●	●	●	●	5.8
5.9	Heart, blood vessels & circulatory system	●	●	●	●	●	●	●	●	●	●	●	5.9
5.10	Changes in blood around the circulatory system	●	●	●	●	●	●	●	●	●	●	●	5.10
5.11	Lymphatic system	●	●		●	●	●	●	(●)	●	●	●	5.11
	Respiration												
6.1	Breathing, gaseous exchange & cellular respiration	●	●	●	●	●	●	(●)	●	●	●	●	6.1
6.2	Internal respiration (aerobic & anaerobic)	●	●	(●)	●	●	●	●	●	●	●	●	6.2
6.3	External respiration (gaseous exchange)		●	●	●	●	●	●	●	●	●	●	6.3
6.4	Organisms respiring in water & air	●	●	●	●	(●)	(●)	(●)	(●)	●	(●)	●	6.4
6.5	Bird respiration							(●)		●		●	6.5
6.6	Mammal respiration	●	●	●	●	●	●	●	●	●	●	●	6.6
6.7	Gaseous exchange in angiosperms	●	●	●	●	●	●	●	●	●	●	●	6.7
6.8	Uses for energy from respiration	●	●						●				6.8
6.9	ATP (Adenosine tri-phosphate)		●						●	●			6.9
	Excretion, temperature regulation & homeostasis												
7.1	Wastes & means of excretion	●	●	●	●	●	●	●	●	●	●	●	7.1
7.2	Mammal urinary system	●	●	●	●	●	●	●	●	●	●	●	7.2
7.3	Abnormal kidney function		●		(●)		●		●			●	7.3
7.4	Body temperature in organisms		●	●		●	●	●		●	●	●	7.4
7.5	Mammal temperature control		●	●	●	(●)	●	(●)	●	●	●	●	7.5

ALSEB	EAEB North	EAEB South	EMREB Syll. 1	EMREB Syll. 2	LREB Opt. A	LREB Opt. B	LREB Opt. C	NREB	NWREB	SEREB	SREB Syll. R.	SWEB	WMEB	YHREB Syll. A	YHREB Syll. B	ALSEB/JMB/ NWREB/ YHREB	EAEB/ UCLES	
CSE	CSE	CSE	CSE	CSE	CSE	CSE	CSE	CSE	CSE	CSE	CSE	CSE	CSE	CSE	CSE	16+	16+	
2	2	2	2	1	1	1	2	2	1	2	1	2	2	1	1	1	2	
1½	2	1½	1½	2	2	2	2	1	2	1	2	2	1½	2	2	2	1	
1½	2	¾	1		0	0	1½	2		1½		1½	2				1½	
Ass. (30%)	No	Opt. in Ass.	1½ hr Prac. OR 5 Practical Assignments (30%)	Ass. (OR 30%)	1½ hr Prac. Yes Ass.	0 Prac. Yes Ass.	0 Prac. No Ass. (35%)	Ass. 40%	Prac. (30%) OR Ass. (30%)	No 60%	No 20%	No No	No 20%	Ass. (25%) No	No Yes	Ass. on extra syll. 30%	1 hr OR Ass. 20%	
100	100	100	57	100	—	—	—	100	100	—	—	60	38	—	100	100	100	
0	0	0	43	0	—	—	—	0	0	—	—	40	62	—	0	0	0	
●	●	●	●		●	●	●	●	●	●	●	●	●	●	●	●	●	2.1
(●)		(●)			(●)						●	(●)				●	(●)	2.2
														●		(●)		2.3
●	●	●	●	●	●	●	●	(●)	●	●	●	●	●	(●)	●	●	●	2.4
●					●	●	●	●	●		●					●		2.5
	(●)	●			(●)	(●)	(●)	(●)		(●)	(●)						●	3.1
●	●	●			●	●	●			●	●	●	●		●	●	●	3.2
●	●	●			(●)	●	●			●	●	(●)	(●)		(●)	(●)	●	3.3
●	●	●			(●)	●	●			●	●	(●)	(●)		(●)	(●)	●	3.4
●	●	●	●		●	●	●		●	●	●	●	●	●	●	●	●	4.1
●	●	●			●				●	●					●	●	●	4.2
(●)	(●)	(●)	●	(●)	(●)	(●)	(●)	(●)	●	●		(●)	●	(●)	(●)	●	●	4.3
●	●	●	●	●	●	●	●	●	●	●	●	●	●	●	●	●	●	4.4
(●)	●	●	(●)	(●)	(●)	(●)	●	(●)	(●)	●	●	(●)	●	●	●	(●)	●	4.5
●	●	●	●	●	●	●	●	●	●	●	●	●	●	●	●	●	●	4.6
																●		4.7
●	●	●	●	●	●	●	●	●		●		●		(●)	●	●	●	4.8
●	●	●	●		●	●	●	●	(●)	●			●	●		●	●	4.9
●		(●)		(●)	(●)	(●)	(●)	●		(●)			●	●			●	4.10
●		Ⓑ									●			(●)		(●)		4.11
●	●	●	●	●	●	●	●	●	●	●	●	●	●	●	●	●	●	4.12
●	●	●	●	●	●	●	●	(●)	●	●	●	●	●	●	●	●	●	4.13
●	●	●	●	●	●	●	●	●	●	●	●	●	●	(●)	●	●	●	4.14
●	●	●	●	●	●	●	●	●	●	●	●	●	●	(●)	●	●	●	4.15
●					●	●	●		●		●			(●)			●	4.16
					●	●					●					(●)		4.17
●	●	●	●	●	●	●	●	●	●	●	●	●		●	●	●	●	4.18
●	●	●	●		●	●	●	●	●	●	●		●	●		●	●	4.19
(●)	●	(●)	(●)		(●)	(●)	(●)	(●)			●			(●)	(●)	(●)	(●)	4.20
●	●	●	●	●	●	●	●	●		●		●	●		●	●	●	4.21
●	●			●	●	●	●	●		●		●	●		●	●		4.22
		(●)								●						●	●	5.1
●	●	●	●	●	●	●	●	●	●	(●)	●	(●)	●	●	●	●	●	5.2
●	●	●	●	●	●	●	●	●	●	●	●	(●)	●	●	●	●	●	5.3
●	●	●	●	●	●	●	●	●	●	Ⓓ	●	●	●	●	●	●	●	5.4
●	●	●	●	●	●	●	●		(●)		●			●	(●)	●	●	5.5
(●)				●		●	●				●						●	5.6
●	(●)	(●)	(●)	●	●	●	●	●	(●)	(●)	(●)	●	●	(●)	(●)	●	●	5.7
(●)	●	●	●	●	●	(●)	(●)	●	●	●	●	●	●	●	●	●	●	5.8
●	●	●	●	(●)	●	●	●	●	●	●	●	●	●	●	●	●	●	5.9
●	●	●	●	●	●	●	●	●	(●)		●	●	●	●	●	●	●	5.10
	●	(●)			●	●	●	●						(●)	●	●	●	5.11
●	●	●	●	●	●			●	●	●	●	●	●	●	●	●	●	6.1
●	(●)	●	●	●	●			●	●	(●)	●	(●)	●	●	(●)	●	●	6.2
●	●	●	●	●	●			●	●	●	●	●	●	●	●	●	●	6.3
(●)	(●)		(●)Ⓑ										●	(●)	(●)			6.4
																		6.5
●	●							●	●	●	●	●	●		●		●	6.6
●	●				●	●	●	●			●	●			●		●	6.7
●	●				●	●					●				●			6.8
					●	●					●							6.9
●	●	●	●	●	●			●	●	●	●	●	●	●	●	●	●	7.1
●	●	●	●	●	●	●	●	●	●	●	●	●	(●)	●	●	●	●	7.2
						(●)	(●)									(●)		7.3
●	●				●				●					●		(●)	(●)	7.4
●	●	●	●	●	●	●	●	●	●	●	●	●	●	●	●	●	●	7.5

Table of analysis of examination syllabuses – *continued*

	Level	SEB	AEB	Cambridge	JMB	London	NIEC	Oxford	O and C	SUJB	WJEC	O and C 'Combined Science'	
		O	O	O	O	O	O	O	O	O	O & CSE	⅓O	
7.6	Homeostasis				●			●				●	7.6
7.7	Skin functions			●	●	●	●	●	●	●	●	●	7.7
	Sensitivity												
8.1	Sensitivity in plants & animals	●	●	●	●	●	●	●	●	●	●	●	8.1
8.2	Mammal sense organs	●	●	●	●	●	●	●	●	●	●	●	8.2
8.3	The eye	●	●	●	●	●	●	●	●	●	●	●	8.3
8.4	Abnormalities in focusing	●		●	●			●					8.4
8.5	The ear	●	●	●	●	●	●	●	●	●	●	●	8.5
8.6	Insect antennae & eyes				●								8.6
	Co-ordination & response												
9.1	Information, messages & action	●	●	●	●	●	●	●	●	●	●	●	9.1
9.2	Mammal nervous system	●	●	●	●	●	●	●	●	●	●	●	9.2
9.3	Nervous impulse			●	(●)								9.3
9.4	Types of nervous system												9.4
9.5	Reflex & intelligent action	●	●	●	●	●	●	●	●	●	●	●	9.5
9.6	Instinctive behaviour									●		●	9.6
9.7	The brain	●	●	●		●	●	●	●	●	●	●	9.7
9.8	Endocrine system	●	●	●	(●)	●	(●)	(●)	(●)	●	(●)	●	9.8
9.9	Nervous & hormonal systems compared			●	●	●	(●)	●	●	●	●	●	9.9
9.10	Feed-back			●	●			●					9.10
9.11	Taxis	●	●	●	●	●		●				●	9.11
9.12	Tropisms	●	●	●	●	●	●	●		●	(●)	●	9.12
9.13	Photoperiodism			●		●							9.13
	Support and locomotion												
10.1	Principles of support	●	●	●	●	●	●	●	●	●	●	●	10.1
10.2	Skeletons used in water, land & air	●	●										10.2
10.3	Exo-, endo- & hydrostatic skeletons	●	●	●								●	10.3
10.4	Principles of movement	●	●	●	●	●	●	●	●	●	●	●	10.4
10.5	Earthworm movement		●	●								●	10.5
10.6	Insect movement (walking (**W**) & flight (**F**))	●	●	W	●							W	10.6
10.7	Mammal movement (tissues)	●	●	(●)		(●)				(●)	(●)	(●)	10.7
10.8	Joints	●	●	●	●	●	(●)	●	●	●	●	●	10.8
10.9	Mammal skeleton	●		●	(●)	(●)	(●)	●	●	●	●	●	10.9
10.10	Insect & mammal skeleton compared		●	●	●							●	10.10
	Growth												
11.1	Growth in plants & animals	●	●	●	●		●	●	●	●		●	11.1
11.2	Growth in angiosperms (primary)			●			●		(●)	●	●		11.2
11.3	Secondary thickening	●								●	●		11.3
11.4	Factors affecting growth		●		●				●	●	●		11.4
11.5	Animal growth patterns	●	●	●			●			●		●	11.5
11.6	Seeds (structure & germination)	●	●	●	(●)	●	●	●	●	●	●	●	11.6
11.7	Growth measurement		●		●					●	●		11.7
	Reproduction												
12.1	Asexual & sexual reproduction compared	●	●	●	●	●	●	●	●	●		●	12.1
12.2	Asexual methods of reproduction	●	(●)	●	●	(●)	●	●	●	●		(●)	12.2
12.3	Winter twig				●	(●)		●	●	●	●		12.3
12.4	Perennial, biennial & annual seed-plants		●		(●)			(●)	(●)				12.4
12.5	Grafting (**G**) & cutting (**C**)	●	G	ONE		C						●	12.5
12.6	Sexual reproduction in plants	●	●	●	●	●	●	●	●	●		●	12.6
12.7	Flowers	●	●	●	●	●	●	●	●	●		●	12.7
12.8	Wind & insect-pollination	●	ONE	●	ONE	●	●	ONE	●	●		ONE	12.8
12.9	Self & cross-pollination			●	●	●	●	●	●	●		●	12.9
12.10	Adaptations for cross-pollination		●				(●)						12.10
12.11	Fertilisation & its consequences	●	●	●	●	●	●	●	●	●	●	●	12.11
12.12	Fruits	●	●	●	●	●	●	(●)	(●)	(●)	(●)	●	12.12
12.13	Dispersal of seeds by fruits	●	ONE	●	●	●	(●)	(●)	●	●	(●)	TWO	12.13
12.14	Sexual reproduction in mammals	●	●	●	●	●	●	●	●	●	●	●	12.14
12.15	Placenta	●	●	●	●	●	●	●	●	●	●	●	12.15
12.16	Parental care	●	●	●	●	●	●	●	●	●	●	●	12.16
12.17	Breeding success in vertebrates compared	●		●			(●)	(●)	(●)			●	12.17
12.18	Menstrual cycle	●	●			(●)		●			(●)		12.18
12.19	Contraception		●					●				●	12.19
12.20	Venereal diseases			●			(●)		(●)	(●)		●	12.20
	Genes, chromosomes & heredity												
13.1	The nucleus, chromosomes & genes		●	●	●	●	●	●	●	●	●	●	13.1
13.2	Genes & characteristics	●	●	●	●	●	●	●	●	●	●	●	13.2
13.3	Human blood groups: co-dominance			●		(●)		(●)					13.3
13.4	Mendel's experiments	●	●	●	●	●	●	●	●	●	●	●	13.4
13.5	Hints on tackling genetics problems	●	●	●	●	●	●	●	●	●	●	●	13.5
13.6	Back-cross test	●	●		●	●	●	●	●	●		●	13.6
13.7	Ratios of phenotypes	●	●	●	●	●	●	●	●	●	●	●	13.7

ALSEB	EAEB North	EAEB South	EMREB Syll. 1	EMREB Syll. 2	LREB Opt. A	LREB Opt. B	LREB Opt. C	NREB	NWREB	SEREB	SREB Syll. R.	SWEB	WMEB	YHREB Syll. A	YHREB Syll. B	ALSEB/JMB/NWREB/YHREB	EAEB/UCLES	
CSE	CSE	CSE	CSE	CSE	CSE	CSE	CSE	CSE	CSE	CSE	CSE	CSE	CSE	CSE	CSE	16+	16+	
(●)	●			(●)				(●)					(●)			●		7.6
●		●	(●) Ⓓ		●	●	●	(●)	(●)	(●)	●	(●)	●	(●)	●	●	●	7.7
●	●	●	●	●	●	●	●	●	●		●	●			●	●	●	8.1
●	●	●	●	●	●	●	●	●	●		●	(●)			●	●	●	8.2
●	●	●	●	●	●	●	●	●	●		●	●		●	●	●	●	8.3
			●								●				●			8.4
●	●	●	●	●	●	●	●	(●)	●	(●)	●	●		●	●	●	●	8.5
			Ⓓ															8.6
●	●	●	●	●	●	●	●	●	●	●	●	●		●	●	●	●	9.1
●	●	●	●	●	●	●	●	●	(●)	●	●	(●)		●	●	●	●	9.2
																		9.3
																		9.4
●	●	●	●	(●)	●	●	●	(●)	●	●	(●)	●		●	●	●	●	9.5
			Ⓓ								●			(●)				9.6
	(●)	(●)	●		●	●	●	(●)		(●)	(●)			(●)		(●)	●	9.7
●	(●)	(●)	●	(●)	●	●	●	(●)		(●)	●	(●)		(●)	●	●	●	9.8
(●)	(●)	(●)	(●)	(●)	(●)	(●)	(●)			(●)	(●)	(●)		●		●	●	9.9
●						●	●				●						●	9.10
●	●		Ⓑ Ⓓ	●					●							●	●	9.11
●	●	●	●	●	●	●	●		(●)	●	●	(●)		●	(●)	●	●	9.12
											(●)							9.13
●	●	●	●		●	●	●	●	●	●	●	●		●	●	●	●	10.1
								●	●		●							10.2
(●)			(●)					(●)	(●)		(●)			●		(●)		10.3
●	●	●	●	●	●	●	●	●	●	●	●	●		●	●	●	●	10.4
			Ⓑ								●			●				10.5
			Ⓑ							●				●		W		10.6
		(●)						(●)			(●)				(●)	(●)		10.7
●	●	●	●	●	●	●	●	●	●	●	●	●		●	●	●	●	10.8
●		●	●		●	●	●	●	●	●	●	(●)		●	●		●	10.9
●		●	●		●			●	●		●			●			(●)	10.10
		●	●	●		●	●	●	●					●	●	●	●	11.1
(●)		●	●		●	●	●							(●)	(●)	(●)	●	11.2
			●															11.3
						●	●							●		●		11.4
	(●)	(●)	●	●	●	●	●	(●)	●					●		(●)		11.5
(●)	(●)	●	●		●	(●)	(●)	●	ONE	●	(●)	ONE		(●)	(●)	●	●	11.6
	(●)	(●)	●	●		●	●		●					●		●	●	11.7
●	●	(●)	●	●	●	●	●	●	●		●			●	●	(●)	●	12.1
(●)	(●)	(●)	(●)	●	(●)	(●)	(●)		(●)	Ⓓ	●		(●)	●	●	(●)	(●)	12.2
(●)						●	●										(●)	12.3
			●												●			12.4
						C	C				●			●	●		C	12.5
●			(●)		●									●			●	12.6
●	●	●	(●)		●	●	●	●	●	●	●	●			●	●	●	12.7
●	ONE	ONE	●		●	●	●	ONE	●	Ⓓ	●	ONE			●	●	●	12.8
●			●	●	(●)	(●)	(●)		(●)	(●)	●			●	●	(●)	(●)	12.9
			(●)							Ⓓ								12.10
(●)	(●)	(●)	●		(●)	(●)	(●)	(●)	●	●	●	●		(●)	●	(●)	(●)	12.11
(●)	(●)	●	(●)		(●)			●	(●)	Ⓓ	(●)	(●)		(●)				12.12
●	●	●	(●)	(●)	(●)	●	●	●	(●)	●	●	(●)		(●)	(●)	●	●	12.13
●	●	●	●	(●)	●	●	●	●	●	●	●	●		●	●	●	●	12.14
●	●	●	●		●	●	●	●	●	●	●	●		●	●		●	12.15
●	●	●	●		●	●	●	●	●	●	●	●		●	●	(●)	●	12.16
	(●)							(●)	●	Ⓒ	●		(●)		(●)	(●)	●	12.17
	●	●	●		●						●			●	●	(●)	●	12.18
			●			●	●				●			●				12.19
	●	(●)	●										●				(●)	12.20
●	●		●	●	●	●	●	●	●	●	●	●		●	●	●	●	13.1
●	●		(●)	●	●	●	●			(●)	●	(●)		●	●	(●)	●	13.2
			(●)	(●)	(●)						●			(●)			●	13.3
●			●	●	●			●		●	●	●		●	●		●	13.4
●					●												●	13.5
																		13.6
●					●												●	13.7

	Table of analysis of examination syllabuses – *continued*	SEB	AEB	Cambridge	JMB	London	NIEC	Oxford	O and C	SUJB	WJEC	O and C 'Combined Science'	
	Level	O	O	O	O	O	O	O	O	O	O & CSE	½O	
13.8	Variation in populations	●	●	●	●	●	●	●	●	●		(●)	13.8
13.9	Sex determination in mammals		●	●	●	●	●	●	●				13.9
13.10	Sex linkage						●	●					13.10
13.11	Mutation		●	●			●	●	●	●		●	13.11
13.12	Mitosis & meiosis in the life cycle		●	●	●	●	●	●	●		●	●	13.12
13.13	Mechanism for separating chromosomes		●	●		(●)	●	●					13.13
13.14	Chromosome behaviour		●	●	(●)	(●)	●	●					13.14
13.15	Nucleic acids & the genetic code												13.15
	Evolution												
14.1	Organic evolution		●	●	●		●	○	●	●		●	14.1
14.2	Charles Darwin		(●)	(●)	(●)		●	○	●			(●)	14.2
14.3	Summary of the neo-Darwinian theory		●	●	●		●	○	●	(●)		●	14.3
14.4	Evidence for evolution		●				●	○	●				14.4
14.5	Other theories of evolution		(●)	(●)	(●)		●	○	(●)	(●)		(●)	14.5
14.6	Artificial selection		●		●		●		●			●	14.6
	Ecology												
15.1	The biosphere	●	(●)	(●)		●	●	○				●	15.1
15.2	Food chains, food webs, & food cycles	●	●	●	●	●	●	○	●	●	●	●	15.2
15.3	Feeding relationships between species	●	●	●	●	●	●	○	●	●	(●)	●	15.3
15.4	Stable & unstable ecosystems	●	●	●		●	●	○	●	●		●	15.4
15.5	Soil	●	●	●	●	●	●	○	●	●	●	●	15.5
15.6	Nitrogen cycle	●	●	●	●	●	●	●	●	●	●	●	15.6
15.7	Carbon cycle	●	●	●	●	●	●	●	●	●	●	●	15.7
15.8	Earthworm & soil	●	(●)	(●)		●	(●)	●	●	●	●	●	15.8
15.9	Water cycle						●	(●)			●	(●)	15.9
	Man & his environment												
16.1	Ploughing	●	●	●	●	●	●	○	●	●	(●)	●	16.1
16.2	Liming & fertilising	●	●	●	●	●	●	○	●	●	(●)	●	16.2
16.3	Crop rotation	●	(●)	(●)	●	●	●	○	●	●		●	16.3
16.4	Pest control					●	(●)	○	●		●	(●)	16.4
16.5	Human population crisis (problems)		●			●	(●)	○	●		(●)	●	16.5
16.6	Pollution	●		(●)		●	●	○	●		●	●	16.6
16.7	Depletion of resources					●	●	○	●		●	●	16.7
16.8	Human population crisis (solutions)	●				●	(●)	○	●		(●)	●	16.8
16.9	Predictions for mankind's future					(●)	(●)		(●)		(●)	(●)	16.9
16.10	Types of disease in man		(●)		(●)	(●)	●	(●)	●	●		(●)	16.10
16.11	Natural defences of the body		●		●	●	●	●	●	●		●	16.11
16.12	Notable contributors to health & hygiene						(●)			●			16.12
	A variety of life												
17.1	Viruses	●	(●)	●			(●)	●	(●)	●		●	17.1
17.2	Bacteria	●	●	●		●	●	●	●	●	(●)	●	17.2
17.3	*Spirogyra* & algae		●			●		●		●		●	17.3
17.4	*Amoeba* & protozoa	●	●	●	●	●		●	(●)	●		●	17.4
17.5	*Rhizopus* & *Mucor* – fungi	(●)	●	●	(●)	●	(●)	●	●	●		●	17.5
17.6	*Hydra*												17.6
17.7	Earthworm					●		●		●			17.7
17.8	Moss (**M**) and fern (**F**)					ONE							17.8
17.9	Angiosperms (general structure)	●	●	●	●	●	●	●	●	●	●	●	17.9
17.10	Parasitic adaptations		●			●			●				17.10
17.11	Pork tapeworm	(●)	●			●			(●)				17.11
17.12	*Pythium debaryanum*	(●)	—OR—	(●)									17.12
17.13	Dodder	(●)	—OR—										17.13
17.14	Insects (life cycles, external features)	●	●			●		●	●	●		●	17.14
17.15	Locust	(●)					●						17.15
17.16	House-fly	—OR—	—OR—	●			●	—OR—	—OR—				17.16
17.17	Large cabbage white butterfly									●			17.17
17.18	Honey bee					●				●			17.18
17.19	Importance of insects to man					●			(●)			●	17.19
17.20	Bony fish		(●)		(●)	●	(●)	●		●	●	(●)	17.20
17.21	Three-spined stickleback	(●)											17.21
17.22	Frog	●		(●)	(●)	●	(●)		●	●			17.22
17.23	Birds – flight (**F**) & reproduction (**R**)	R	F	R	F	R	●	R	●		F		17.23
17.24	Mammal characteristics					●	(●)	●			●	●	17.24
17.25	Rabbit					●		●		(●)	(●)		17.25

ALSEB	EAEB North	EAEB South	EMREB Syll. 1	EMREB Syll. 2	LREB Opt. A	LREB Opt. B	LREB Opt. C	NREB	NWREB	SEREB	SREB Syll. R.	SWEB	WMEB	YHREB Syll. A	YHREB Syll. B	ALSEB/JMB/NWREB/YHREB 16+	EAEB/UCLES 16+	
CSE	CSE	CSE	CSE	CSE	CSE	CSE	CSE	CSE	CSE	CSE	CSE	CSE	CSE	CSE	CSE	16+	16+	
●			●	●	●	●	●	●			(●)			●	●	●	●	13.8
	●		●		●			●							●	●	●	13.9
																		13.10
(●)			●								(●)	●			●	●		13.11
●	●		●		●	●	●	●	●		●				●	●	●	13.12
(●)			●		(●)						●					(●)	(●)	13.13
(●)			●		(●)						●					(●)	(●)	13.14
			(●)															13.15
	●		●	(●)		●	●	●	●	●	●	●		●	●	●		14.1
											(●)			●				14.2
	(●)							(●)		(●)	●	(●)		●	●	●		14.3
	(●)		(●)	(●)				●			(●)	●		●				14.4
											●							14.5
			(●)			●	●	●		Ⓑ Ⓓ	●				●	●		14.6
(●)	(●)				●					●	Ⓐ							15.1
●	●	●	●	●	●	●	●	●	●		Ⓐ	●	(●)		●	●	●	15.2
●	●	●	●	●	●	●	●	●	●		Ⓐ	●			●	●	(●)	15.3
●	●	●	●	●	●	●	●	●	●		Ⓐ	●			(●)		●	15.4
●	●	●	●	●	●	●	●	●	●	●	●	●			(●)		●	15.5
●	(●)		●		●	●	●			(●)	●				●		●	15.6
●	●		●		●	●	●			●	●	●			●		●	15.7
		(●)							●		(●)				●		●	15.8
●										●	●				●			15.9
●		(●)			●						(●)						●	16.1
●	●	●		(●)	●	●	●			●	(●)				●		●	16.2
●	(●)		(●)			(●)	(●)			(●)	(●)				●		●	16.3
●			●		●	●	●				(●)	(●)		(●)			●	16.4
●	●				●				●					●				16.5
●	●	(●)	Ⓐ Ⓒ	●	●	●	●	●	●	(●)		●		●	●		(●)	16.6
●	(●)		Ⓒ	(●)	●	(●)	(●)	(●)				(●)						16.7
●	●		Ⓒ		●									●				16.8
(●)	(●)				(●)									●				16.9
	●	●	Ⓐ		(●)	●	●	(●)		Ⓑ	●	(●)		●	●		(●)	16.10
	●	●	Ⓐ		●	●	●	(●)		Ⓑ	●			●	●		●	16.11
					●	●				Ⓑ	(●)			(●)	●		(●)	16.12
	(●)	●	Ⓐ			(●)	(●)			Ⓑ	●		(●)	(●)	(●)		(●)	17.1
	(●)	●	Ⓐ		●	(●)	(●)			Ⓑ	(●)	(●)	(●)	(●)	(●)		●	17.2
					●										(●)			17.3
(●)	(●)	(●)			●	(●)	(●)			Ⓒ	●		(●)	(●)		(●)	(●)	17.4
(●)	(●)	(●)	(●)		●	(●)	(●)		●	(●)	(●)	(●)	(●)	●	●		(●)	17.5
										Ⓒ					(●)			17.6
			(●)							Ⓒ			(●)		●			17.7
			(●)								●				(●)			17.8
●	●	●	●		●	●	●	●	●	●	●	●		(●)	●	●	●	17.9
					●					(●)				(●)	●	(●)	●	17.10
			(●)		●									(●)	(●)	(●)		17.11
										ONE				(●)				17.12
															OR			17.13
(●)	(●)	(●)	(●)		●	●	●	(●)	(●)		●		●	(●)	●			17.14
			(●)								●							17.15
	●	●	Ⓐ		OR	OR	OR	OR		Ⓒ ONE	●	ONE					●	17.16
			●															17.17
										Ⓓ							(●)	17.18
										Ⓓ	●			(●)			(●)	17.19
			(●)		●	●	●	●					(●)					17.20
			(●)													(●)		17.21
			(●)		●					(●)	(●)		(●)		(●)		●	17.22
						●	●	●										17.23
●	(●)	(●)			●	●	●	●		●		●			●			17.24
					(●)	(●)	(●)			Ⓒ					(●)			17.25

EXAMINING BOARDS

GCE Boards

AEB Associated Examining Board
Wellington House, Aldershot, Hampshire GU11 1BQ

Cambridge University of Cambridge Local Examinations Syndicate
Syndicate Buildings, 17 Harvey Road, Cambridge CB1 2EU

JMB Joint Matriculation Board
Manchester M15 6EU

London University Entrance and School Examinations Council
University of London, 66–72 Gower Street, London WC1E 6E

NIEC Northern Ireland Schools GCE Examinations Council
Beechill House, 42 Beechill Road, Belfast BT8 4RS

Oxford Oxford Local Examinations
Delegacy of Local Examinations, Ewert Place, Summertown, Oxford OX2 7BX

O and C Oxford and Cambridge Schools Examination Board
10 Trumpington Street, Cambridge; and Elsfield Way, Oxford

SUJB Southern Universities' Joint Board for School Examinations
Cotham Road, Bristol BS6 6DD

WJEC Welsh Joint Education Committee
245 Western Avenue, Cardiff CF5 2YX

SCE Board

SEB Scottish Examination Board
Ironmills Road, Dalkeith, Midlothian EH22 1BR

CSE Boards

ALSEB Associated Lancashire Schools Examining Board
77 Whitworth Street, Manchester M1 6HA

EAEB East Anglian Examinations Board
The Lindens Lexden Road, Colchester, Essex CO3 3RL

EMREB East Midland Regional Examinations Board
Robins Wood House, Robins Wood Road, Apsley, Nottingham NG8 3NH

LREB London Regional Examinations Board
Lyon House, 104 Wandsworth High Street, London SW18 4LF

NREB North Regional Examinations Board
Wheatfield Road, Westerhope, Newcastle upon Tyne NE5 5JZ

NWREB North West Regional Examinations Board
Orbit House, Albert Street, Eccles, Manchester M30 0WL

SREB Southern Regional Examinations Board
53 London Road, Southampton SO9 4YL

SEREB South East Regional Examinations Board
Beloe House, 2/4 Mount Ephraim Road, Royal Tunbridge Wells, Kent TN1 1EU

SWEB South Western Examinations Board
23–29 Marsh Street, Bristol BS1 4BP

WJEC Welsh Joint Education Committee
245 Western Avenue, Cardiff CF5 2YX

WMEB West Midlands Examination Board
Norfolk House, Smallbrook Queensway, Birmingham B5 4NJ

YHREB Yorkshire and Humberside Regional Examinations Board
31–33 Springfield Avenue, Harrogate, North Yorkshire HG1 2HW

16+ Boards See above Boards for addresses
ALSEB/JMB/
NWREB/YHREB

EAEB/UCLES See above Boards for addresses
(*Cambridge*)

1 Academic success

1.1 INTRODUCTION

Successful students are those who can organise their work. In particular, they must be able to work effectively on their own. If you are to be successful you need determination to succeed, a work plan fitted to a time schedule and determination to keep to that schedule. Unfortunately, few students are told *how* to devise that plan and carry it out – that is where this book comes in.

This chapter contains some advice that will help you to succeed in school. It also gives reasons for this advice. The rest of the book concerns itself with presenting biological facts in a form that makes it easy to revise.

The first three steps in the learning process are planned by your teacher who knows the sort of examination you will be sitting (stage 5 in Fig. 1.1) and plans accordingly. Where so many students fail, needlessly, is at stage 4 (revision) – because they do not know how to go about it. **Revision** is what this book is all about – leave out stage 4 in the diagram below and you have F for failure.

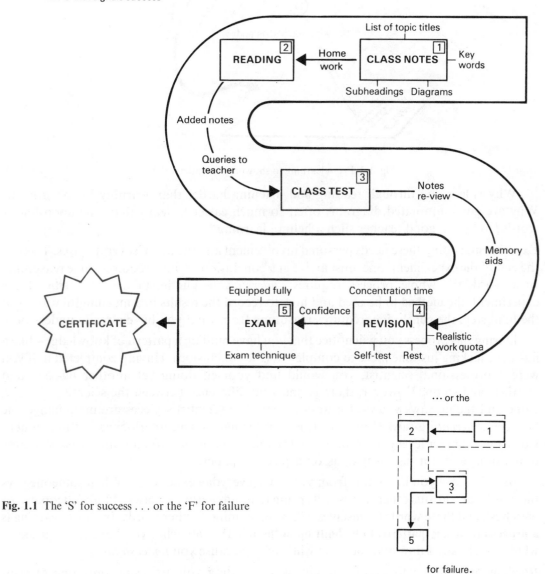

Fig. 1.1 The 'S' for success . . . or the 'F' for failure

1.2 THE LEARNING PROCESS: PATTERNS IN THE MIND

In science you learn from experiments – your own or those reported by others. It is well known that students tend to remember far better the 'facts' they have learned by doing experiments themselves. Unfortunately there is not enough time to learn everything this way, so that the rest has to be learned by reading and listening.

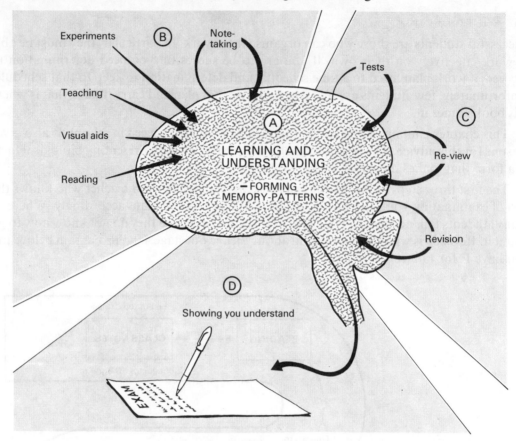

Fig. 1.2 From learning to showing you understand

Why is learning through reading and listening harder than learning by experiment? Why are good annotated diagrams often so much easier to learn than line upon line of words? Why is a good teacher such a help in learning?

Experiments: doing these needs personal involvement and the use of several senses. Then, at the end of the experiment, one must arrive at a conclusion – which requires some reasoning. In a word, the whole process requires *understanding* – understanding the **aim** of the experiment, the **method** to be used and how to record the **results** in a meaningful way. And the final step, the **conclusion,** requires reasoning from what you have already understood.

During this process you will notice that you have built up a pattern of knowledge – like a jig-saw – lacking just one piece to complete it (the conclusion). Having completed it, if you were a professional scientist, you would find yourself doing yet another jig-saw, and another, and so on. However, there is one vital difference between the scientist's jig-saw game and the jig-saws you do for amusement. The scientist's pieces are interchangeable between *different* jig-saws (Fig. 1.3). It is as if his jig-saws all interlocked in three dimensions. On a simpler level you probably realise that you can play noughts and crosses in three dimensions and not just in two, as on a piece of paper.

But of course you know this from your own everyday experience. When someone says the word 'cat' various other words will spring to mind. Perhaps 'claws', 'fluffy', 'leopard' or 'witches', and these words themselves will bring to mind further words. In short, **learning is a process requiring patterns to be built up in the mind:** relate what you have just learned to what you already know and the facts will stick – because you *understand.*

Reading: in contrast to experimenting, when reading you are using only one of your senses – sight – and you are not *involved*, as you are in an experiment, unless you make a mental effort. Nor do you feel the same sense of discovery. Worst of all, the information is presented as a series of facts. In well-written books the facts *are* written to form patterns;

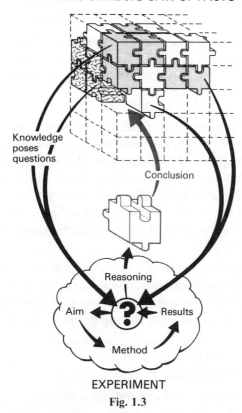

Fig. 1.3

but it is you, the reader, who has to concentrate hard enough to pick them out. If you can do this and fit your newly acquired jig-saw of facts into the system of jig-saws already in your brain, you have learned to learn by reading. This is initially much harder to do than by experiment.

Pictures and diagrams: one method of learning from books goes half-way towards experimental learning. Do you enjoy strip cartoons? At any rate you will agree that they are easy reading and convey much more than the few words appearing with the pictures. Pictures and diagrams, like words, require eyes alone to see them. But, unlike words, pictures build up patterns in the brain more readily and understanding is more immediate. So, well-constructed diagrams are an invaluable learning aid. If you learn the art of diagram-drawing you will reinforce both your memory and your understanding. Ultimately you should be able to construct your own original topic-summary diagrams, and there is a definite stage in the learning process when you should do this (see unit 1.4)

Teachers: have you ever thought about the role of teachers in the learning process? They attempt to activate more senses in you than just your hearing. By showing films and slides, by drawing diagrams or asking your opinions and by giving you definite learning objectives, they try to keep you personally involved. It is for you to respond – if you are going to learn. Amidst it all you must carefully latch onto the *pattern* of facts that the teacher explains. A teacher usually explains what the *whole* lesson is to be about during the first few minutes. Listen hard to that outline and the rest of the lesson will be easier to absorb. The outline is the basic skeleton upon which the teacher will build up the flesh and features of his subject, as the lesson proceeds. If you miss the description of the skeleton, the subject may turn out to be a monster for you!

1.3 CAPTURING FACTS

1 Class notes: your teacher has probably advised you on how to make these. For easy revision it is essential that they include:

(*a*) a topic list referring to numbered pages in your notebook;
(*b*) clear, underlined topic titles and sub-titles;
(*c*) underlined 'key words';

(*d*) clear diagrams with titles;

(*e*) space for topic-summary diagrams made during revision.

2   Reading texts: your teacher may advise you what to read. Realise too that a text has an index at the back; use it to look up things for yourself. At this stage many students get bogged down because they read slowly and give up. If you are someone with this problem, try this:

The cat sat on the mat.

Because of the way you were taught to read, for example 'c-a-t' or 'cat' you have been 'brainwashed' into thinking that you can only read one word at a time. Now bring your head back further from the page. Notice that now you can have more than one word in focus at a time – without having to move your eyes at all. With practice you will find that not only 'cat' is in focus but also 'The' and perhaps even 'sat' as well. It does need practice but soon you will find that the whole of 'The cat sat on' is in focus at one glance and that you can take it *all* in. Four words instead of one at each glance – four times your original reading speed!

Time how long it takes you to read a page now. Repeat the test after each week of practising the new method. Some people can read 800 words per minute with ease, understanding as they go. No wonder this method is called speed-reading! Reading the text should be done after you have been taught the topic – say during home-work. Your reading:

(*a*) reinforces in your mind the facts recorded in class notes;

(*b*) allows you to add extra bits to your notes;

(*c*) should clear up misunderstandings.

Ask your teacher if you still do not understand something.

3   Class tests: these are designed to help you to recall facts and to reason from them. In this process you and the teacher are on the *same* side; together you will succeed. The teacher is *not* putting you to the torture. Tests:

(*a*) help you to assess your progress (should you work harder?);

(*b*) help the teacher to clear up your difficulties (adjust your notes?);

(*c*) help you to remember facts better;

(*d*) give you exam practice.

1.4   RETAINING FACTS

Revision: this is the vital last stage in the learning process, the stage when you are finally on your own. You must understand clearly how to go about it. Look at the graph in Fig. 1.4.

All of us have different **'concentration times'**. How long is yours? Go to a quiet working place indoors, without distractions, and note the time. Read a part of your text-book that is new to you, making a determined effort to take in all you read. When your mind begins to

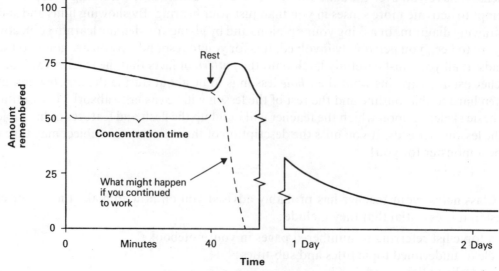

Fig. 1.4 Concentration time graph

wander, look again at your watch; you are at the end of your concentration time. It should be around 20–40 minutes and will differ according to the amount of sleep you have had, what else is on your mind, and even on the subject matter. Never revise for longer than your concentration time. If you do, you will waste your time. You may still be reading but you will not understand. So **rest** for five minutes.

After the rest, surprisingly enough, the facts you read in the text-book will come back to you more easily still. During the rest, the brain was 'organising' the facts you took in. Note-taking would have assisted this organising process. Unfortunately most of these facts go into what is called your 'short-term memory'. Within 48 hours you will retain as little as 10% of what you thought you knew so well. Don't be depressed. You can push these facts into your 'long-term memory', which is essential for examination purposes, by **reviewing**.

Reviewing is a *quick* re-read of your notes, taking only a few minutes. If your notes are disorganised you will not gain much. But with clear summaries, such as you will find in this book, you should dramatically increase the number of facts going into your long-term memory. Do this re-reading after a week and then again two weeks later after having learned the topic for the first time in class. Fig. 1.5 shows the sort of result that can be obtained by thorough reviewing and revision.

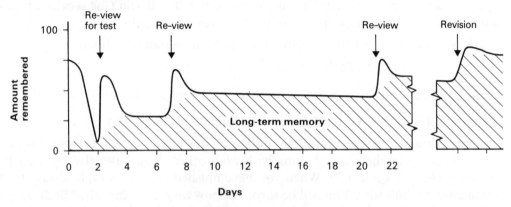

Fig. 1.5 Review and revision graph

Revision is just an extension of reviewing. If you have followed the learning plan so far, there will be relatively little to do. During revision whole chunks of your notes will not need to be read because sub-titles and key-words alone will trigger off a mass of facts already in your long-term memory. For the rest of the plan, follow these principles:

(*i*) Months ahead of the examinations plan how much to revise each week.

(*ii*) Have a regular time for work and stick to it.

(*iii*) With your concentration time in mind, plan a *realistic* amount of work for each 20–40 minute session. You must get up from your task with a sense of achievement, i.e. that you have completed what you set out to do. Otherwise you will get depressed 'at the hopelessness of it all'.

(*iv*) Take those 5-minute breaks. But do not exceed them.

(*v*) Use the memory aids and summary diagrams in this book to help you.

(*vi*) Check your knowledge by using the self-test units (pages 158–186).

Memory aids

(*i*) Repetition   (*ii*) Mnemonics   (*iii*) Pattern-diagrams

(**i**) **Repetition:** By chanting something over and over again you can learn it 'parrot-fashion'. Many people learn their times-tables or poetry in this way. The method has its uses. But though you can remember in this way you do not necessarily *understand*.

(**ii**) **Mnemonics:** These are words, sentences or little rhymes chosen from everyday language to help you to remember technical words that you find difficult to memorise. This book provides you with a few examples; but you may be able to do better. Make your own mnemonics funny, outrageously absurd – even rude – if you are going to remember them. Dull mnemonics are difficult to remember. The words you choose must be sufficiently similar to the technical words to remind you of them. For example:

'How do I remember the words on the Royal Garter when I don't know enough French? Look at Fig. 1.6 and try:

On his way he madly puns.

Fig. 1.6 The Royal Garter

'How can I remember the characteristics of living things – which I *do* understand but may not be able to remember fully in an exam?' Try **Berlin God sees** and turn to unit 2.1. This example uses initial letters of the key words only.

'How do I remember the principal regions of the vertebral column?'

Try   **The servant   attacks with saw and axe the lumber   stack and cord**

against   Cervical (atlas, axis)   Thoracic   Lumbar Sacral   Caudal

and turn to Fig. 10.10. You will find another mnemonic in unit 3.1

(iii) **Pattern-diagrams:** these are important or 'key' words written down and joined up with lines according to their connections with each other. You have already seen two examples (Figs. 1.1 and 1.2). When you have finished revising a topic always try to summarise it in this way. You will be surprised how easy it is. And why? Because, you will remember (Fig. 1.3), your mind thinks in patterns and not in lists. When you come to the examination you will be able to remember your pattern-diagrams and even create new ones when planning your answers to essay questions (see page 194).

Section IV of this book (pages 193–198) contains valuable advice on how to do your best in the examination. It also tells you about the types of question you might expect to find in an examination and gives hints on how to answer them.

Section V gives you the opportunity to practise the techniques you have learned.

Section II Core units 2—17

2 Life

2.1 CHARACTERISTICS OF ORGANISMS

Living things are called **organisms**. Three large groups of organisms are the **green plants**, e.g. grass; **non-green plants**, e.g. mushrooms; and the **animals** (see units 3.3 and 3.4). All organisms perform *all* the 9 'vital functions' at some time during their existence; and their bodies are made of cells. Some organisms remain, for a time, **dormant** (inactive), e.g. as seeds, spores or cysts. These bodies appear not to perform vital functions but are activated by suitable stimulation to do so e.g. by germinating.

10 characteristics of organisms   (*Mnemonic:* **BERLIN GOD SEES**

Breathing (= Respiration)
Excreting
Reproducing
Locomotion (= Moving)
Irritability (= Sensitivity and response)
Nutrition
Growing
Osmoregulation
Death
Cells

B   Respiration: release of energy within cells from food so as to power other vital functions. In most organisms, requires oxygen and releases carbon dioxide and heat. (See unit 6.)

E   Excretion: removal of waste products from **metabolism** (all the chemical reactions within the body). (See unit 7.)

N.B. Do not confuse this with 'egestion' (Removal of **indigestible** matter – which has thus never entered cells to be metabolised).

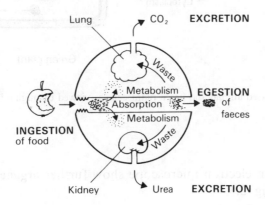

Fig. 2.1 The distinction between excretion and egestion

R   Reproduction: formation of more individuals either from one parent (asexually) or two (sexually). (See unit 12.)

L   Movement: an animal moves its whole body, using limbs or their equivalent. A plant 'moves' only by *growing* parts of itself towards or away from influences important to it. (See units 9.11 and 9.12.)

I   **Sensitivity and response:** influences (**stimuli**) in the surroundings (**environment**) stimulate certain areas of an organism so that they send messages to other parts which respond, e.g. by movement, growth or secretion. (See unit 8.)

N   **Nutrition:** intake of food materials from the environment for building up and maintaining living matter. (See unit 4.2.)

G   **Growth:** cells divide and then get larger again by adding more living material (made from their food) until they repeat the process. (See unit 11.)

O   **Osmoregulation:** maintenance of the water content of cells at a suitable level. (See unit 5.6.)

D   **Death:** when metabolism ceases completely.

C   **Cells:** the simplest units of life. All cells, when young, have at the very least three parts: a *membrane* enclosing jelly-like *cytoplasm,* in which lies a *nucleus* which controls their life. (See unit 2.2.) These three parts make up *protoplasm* (living matter). The cell wall secreted outside the protoplasm by plant cells only, is non-living. Cells cannot live without supplies of energy, food, water and O_2 and a suitable environmental temperature and pH.

Cells from animals and green plants show differences, as seen in Fig. 2.2.

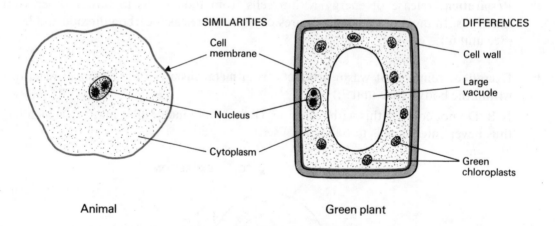

Fig. 2.2 Generalised animal and green plant cells as viewed through a light microscope

2.2   ORGANELLES

Cells examined with an electron microscope show further **organelles** (parts with special functions) as seen in Fig. 2.3.

(a) **Cell wall**
Made of cellulose.
Freely permeable (porous) to all kinds of molecules.
Supports and protects the cell.
Supports non-woody plant organs, e.g. leaves, by turgor pressure (water pressure within vacuole distending cell wall).
Osmoregulates by resisting entry of excess water into cell. (See Fig. 5.4C)

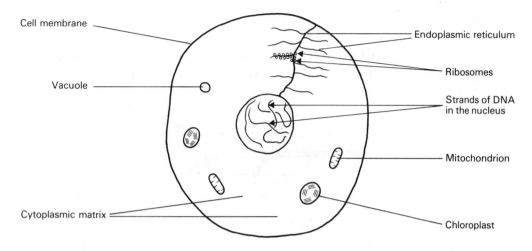

Fig. 2.3 Protoplasm of a generalised cell as viewed through an electron microscope

(*b*) **Cell membrane**
Exterior of all protoplasm.
Very thin layer of protein and oil.
Freely permeable to water and gases only.
Selectively permeable to other molecules (e.g. allows foods in but keeps unwanted molecules out).

(*c*) **Endoplasmic reticulum (ER)**
Maze of fine tubes, made of cell membrane material, throughout the cytoplasm.
Allows transport of materials across cell.
Allows export of materials out of cell, e.g. digestive enzymes.

(*d*) **Ribosomes**
Minute bodies in thousands; most attached to membranes of ER.
Assemble proteins under 'instructions' from nucleus

(*e*) **Vacuoles**
Spaces for various functions, e.g. food storage, osmoregulation.

(*f*) **Chloroplasts** (for photosynthesis)
Large bodies containing chlorophyll (green).
Chlorophyll converts sunlight energy into chemical energy (ATP).
ATP is used to combine CO_2 with H_2O, making glucose; by-product is O_2.

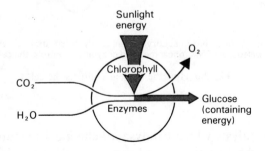

Fig. 2.4 Photosynthesis

(*g*) **Mitochondria** (for internal respiration)

Absorb O_2 and glucose.

Break down glucose to CO_2 and H_2O. This releases energy from glucose bonds to form ATP (for use in other vital functions, e.g. growth, see unit 6.9.)

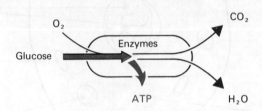

Fig. 2.5 Internal respiration

(*h*) **Cytoplasmic matrix**

Supports organelles.

Consistency of raw egg-white.

Up to 80% water; remainder mainly protein.

(*i*) **Nucleus**

Stores and passes on cell 'information'.

Contains many long strands of DNA (invisible by light microscope).

When cell divides, DNA coils up to form chromosomes (visible). (See unit 13.1)

Segments of DNA are called **genes**.

Genes are responsible for characteristics of organisms, e.g. blood group and eye colour.

2.3   How the nucleus controls the cell

DNA makes RNA and RNA makes proteins. (See Fig. 2.6.)

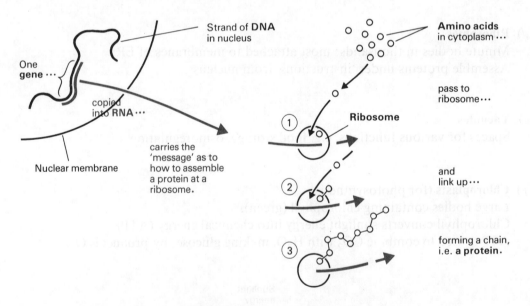

The protein may be an enzyme. Enzymes are catalysts 'controlling' cell metabolism.
Thus the nucleus, via RNA, ribosomes and enzymes, 'controls' the cell.

Fig. 2.6 How the nucleus controls the cell

Enzymes are protein catalysts which catalyse *all* chemical reactions (metabolism) of the body, e.g. respiration, photosynthesis, and digestion. Without enzymes, reactions would not go fast enough for life to exist.

Each enzyme works at a preferred *temperature* (boiling stops its action for good; cooling only slows its action) and at a preferred *pH*, e.g. pepsin works only in acid conditions. (See unit 4.13.)

Each enzyme is specific in action, e.g. ptyalin digests starch only, never protein. (See unit 4.13.)

2.5 UNITS OF LIFE BEYOND THE CELL

Just as inorganic molecules are built up into organic molecules; which in turn are built into organelles (see unit 2.2), so cells are sub-units of organisms. There is a great variety of types of cell. (See units 4.8, 5.5, 5.8, 9.2, 10.7, 12.14.)

Tissues are groups of cells, usually of the same type, specialised to carry out certain functions, e.g. muscle, nerve, epithelium, xylem, bone.

Organs are made up of tissues co-ordinated to perform certain functions, e.g. eye, leaf, kidney.

Organ systems are groups of organs which combine to perform their functions, e.g. gut, endocrine system, nervous system.

Organisms, depending on their complexity, may each be just one cell, e.g. a bacterium, or *Amoeba*, or millions of cells with a variety of functional units as above, e.g. an oak tree or man. An organism which reproduces sexually is not much use on its own, unless it self-fertilises. The basic unit of reproduction is thus usually a **breeding pair**. From this stem **populations** – as small as herds or as large as hundreds of herds occupying an island or a continent. A number of populations forms a **species** (see Fig. 2.7). Populations of different species living in balance in nature are called **communities**. Communities form part of **ecosystems** in the **biosphere**. (See unit 15.1.)

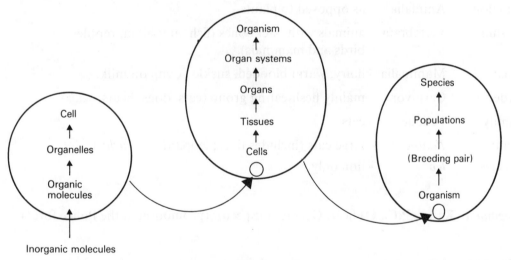

Fig. 2.7 Units of life

3 Classification

3.1   Linnaeus and his classification system

Carl Linnaeus of Sweden in 1735 introduced the basis of modern **taxonomy** (classification):
All species are given two names in Latin – the **binomial system** of naming:
(*a*) genus name, written first, with an initial *capital* letter, e.g. *Homo* (man).
(*b*) species name, written second, with a *small* initial letter, e.g. *sapiens* (modern).

The binomial ought to be printed in italics but is underlined when handwritten or typed by
scientists, e.g. <u>Panthera</u> <u>tigris</u> (tiger).

Species: a group of organisms with a very large number of similarities in structure and
physiology, capable of breeding to produce fertile offspring.

Genus: a group of organisms with a large number of similarities but whose different sub-
groups (species) are usually unable to inter-breed successfully.

Taxons: just as species are sub-groups of genera, so genera are grouped together into larger
and larger groups forming a **hierarchy of taxons** (groups), each group including as many
similarities as possible. The largest taxon is a kingdom, the smallest a species. The lion can
be classified as follows:

Kingdom	Animalia	– as opposed to plants.
Phylum	Vertebrata	– animals with backbones (fish, amphibia, reptiles, birds and mammals).
Class	Mammalia	– hairy, warm blooded, suckle young on milk.
Order	Carnivora	– mainly flesh-eating group (cats, dogs, bears, seals).
Family	Felidae	– cats.
Genus	*Panthera*	– large cats (includes tiger; leopard, *P. pardus*).
Species	*leo*	– lion only.

Mnemonic: **K**adet, **P.C.**, **OF**ficer, **G**eneral in**S**pector (promotion in the Police force).

Advantages of the system

1   Universal: Japanese, Bantu or Russian biologists all understand that *Felis domestica*
means 'house cat' without having to resort to a dictionary.

2   Shorthand information: one word, e.g. mammal, conveys a mass of information to all
biologists. (See unit 17.24.)

3   Reflects evolutionary relationships: e.g. the five classes of vertebrate are very different
(see unit 3.4), yet all have a common body plan. The basic plan (in Fish) (see p. 23), was
improved upon, permitting land colonisation (Amphibia) and exploitation (Reptiles and
Mammals), and even conquering of the air (Birds). The classification of vertebrates thus
probably reflects the evolutionary process.

3.2 KEYS

Keys are a means of identifying organisms in *local* situations, e.g. in stream or woodland. The user of the key selects one of two contrasting descriptions, choosing the one that fits the organism being identified. The chosen description leads to a number, alongside which are further descriptions from which to choose. The final choice leads to the organism's name.

Example: Choose one of the organisms in Fig. 3.1 and use the key below the diagram to identify it.

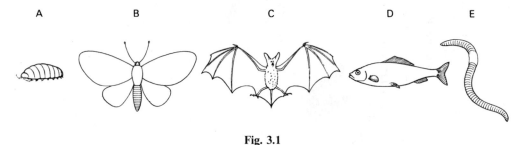

Fig. 3.1

With wings	**1**	*(Now look at descriptions by **1** below)*
Without wings	**2**	*(Now look at descriptions by **2** below)*
1 { Two legs	C – Bat	
Six legs	B – Butterfly	
2 { With legs	A – Woodlouse	
Without legs	**3**	*(Now look at description by **3** below)*
3 { With eyes	D – Fish	
Without eyes	E – Earthworm	

In the example above, use of internal characteristics (e.g. vertebrae) or confusing ones (e.g. hairiness) would delay identification – some butterflies are as hairy as bats!

Your key of the organisms above could be different but still be 'correct' – if it works.

3.3 PLANT KINGDOM

Classification of the main members of the plant kingdom can be seen on page 22 overleaf.

3.4 ANIMAL KINGDOM

Classification of the main members of the animal kingdom can be seen on page 23.

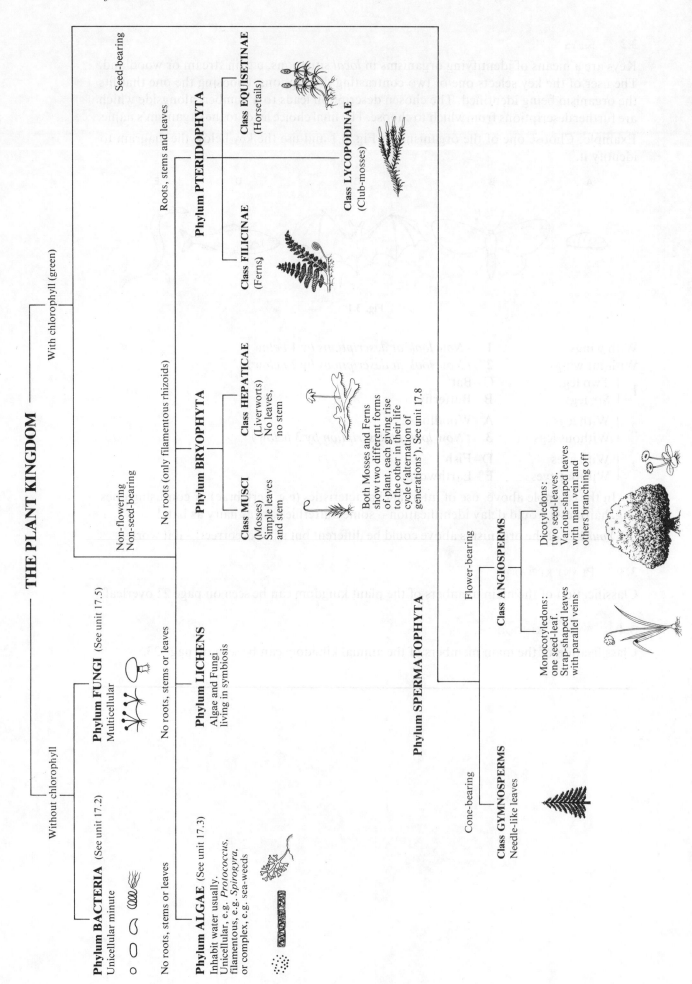

THE PLANT KINGDOM

Without chlorophyll

Phylum BACTERIA (See unit 17.2)
Unicellular minute

No roots, stems or leaves

Phylum FUNGI (See unit 17.5)
Multicellular

No roots, stems or leaves

Phylum LICHENS
Algae and Fungi
living in symbiosis

Phylum ALGAE (See unit 17.3)
Inhabit water usually.
Unicellular, e.g. *Protococcus*,
filamentous, e.g. *Spirogyra*,
or complex, e.g. *sea-weeds*

With chlorophyll (green)

**Non-flowering.
Non-seed-bearing**

No roots (only filamentous rhizoids)

Phylum BRYOPHYTA

Class MUSCI
(Mosses)
Simple leaves
and stem

Class HEPATICAE
(Liverworts)
No leaves,
no stem

Both Mosses and Ferns
show two different forms
of plant, each giving rise
to the other in their life
cycle ('alternation of
generations'). See unit 17.8

Roots, stems and leaves

Phylum PTERIDOPHYTA

Class FILICINAE
(Ferns)

Class EQUISETINAE
(Horsetails)

Class LYCOPODINAE
(Club-mosses)

Seed-bearing

Phylum SPERMATOPHYTA

Cone-bearing

Class GYMNOSPERMS
Needle-like leaves

Flower-bearing

Class ANGIOSPERMS

Monocotyledons:
one seed-leaf.
Strap-shaped leaves
with parallel veins

Dicotyledons:
two seed-leaves.
Various-shaped leaves
with main vein and
others branching off

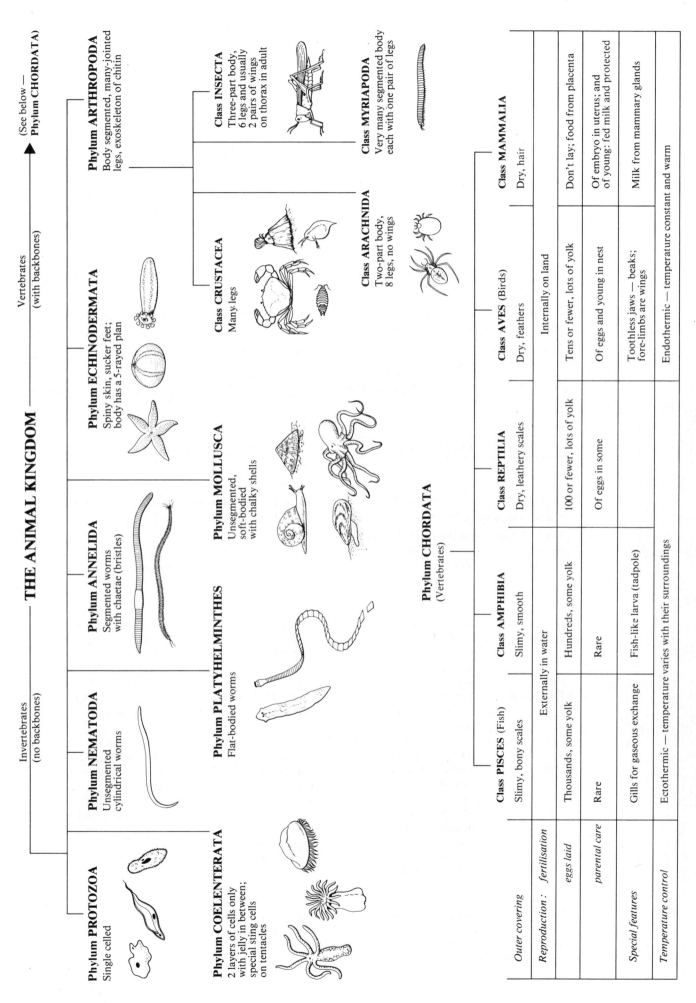

THE ANIMAL KINGDOM

Invertebrates (no backbones) — Vertebrates (with backbones) (See below — Phylum CHORDATA)

Phylum PROTOZOA
Single celled

Phylum NEMATODA
Unsegmented cylindrical worms

Phylum ANNELIDA
Segmented worms with chaetae (bristles)

Phylum ECHINODERMATA
Spiny skin, sucker feet; body has a 5-rayed plan

Phylum ARTHROPODA
Body segmented, many-jointed legs, exoskeleton of chitin

Phylum COELENTERATA
2 layers of cells only with jelly in between; special sting cells on tentacles

Phylum PLATYHELMINTHES
Flat-bodied worms

Phylum MOLLUSCA
Unsegmented, soft-bodied with chalky shells

Class INSECTA
Three-part body, 6 legs and usually 2 pairs of wings on thorax in adult

Class MYRIAPODA
Very many segmented body each with one pair of legs

Class CRUSTACEA
Many legs

Class ARACHNIDA
Two-part body, 8 legs, no wings

Phylum CHORDATA
(Vertebrates)

		Class PISCES (Fish)	**Class AMPHIBIA**	**Class REPTILIA**	**Class AVES** (Birds)	**Class MAMMALIA**
Outer covering		Slimy, bony scales	Slimy, smooth	Dry, leathery scales	Dry, feathers	Dry, hair
Reproduction :	*fertilisation*	Externally in water		Internally on land		
	eggs laid	Thousands, some yolk	Hundreds, some yolk	100 or fewer, lots of yolk	Tens or fewer, lots of yolk	Don't lay; food from placenta
	parental care	Rare	Rare	Of eggs in some	Of eggs and young in nest	Of embryo in uterus; and of young: fed milk and protected
Special features		Gills for gaseous exchange	Fish-like larva (tadpole)		Toothless jaws — beaks; fore-limbs are wings	Milk from mammary glands
Temperature control		Ectothermic — temperature varies with their surroundings			Endothermic — temperature constant and warm	

4 Foods and feeding

4.1 FOOD

Food (material for building up protoplasm) is of two types:

1 Inorganic: (simple molecules common to non-living matter), e.g. carbon dioxide, mineral salts and water.

2 Organic: (complex, carbon-containing compounds), e.g. carbohydrates, fats, proteins and vitamins. These classes of molecules are characteristic of living matter.

4.2 HOLOPHYTIC, HOLOZOIC AND SAPROPHYTIC NUTRITION COMPARED

There are two fundamentally different methods of nutrition:

1 Autotrophic organisms (plants containing green chlorophyll) need *only inorganic food* from which they synthesise organic molecules, using *energy trapped from sunlight* to drive the reactions.

2 Heterotrophic organisms (animals and non-green plants, e.g. fungi) have to feed on ready made *organic food*. From this food they derive their *energy, released by respiration.* They also need some inorganic food.

Organic food can be obtained from living organisms (**holozoic** nutrition) or from dead matter (**saprophytic** nutrition). (For other variations see unit 4.11.)

Table 4.1 Comparison of types of nutrition

Type of nutrition	Autotrophic	Heterotrophic	
	Holophytic	Holozoic	Saprophytic
Examples of organisms	Typical green plants e.g. *Spirogyra* (Unit 17.3) and angiosperms	Typical animals e.g. *Amoeba* (Unit 17.4) and mammals	Bacteria and fungi of decay e.g. *Mucor* (Unit 17.5) and mushrooms
Type of food	Inorganic only: CO_2, H_2O and mineral salts	Organic, H_2O and mineral salts	Dead organic, H_2O and mineral salts
How the food is used	(*i*) CO_2 and water are combined in **photosynthesis** to make carbohydrates (*ii*) carbohydrates are modified and also often combined with salts to **form other organic molecules,** e.g. protein	Food organisms are killed; *ingested* into a **gut**; *digested* by enzymes secreted internally; soluble products *absorbed*; indigestible waste *egested* (eliminated)	Dead organisms or excreta are digested by enzymes secreted **externally** onto them; soluble products absorbed
Source of energy for vital functions	**Sunlight** – trapped by chlorophyll during photosynthesis	Cannot trap sunlight energy since they lack chlorophyll. Rely on **respiration** of organic molecules (the bonds of which contain energy)	

Thus the kinds of organism practising these three forms of nutrition provide food for each other:

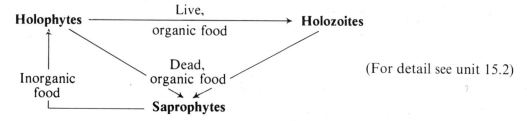

(For detail see unit 15.2)

The principles outlined in Table 4.1 are best studied in detail by reference to simple organisms such as those named (see units 17.3–17.5). Complex organisms, however, have complex requirements and uses for the molecules they absorb. This is taken into account below.

INORGANIC FOOD

1   Water (see unit 5.1)   **2   Mineral salts**

4.3   MINERAL SALTS FOR MAMMALS AND ANGIOSPERMS

(Angiosperms are flowering plants)

Table 4.2 Mammal requirements (especially man)

Element	Good sources	Uses	Deficiency effects
Ca (*Calcium*)	Milk; cheese; bread (chalk added by law)	Bones and teeth are about $\frac{2}{3}$ calcium phosphate	Brittle bones and teeth
P (*Phosphorus*)	Milk	Bones and teeth; ATP the energy molecule (Unit 6.9); nucleic acids–genes and their functions (Unit 3.5)	As above
Fe (*Iron*)	Liver, egg yolk	Part of haemoglobin, the oxygen-carrying molecule	Anaemia (lack of red blood cells)
I (*Iodine*)	Sea foods Table salt (iodised by law)	Part of thyroxin, the hormone controlling metabolic rate (Unit 9.8)	Goitre – thyroid swelling in adults
F (*Fluorine*)	Toothpaste or tap water that have been fluoridated	Ensures hard tooth enamel, therefore less tooth decay (caries)	Dental caries more likely
Na (*Sodium*)	Table salt (NaCl)	A correct balance of these is required, particularly for proper function of nerves and muscles	
K (*Potassium*)	Plant food		

Table 4.3 Angiosperm requirements (See unit 4.10)

Element	Sources	Uses	Deficiency effects
N (*Nitrogen*)	Nitrates	Protein and nucleic acid synthesis	Poor growth – little protoplasm made
S (*Sulphur*)	Sulphates		
P (*Phosphorus*)	Phosphates	ATP (energy molecule) in photosynthesis and respiration; nucleic acid synthesis	Poor growth – little energy for synthesis of protoplasm

Table 4.3 – *(cont'd)*

Element	Sources	Uses	Deficiency effects
K *(Potassium)*	Potassium salts	Functions not clear	Poor growth – dehydration
Ca *(Calcium)*	Lime ($CaCO_3$)	'Gum' (middle lamella) between adjacent cell walls	Faulty cell division
Fe *(Iron)*	Iron salts	Enzymes for making chlorophyll	Pale leaves (chlorosis)
Mg *(Magnesium)*	Magnesium salts	Part of chlorophyll molecule	

Trace elements include Zinc (**Zn**), Copper (**Cu**) and Manganese (**Mn**). Required in very minute quantities for healthy growth (larger quantities are often poisonous).

Although green plants absorb mineral salts as ions, man does not always give them to his crops by way of inorganic fertilisers (see unit 16.2). Organic fertilisers, such as dung, also yield salts, once they have been broken down by bacteria and fungi (see units 15.6, 17.2, 17.5).

ORGANIC FOOD
1   Carbohydrates, fats and proteins   2   Vitamins

4.4   CARBOHYDRATES, FATS AND PROTEINS

Table 4.4 Carbohydrates, fats, oils and proteins

	Carbohydrates	*Fats* (solids), *oils* (liquid)	*Proteins*
Elements	C, H, O Ratio of H:O is 2:1 (as in H_2O)	C, H, O Ratio of H:O is very high, i.e. very little O	C, H, O, N, often S
Examples	Glucose, $C_6H_{12}O_6$ Sucrose, $C_{12}H_{22}O_{11}$	Mutton fat: ($C_{57}H_{110}O_6$)	Haemoglobin, ptyalin, insulin $C_{254}H_{377}N_{65}O_{75}S_6$
Units	Mono-saccharides (simple sugars, like glucose)	Glycerol + fatty acids	Amino acids
	These are the smallest units into which these three classes of food can be broken down by digestion (*hydrolysis*). The units can be reassembled into larger molecules again by *condensation*, e.g. when food needs to be stored (see unit 4.12).		
Larger molecules	Di-saccharides (2 units) e.g. sucrose, maltose		Di-peptides (*two linked amino acids*)
	Poly-saccharides, e.g. starch, glycogen, cellulose		Poly-peptides (*many*)
Chemical tests	1 Blue **Benedict's** solution* + **reducing sugar** $\xrightarrow{boiled}$ *orange* precipitate **Clinistix + glucose** $\xrightarrow{cold}$ mauve or *purple*	1 The clear filtrate obtained from mixing **absolute ethanol** with crushed food, when added to an equal quantity of water, gives a white emulsion.	1 Colourless **Millons** solution + protein $\xrightarrow{boiled}$ *brick-red* clotted protein

* *Note:* **Fehling's** solutions I and II, if mixed to give a *royal blue* solution, give similar results to Benedict's solution.

Table 4.4 – (*cont'd*)

	Carbohydrates	*Fats* (solids), *oils* (liquid)	*Proteins*
Chemical tests (cont'd)	**2** Colourless conc. **HCl** + **sucrose** <u>boiled for 10 minutes</u>→ *urine-coloured* solution **3** Brown **iodine** solution + **starch** <u>must be cold</u>→ *blue-black*	**2** **Translucency:** when warmed on paper, makes paper permanently translucent ('grease spot')	**2** Colourless 40% **NaOH** + protein extract, add 2 drops blue **CuSO₄** → *mauve* **Biuret** colour **(Biuret test)**
Functions	**Energy supply** when respired: 17 kJ/g. Used first. Stored as *starch* (green plants) and *glycogen* (animals, colourless plants). Transported as sugars **Structural:** cellulose cell walls **Origin of other organic molecules:** e.g. sugar + nitrate → amino acid	**Energy supply** when respired: 39 kJ/g. Used after carbohydrates. Important in flying, migrating and hibernating animals. (More energy per unit mass than glycogen) **Heat insulation:** subcutaneous fat in mammals **Waterproofing:** of skin, fur, feathers **Buoyancy:** e.g. fish larvae in the sea	**Energy supply** when respired: 17 kJ/g. Important in carnivores otherwise only respired extensively in starvation **Movement:** *muscles* contract; *tendons* connect muscles to bones; *ligaments* connect bone to bone at joints – all are protein **Catalysts:** *enzymes* make metabolism reactions possible (see unit 2.4) **Hormones** regulate metabolism (see unit 9.8). Many, e.g. insulin, are protein

4.5 VITAMINS

Vitamins: organic substances (of a variety of kinds) required in *minute* amounts to maintain health of heterotrophs. Autotrophs make all they need.

Lack of a vitamin in the diet results in a *deficiency disease,* e.g. scurvy. A vitamin for one organism is not necessarily a vitamin for another, e.g. man suffers scurvy from lack of vitamin C but rats do not because they synthesise their own.

Fat-soluble vitamins (**A, D, E, K**) are ingested in fats and oils.

Water-soluble vitamins (**B, C**) are present in other materials.

Table 4.5 Vitamins

Vitamins	*Good sources*	*Functions*	*Deficiency diseases*
A	Vegetables, butter, egg yolk. Liver oils, e.g. cod-liver oil, contain both A and D	**1** Healthy epithelia **2** Part of 'visual purple' in rod cells of retina (Unit 8.2)	Susceptibility to *invasion by disease organisms* *Poor night-vision*
D *'sunshine vitamin'*	Butter, egg yolk. (Can be synthesised in the skin from oils irradiated by ultraviolet light)	Regulation of calcium and phosphate absorption from gut and their deposition in bone	*Rickets:* poor bone formation, weak and often deformed, e.g. 'bow legs' in children

Table 4.5 – *(cont'd)*

Vitamins	Good sources	Functions	Deficiency diseases
E	Butter, wholemeal bread	Not important to man. (Rats: in reproduction)	Male rat sterility; death and resorption of embryos of rat
K	Cabbage, spinach. Made abundantly by bacteria in intestine	Aids blood clotting	Longer bleeding time before clotting
B_1 *(Thiamine)*	Wholemeal bread	Efficient respiration	*Beri-beri:* inflamed nerves; and swollen heart muscle
B_2 complex *(9 vitamins)*	Yeast and 'Marmite' (= yeast extract) Liver	A variety of roles in metabolism	Skin, eye lesions (riboflavin); *pellagra:* gut problems, paralysis etc. (nicotinic acid)
B_{12} *(Cobalamine)*	Liver	Aids formation of red blood cells	*Pernicious anaemia:* lack of red blood cells
C 'Sailors' vitamin'	Citrus fruit, milk and *fresh* vegetables (destroyed by cooking)	Tissue-damage repair	*Scurvy:* capillary bleeding, poor healing of wounds

HOLOPHYTIC NUTRITION

Unique features: uses only inorganic food molecules to photosynthesise sugars and synthesise amino acids.

4.6   PHOTOSYNTHESIS

Photosynthesis: makes sugars and the by-product oxygen, from CO_2 and water using the energy of sunlight, trapped by chlorophyll. Occurs in chloroplasts (see unit 2.2). Two stages:

(*a*) **photolysis** – water is split to give

(*i*) oxygen gas (by-product)
(*ii*) hydrogen for reducing CO_2 } only in the *light*

(*b*) **reduction** – of CO_2 to form sugars, e.g. glucose.

Evidence: if heavy isotope of oxygen, ^{18}O, is used to 'label' water fed to plants, all the O_2 given off is ^{18}O and none is normal oxygen, ^{16}O. If the CO_2, and not the water, fed to the plants is labelled with ^{18}O, *none* of the O_2 given off is ^{18}O. Therefore all the O_2 by-product comes from water and not CO_2. (This also proves the need for water in photosynthesis.)

To take account of this, the **overall equation** for photosynthesis must be:

$$6CO_2 + 12H_2O \xrightarrow[\text{Chlorophyll}]{\text{Sunlight energy}} \underset{\substack{\text{Glucose} \\ \text{(storing sun-energy)}}}{C_6H_{12}O_6} + 6O_2 + 6H_2O$$

Similarly, if CO_2 'labelled' with ^{14}C is fed to a plant, the ^{14}C ends up in glucose.

Fate of glucose:
(*a*) Condensed to sucrose – for *transport* elsewhere.
(*b*) Condensed to starch – for *storage* in leaf (transported away as sucrose by night). (Basis for leaf starch-test.)
(*c*) Used in *respiration,* or *amino acid synthesis* (see unit 4.9).
(*d*) Condensed to cellulose – making *cell walls.*

Evidence for the four factors necessary for photosynthesis
Plant must be de-starched before any experiment by keeping it in the dark for 48 hours. The presence of starch in the leaves at the end of the experiment is evidence of photosynthesis.
1   The starch test for leaves (Fig. 4.1)

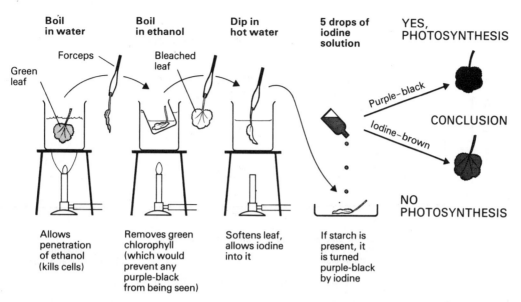

Fig. 4.1 Testing leaves for starch

2 Test the need for: ①**Sunlight.** ②**Carbon dioxide.** ③**Chlorophyll** (Fig. 4.2).

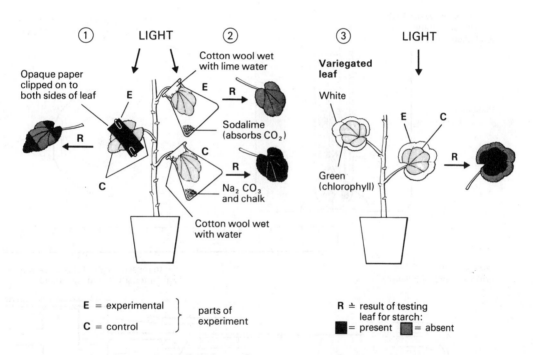

Fig. 4.2 Testing the need for①sunlight,②carbon dioxide,③chlorophyll in photosynthesis

④ **Water** – impossible without use of ^{18}O isotope experiment (see 'photolysis' above) because denying the plant water kills it anyway.

4.7 LIMITING FACTORS

In a physiological process (such as photosynthesis) any factor which is in short supply, so that it reduces the rate of the process from its possible maximum, is said to be the limiting factor. Thus with plants photosynthesising outdoors, *light* is limiting at dusk; CO_2 during most of the day; *water* probably never. *Temperature* can also be limiting (too cold – reactions too slow; too hot – destroys enzymes). *Factors closing stomata* are limiting by reducing flow of CO_2 into leaf. *Lack of Mg* in soil limits the amount of chlorophyll made in the leaf (see Fig. 4.3).

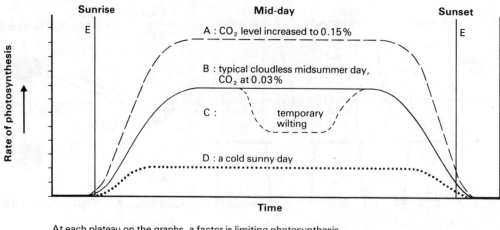

At each plateau on the graphs, a factor is limiting photosynthesis.
A and B : probably CO_2 in air.
C : CO_2 reaching chloroplasts.
D : temperature.
E : at dawn and dusk : light.

Fig. 4.3 Limiting factors for photosynthesis

Rate of photosynthesis in a water plant, e.g. *Elodea*, can be estimated by counting the *number of bubbles* per unit time coming from a cut stem. Alternatively, trap bubbles and measure *volume* per unit time in a capillary tube (see Fig. 4.4).

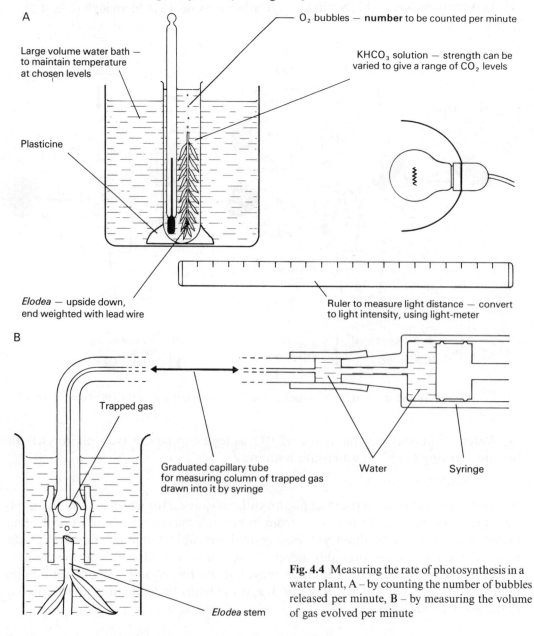

Fig. 4.4 Measuring the rate of photosynthesis in a water plant, A – by counting the number of bubbles released per minute, B – by measuring the volume of gas evolved per minute

4.8   LEAF STRUCTURE AND PHOTOSYNTHESIS

LEAF STRUCTURE

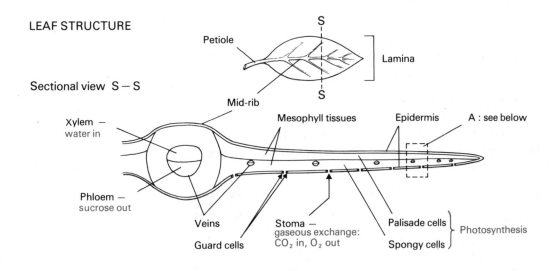

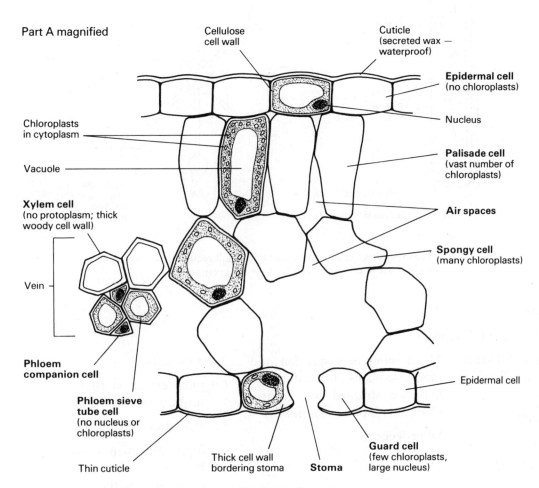

Fig. 4.5 Leaf structure

4.9   AMINO ACID SYNTHESIS

Dependent on photosynthesis.

Nitrates combine with sugar products to from amino acids.

Green plants alone can do this, at root and shoot tips (growing regions).

Amino acids are condensed (see unit 4.12) to form protein.

4.10 MINERAL SALT UPTAKE BY ROOTS

Absorption of salts
Mainly at root tips.
Partly at root hair region (see Fig. 11.1).
Mainly by active transport, partly by diffusion (see unit 5.2). Thus oxygen is needed.
Quite independent of water uptake by osmosis (see unit 5.2).

Evidence for need for salts
Plants are grown with roots in salt-solutions ('water culture').
Control solution contains all salts needed (see unit 4.3).
Test solutions each omit one element, e.g. − N = omit nitrates; − S = omit sulphates.
Solutions aerated to allow efficient salt uptake.

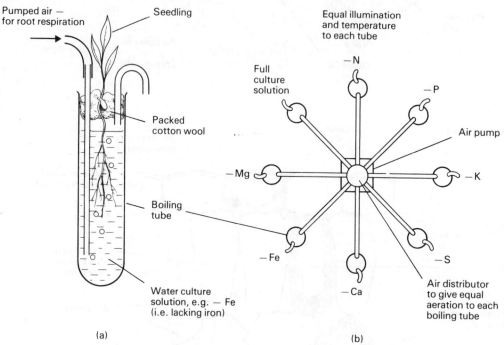

(a)   (b)

Fig. 4.6 Water culture experiment to determine the mineral salt requirements of a plant:
(a) side view of one tube, (b) plan view of experiment

HOLOZOIC NUTRITION

4.11 FEEDING METHODS OF ANIMALS

Animals obtain food in one of three ways:

1 As solids: food-organisms that have to be chewed (Fig. 4.7) small enough to be ingested.

Herbivores – eat plants

Carnivores – eat animals

Omnivores – eat plants and animals

2 As solids in suspension: tiny food-organisms in water that must be strained out of it – plankton (plants and animals)

Filter-feeders

3 As liquids:

(*a*) juices extracted from living hosts, without killing them.

Parasites (see unit 17.10)

(*b*) liquid nutriment produced by digesting dead food externally and then sucking it up

Saprozoites, e.g. housefly (Fig. 4.10)

Adaptations necessary for each feeding method
1 Herbivores: food does not run away, but large quantities must be gathered since food is relatively poor in quality. Herbivores include locusts, deer and sheep.

2 Carnivores: have to capture and overcome prey, e.g. by cunning (dogs), traps (spiders' webs), poisons (cobras) and sharp weapons (claws, teeth). (See Fig. 4.14.)

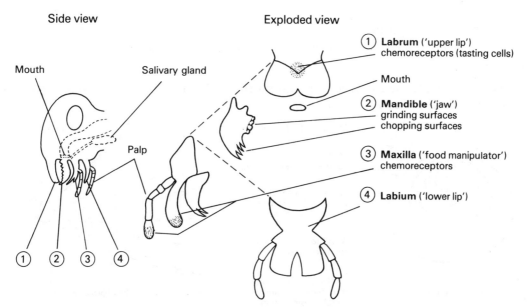

Fig. 4.7 Mouthparts of a chewing insect, e.g. locust (herbivore), cockroach (omnivore), ground beetle (carnivore)

3 Omnivores: adaptations for feeding are intermediate between those of herbivores and carnivores, e.g. human teeth. Often very successful animals since they vary their food according to availability, e.g. cockroaches, rats, pigs and man.

4 Filter feeders: require sieves. (Figs. 4.8a and 4.8b.) Baleen whales trap 'krill' (shrimps) on frayed edges of whale-bone plates hanging down in mouth cavity, open to the sea as they swim.

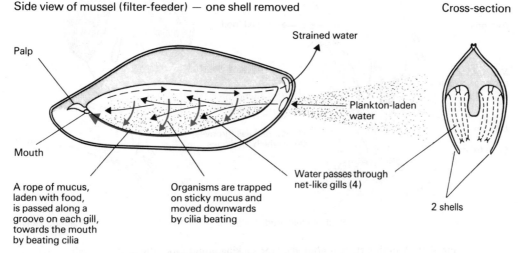

Fig. 4.8a Filter feeding in mussels

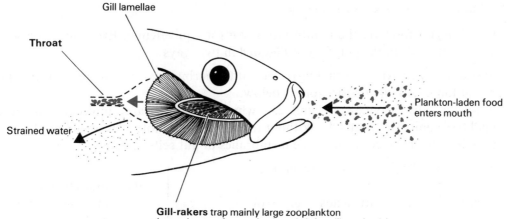

Fig. 4.8b Filter feeding in herring (one gill of its four pairs displayed)

5   Parasites: Endo-parasites bathe in nutritious liquids, e.g. blood or digested food in gut of host, absorbing food directly through 'skin' – no gut, e.g. Trypanosome, tape-worm (see unit 17.11).

Ecto-parasites pierce their host to suck out nutritious liquids, e.g. mosquito, flea (blood); aphid (phloem sap). (See Fig. 4.9.)

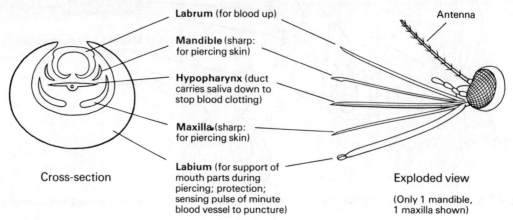

Fig. 4.9 Mouthparts (proboscis) of female mosquito – for piercing skin and sucking blood

6   Saprozoites: need no jaws, only tubes for saliva (down) and liquid food (up), with pumps (see Fig. 4.10).

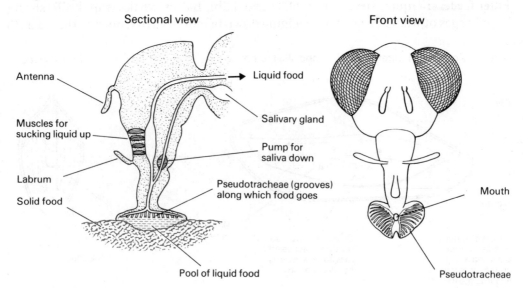

Fig. 4.10 Mouthparts of a housefly – for sucking liquid food (digested externally)

4.12   DIGESTION AND ITS CONSEQUENCES

All animals **ingest** food via the mouth into a gut (or equivalents). Exceptions: parasites which bathe in food. In the gut, food is **digested** in two ways:

(a) *physically* – by chewing or grinding (important in herbivores). This increases the surface area of food, making it easier for (b) below.

(b) *chemically* – by enzymes (see unit 2.4) which hydrolyse large molecules into their small basic units (see unit 4.4). Without this, large food molecules would not be small enough to be **absorbed** through the membranes of gut cells: e.g.

$$\text{starch} + \text{water} \xrightarrow[\text{enzymes}]{\text{hydrolysing}} \text{monosaccharides}$$

$$\text{fat} + \text{water} \xrightarrow[\text{enzymes}]{\text{hydrolysing}} \text{fatty acids} + \text{glycerol}$$

$$\text{protein} + \text{water} \xrightarrow[\text{enzymes}]{\text{hydrolysing}} \text{amino acids}$$

} these molecules are now small enough for absorption

Absorbed food is then **assimilated** (used or stored) into the body. Storage occurs when enzymes condense the small units of foods into large molecules (reverse of hydrolysis). For example:

$$\text{amino acids} \xrightarrow[\text{enzymes}]{\text{condensing}} \text{protein} + \text{water}$$

Indigestible food is **egested** (eliminated) through the anus or equivalent. Most animals have no enzymes to digest cellulose – hence special adaptations of herbivores. (See unit 4.17.)

4.13   EXPERIMENTS WITH DIGESTIVE ENZYMES

Each enzyme works best at a certain temperature and pH (these are its 'optimum' conditions). Outside these conditions enzymes may cease to work or may even be destroyed.

Example 1   Investigating the effect of temperature on digestion of starch by salivary amylase (ptyalin).

Method:

1   Add 5 cm³ of 1% starch solution to each of 5 boiling tubes and 1 cm³ of saliva diluted with water to 4 test tubes as shown in Fig. 4.11a.

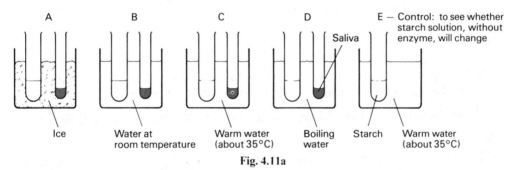

Fig. 4.11a

2   Leave the starch and the enzyme for at least two mintues, to gain the temperature of the water bath.

3   Pour the saliva into the boiling tube next to it, so mixing it with the starch. Note the time immediately.

4   Using a separate dropper for each tube, test one drop from each boiling tube with iodine, as shown in Fig. 4.11b.

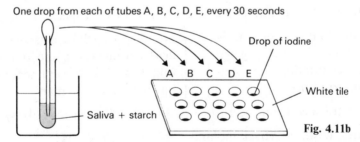

Fig. 4.11b

5   Note the time when each drop no longer turns the iodine blue-black (i.e. starch is digested). Do not test for longer than 15 minutes.

Results:

A – still blue-black after 15 minutes   D – still blue-black after 15 minutes
B – changes to brown at 8 minutes   E – still blue-black after 15 minutes
C – changes to brown at 2 minutes

6   Now put the boiling tubes from A and D into the warm water bath C and test them with iodine after 5 minutes (once only).

Results:

A – brown colour   D – blue-black

Conclusions:

1 Digestion proceeds faster at warm temperatures than at cold (A, B, C).

2 At low temperatures, the enzyme is inactive but not destroyed (A, step **6**).

3 At water's boiling point, the enzyme is destroyed (D, step **6**).

Example 2   Investigating the effect of pH on digestion of egg albumen (protein) by pepsin.

Method:

1 Put in each of 6 tubes a 5 mm cube of cooked egg white and a thymol crystal (to prevent bacteria digesting the egg). Then add 2 cm³ of M/10 solutions to affect the pH. as shown in Fig. 4.12.

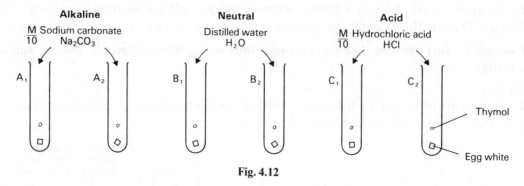

Fig. 4.12

2 Add 2 cm³ pepsin solution to A_1, B_1 and C_1, but not to A_2, B_2 and C_2 (which are controls used to see whether Na_2CO_3, water and HCl alone, digest egg white).

3 Incubate the tubes in a warm place (about 35°C) for 24 hours and then look at the cubes.

Results:

Not digested:
in tubes A_1, A_2, B_2, C_2
Sharp edges

Slightly digested:
in tube B_1
Smaller cube
with fuzzy edges

Totally digested:
in tube C_1
Cube absent

Conclusion: pepsin requires acid conditions to digest cooked albumen.

4.14   MAMMAL TEETH AND DENTAL CARE

Only vertebrate group with *differentiated* teeth (4 types with special uses):

1 Incisors – for obtaining mouthfuls
2 Canines – for stabbing, holding prey
3 Pre-molars – for grinding
4 Molars – for grinding

Number of each kind can be expressed in a **dental formula:** top line for number in upper half-jaw, lower line for lower half-jaw, e.g. for man:

First set of teeth are shed ('milk teeth'): I_2^2 C_1^1 Pm_2^2 (no molars)

Adult set includes 'wisdoms' (back molars): I_2^2 C_1^1 Pm_2^2 M_3^3

Structure of teeth: layers of modified bone nourished from pulp cavity and shaped according to function. (See Fig. 4.13.)

Dental health

1 To grow healthy teeth requires adequate calcium and traces of fluoride (see unit 4.3).

2 To maintain healthy teeth and discourage activities of mouth bacteria:

(*a*) *brush teeth* with fluoride toothpaste after meals to remove food particles and bacteria.

(*b*) *remove sucrose* around teeth. This sugar (in sweets) is turned by bacteria into acids which greatly accelerate tooth decay (caries). Rinse mouth with water.

(*c*) *eat some crisp foods,* e.g. raw carrots. Mild abrasion keeps gums healthy, preventing entry of bacteria to cement allowing teeth to fall out (periodontal disease).

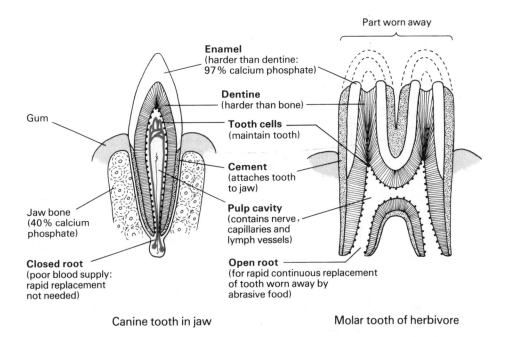

Fig. 4.13 Vertical section through two kinds of teeth

4.15 MAMMAL ALIMENTARY CANAL

See Fig. 4.15 on the next page for the treatment of food from mouth to anus.

4.16 HERBIVORES AND CARNIVORES: TEETH AND JAWS

See Fig. 4.14 for a comparison of teeth and jaws in herbivores and carnivores.

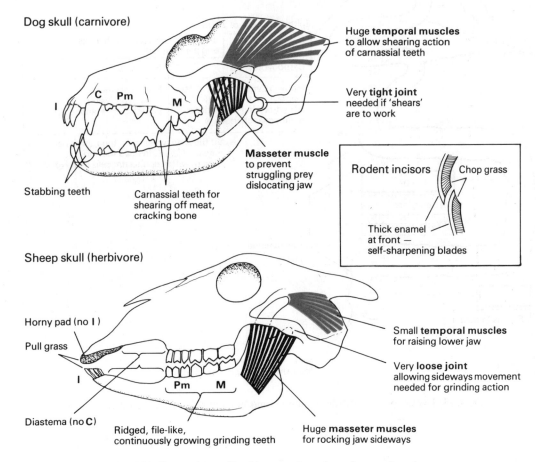

Fig. 4.14 Comparison of herbivore and carnivore jaws and teeth

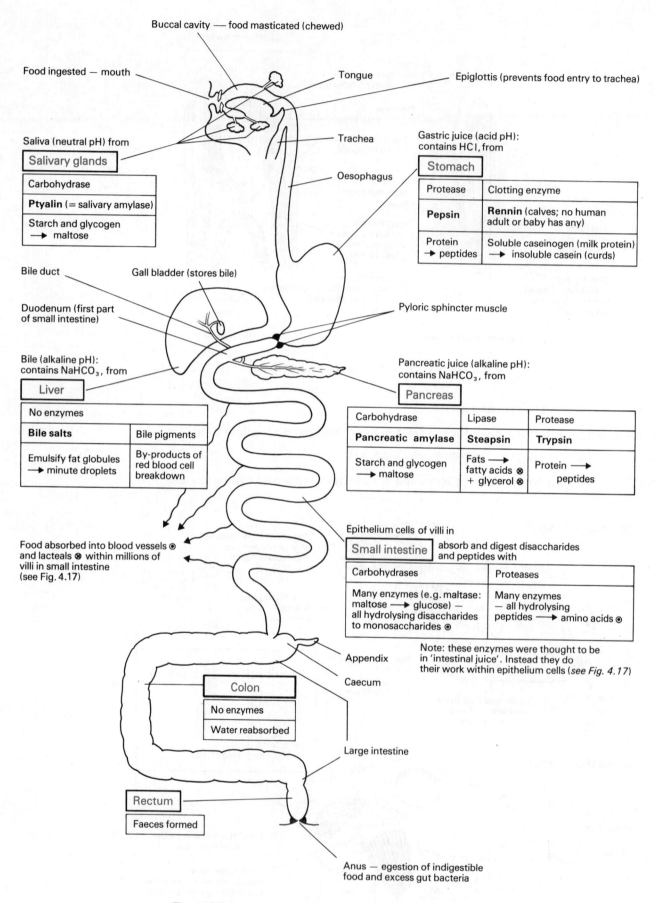

Buccal cavity — food masticated (chewed)

Food ingested — mouth

Tongue

Epiglottis (prevents food entry to trachea)

Trachea

Oesophagus

Saliva (neutral pH) from

Salivary glands
Carbohydrase
Ptyalin (= salivary amylase)
Starch and glycogen $\longrightarrow$ maltose

Gastric juice (acid pH): contains HCl, from

Stomach	
Protease	Clotting enzyme
Pepsin	**Rennin** (calves; no human adult or baby has any)
Protein $\rightarrow$ peptides	Soluble caseinogen (milk protein) $\longrightarrow$ insoluble casein (curds)

Bile duct

Gall bladder (stores bile)

Pyloric sphincter muscle

Duodenum (first part of small intestine)

Pancreatic juice (alkaline pH): contains $NaHCO_3$, from

Bile (alkaline pH): contains $NaHCO_3$, from

Liver	
No enzymes	
Bile salts	Bile pigments
Emulsify fat globules $\longrightarrow$ minute droplets	By-products of red blood cell breakdown

Pancreas		
Carbohydrase	Lipase	Protease
Pancreatic amylase	**Steapsin**	**Trypsin**
Starch and glycogen $\longrightarrow$ maltose	Fats $\longrightarrow$ fatty acids ⊗ + glycerol ⊗	Protein $\longrightarrow$ peptides

Epithelium cells of villi in

Food absorbed into blood vessels ◉ and lacteals ⊗ within millions of villi in small intestine (see Fig. 4.17)

Small intestine	absorb and digest disaccharides and peptides with
Carbohydrases	Proteases
Many enzymes (e.g. maltase: maltose $\longrightarrow$ glucose) — all hydrolysing disaccharides to monosaccharides ◉	Many enzymes — all hydrolysing peptides $\longrightarrow$ amino acids ◉

Appendix

Caecum

Note: these enzymes were thought to be in 'intestinal juice'. Instead they do their work within epithelium cells (*see Fig. 4.17*)

Colon
No enzymes
Water reabsorbed

Large intestine

Rectum
Faeces formed

Anus — egestion of indigestible food and excess gut bacteria

Fig. 4.15 Treatment of food from mouth to anus in mammals (based on man)

4.17 HERBIVORES AND CARNIVORES: THE GUT

Carnivore: gut *short* – food is largely protein so it is easy to digest.

Herbivore: gut *long* – no mammal produces cellulases (cellulose-digesting enzymes). Aid from bacteria which have *cellulases,* living in symbiosis (see unit 15.3) in *rumen* of ruminants, e.g. cows, sheep; or *caecum*, e.g. of horses, rabbits. Rabbits eat their green nutritious faeces from first passage through gut ('refection'), absorbing more food during second passage. Horses do not refect (see Fig. 4.16).

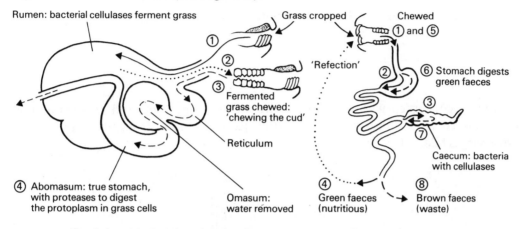

Rumen: bacterial cellulases ferment grass
Grass cropped
Chewed ① and ⑤
'Refection'
② ⑥ Stomach digests green faeces
③
⑦
Fermented grass chewed: 'chewing the cud'
Reticulum
Caecum: bacteria with cellulases
④ Abomasum: true stomach, with proteases to digest the protoplasm in grass cells
Omasum: water removed
④ Green faeces (nutritious)
⑧ Brown faeces (waste)

Cow's large 4-chambered stomach　　　**Rabbit's large caecum**

Fig. 4.16 Adaptations to herbivorous diet

4.18 ABSORPTION OF FOOD AT A VILLUS

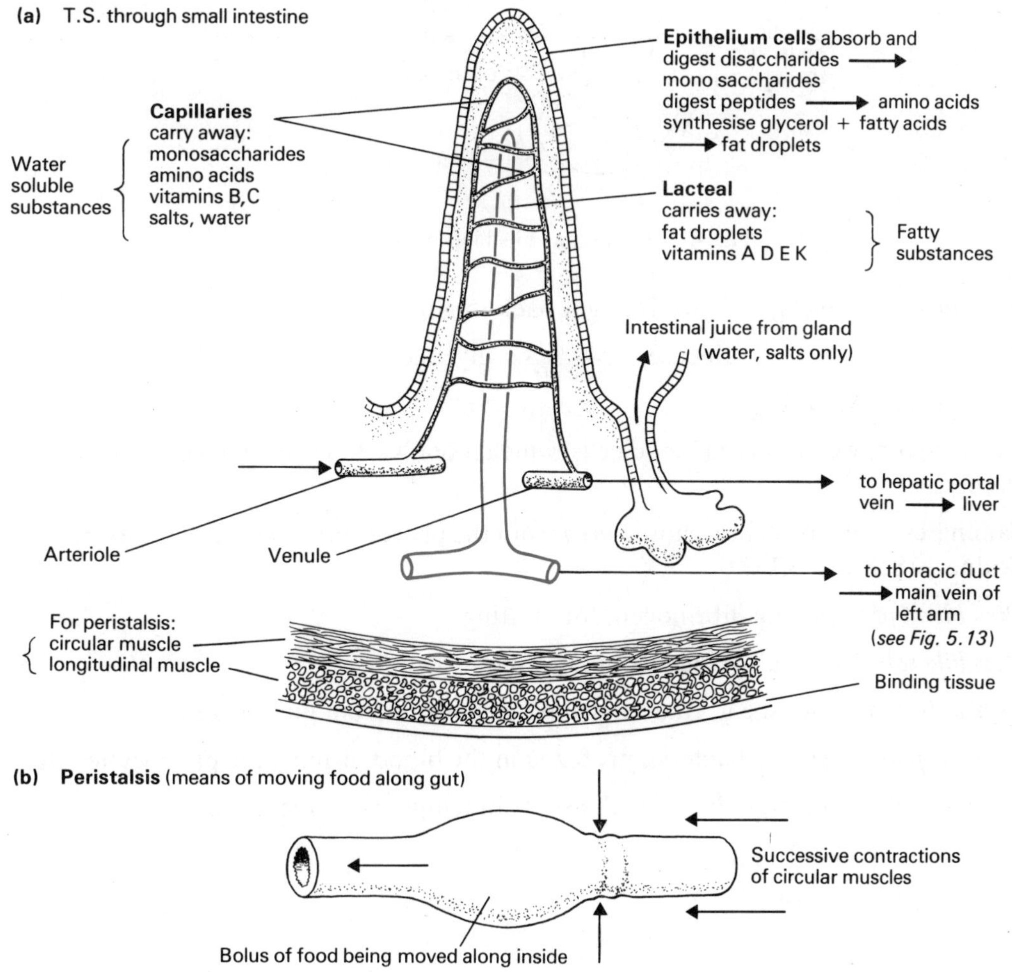

(a) T.S. through small intestine

Epithelium cells absorb and digest disaccharides ⟶ mono saccharides
digest peptides ⟶ amino acids
synthesise glycerol + fatty acids ⟶ fat droplets

Capillaries carry away: monosaccharides amino acids vitamins B,C salts, water

Water soluble substances

Lacteal carries away: fat droplets vitamins A D E K — Fatty substances

Intestinal juice from gland (water, salts only)

Arteriole　　　Venule

to hepatic portal vein ⟶ liver

to thoracic duct ⟶ main vein of left arm (*see Fig. 5.13*)

For peristalsis: circular muscle longitudinal muscle

Binding tissue

(b) **Peristalsis** (means of moving food along gut)

Successive contractions of circular muscles

Bolus of food being moved along inside

Fig. 4.17 (a) Enlarged longitudinal section of a villus (millions lining the small intestine)　(b) Peristalsis

4.19   STORAGE OF FOOD

1 Monosaccharides, e.g. glucose: condensed to glycogen in liver and muscles, excess converted to fats stored under skin.

2 Fatty substances: stored in liver (including vitamins A, D) and under skin.

3 Amino acids: used immediately, *not* stored; excess de-aminated in liver to give two parts:

  (*a*) nitrogen-containing part (amine) becomes urea – excreted by kidneys;
  (*b*) remainder (the acid) can be respired to give energy

4.20   THE LIVER

A large organ, concerned with homeostasis by metabolising food and poisons and re-moving unwanted cells. Stores foods and blood. Receives blood from two sources (Fig. 4.18); discharges bile.

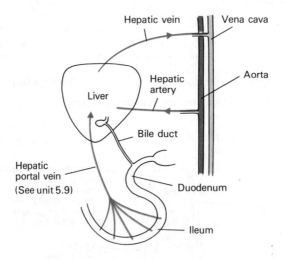

Fig. 4.18 The liver and its blood supply

1 Stores *glucose* as glycogen, hydrolysing it back to glucose when needed:

$$\text{glucose} \underset{\text{adrenalin}}{\overset{\text{insulin}}{\rightleftharpoons}} \text{glycogen}$$

2 Stores *vitamins* A, D, B_{12}.

3 Stores *iron* from worn-out red blood cells, which it breaks down, excreting *bile pigments* in the process.

4 De-aminates excess proteins sending *urea* from the process into the blood for excretion by the kidneys (See unit 4.19).

5 Makes *blood proteins*. e.g. fibrinogen, for clotting.

6 Makes *bile salts* for emulsifying fats in intestine.

7 Makes *poisons* harmless, e.g. ethanol drunk, or poisons from gut bacteria.

8 Filters out *pathogens*, e.g. bacteria, protozoa in the blood, using large phagocytic cells.

9 Produces *heat* from metabolism which assists in temperature regulation.

4.21   DIET

A **balanced diet** is one that maintains health. It differs according to *age* (baby or adult); *oc-cupation* (manual worker or typist); *climate* (Arctic or tropical); *sex*. A diet must provide:

(*a*) energy (carbohydrates and fats). Manual worker uses 24 000 kJ/day, typist uses 12 000 kJ/day

(*b*) materials for growth and repair (proteins). (See note below)

(*c*) co-factors for enzymes to work (vitamins). (See unit 4.5)

(*d*) salts (e.g. for bone growth or to replace those lost in sweat) (See unit 4.3)

(*e*) water (See unit 5.1)

(*f*) roughage (indigestible 'bulk' to help peristalsis), e.g cellulose walls in plant food.

Note: first class proteins contain the 8 amino acids that man cannot make. Animal protein is rich in them, plant protein usually poor. Without them, *kwashiorkor* results (wasting of limbs, pot-belly full of fluid). Occurs in maize-eating Africans eating only second class protein. Beans are richer in first class protein than maize.

SAPROPHYTIC NUTRITION

4.22 SAPROPHYTES

See examples of fungi (unit 17.5) and bacteria (unit 17.2). Note some similarity with saprozoite method of feeding (see unit 14.11).

5 Water and transport systems

5.1 IMPORTANCE OF WATER

Water makes up two-thirds or more of living active protoplasm:

Solvent:

(*a*) all *reactions* of metabolism occur in solution.

(*b*) foods, hormones, etc. are *transported* in solution (in blood, sap).

Reactant:

(*a*) with CO_2 during *photosynthesis*.

(*b*) in *hydrolysis* reactions, e.g. digestion.

Coolant:

(*a*) *absorbs a lot of heat* without much change in temperature, thus keeping habitats like the sea relatively stable in temperature.

(*b*) *removes a lot of heat* when evaporated, keeping bodies cool, e.g. in sweating, transpiration.

Support:

(*a*) aquatic organisms need less strong skeletons than land organisms because *Archimedes force* makes them 'lighter'.

(*b*) *turgor pressure* in plant cells supports leaves and herbaceous plant stems; without it they wilt.

Lubricant:

E.g. synovial fluid in joints; mucus in guts.

5.2 DIFFUSION, ACTIVE TRANSPORT AND OSMOSIS

Substances move into cells by:

1 Diffusion (gases and liquids)

2 Active transport

3 Osmosis (water)

Table 5.1 Comparison of diffusion and active transport

Diffusion	Active transport
Not selective	Selective (cell only absorbs what it wants)
Substances move only *along* a concentration gradient	Substances move in even *against* a concentration gradient
Living membrane not essential	Living membrane essential
Cell provides no energy	Respiration provides energy for absorption

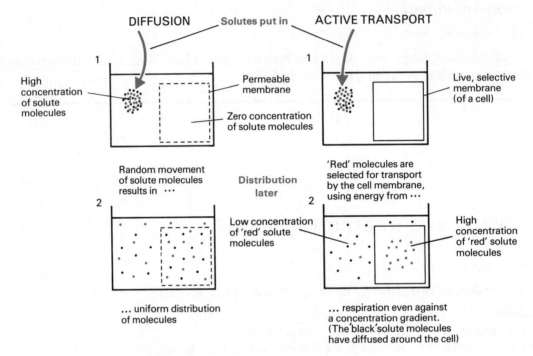

Fig. 5.1 Diffusion contrasted with active transport

Osmosis: the diffusion of water *only*, through a 'semi-permeable' membrane from a weak solution to a strong one (see Fig. 5.2).

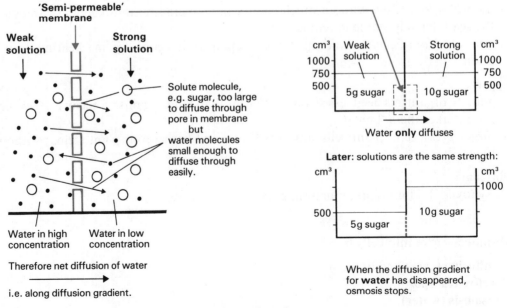

Fig. 5.2 Osmosis

Requires *no* respiration (cf. active uptake of salts in roots).

Requires *live* cell membrane for osmosis to occur in cells, but will happen with suitable non-living membranes.

All solutions have an **osmotic potential** (which can be measured as an **osmotic pressure** using a manometer. See Fig. 5.3).

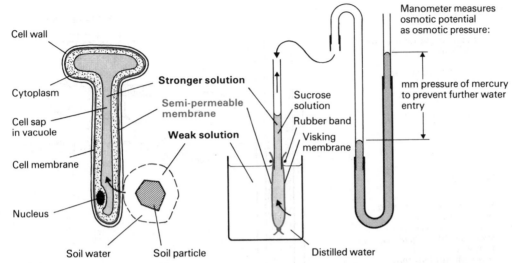

Fig. 5.3 Comparison of osmosis in a living cell (root hair) and a non-living system

Cells prevent continued flow of water into them (which would burst them) by **osmoregulating.**

ANGIOSPERMS

5.3   WATER UPTAKE AND LOSS IN ANGIOSPERMS

Cells

Cells fluctuate between being flaccid and fully turgid in nature. However plasmolysis is relatively rare (except in experiments) and will result in the cell's death if it is prolonged e.g. when the cell suffers prolonged drying (see Fig. 5.4).

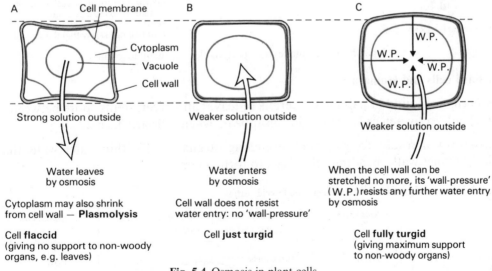

Fig. 5.4 Osmosis in plant cells

Whole plants

1   Leaves and green stems are waterproofed by a waxy *cuticle*, but most keep open *stomata* to get CO_2 for photosynthesis. Through stomata, **transpiration** (the loss of water vapour via the aerial parts of a plant) occurs. This creates a *suction upward* of water from below.

2   Old stems and roots are waterproofed with cork (of bark). Their xylem acts as a conduit for water. Some water-loss occurs via *lenticels* (pores in bark).

3 Young roots – particularly *root-hair* region – absorb water by osmosis. This continues owing to suction generated by transpiration.

If soil water supply dries up, leaf cells become flaccid and leaf *wilts*. Only *after* this will guard cells become flaccid, closing stomata, thus conserving water but also stopping photosynthesis (see unit 4.7 and Fig. 5.5).

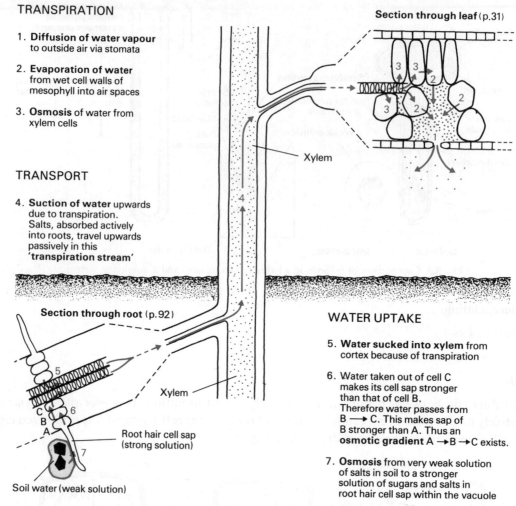

TRANSPIRATION

1. **Diffusion of water vapour** to outside air via stomata

2. **Evaporation of water** from wet cell walls of mesophyll into air spaces

3. **Osmosis** of water from xylem cells

TRANSPORT

4. **Suction of water** upwards due to transpiration. Salts, absorbed actively into roots, travel upwards passively in this **'transpiration stream'**

Section through leaf (p.31)

Xylem

Section through root (p.92)

Xylem

Root hair cell sap (strong solution)

Soil water (weak solution)

WATER UPTAKE

5. **Water sucked into xylem** from cortex because of transpiration

6. Water taken out of cell C makes its cell sap stronger than that of cell B. Therefore water passes from B ⟶ C. This makes sap of B stronger than A. Thus an **osmotic gradient** A ⟶ B ⟶ C exists.

7. **Osmosis** from very weak solution of salts in soil to a stronger solution of sugars and salts in root hair cell sap within the vacuole

Fig. 5.5 Water uptake, transport and loss in an angiosperm

4 Guard cells and stomata

Guard cells are found in pairs in epidermis of leaves and green stems; pore between them (*stoma*) enlarges when cells are turgid; disappears when cells are flaccid.

Open stoma results from greater stretching of guard cells' thin outer walls than of thickened inner walls, bending cells apart to form a pore.

Table 5.2 Features of guard cells in the turgid and flaccid states

	Stoma open	*Surface view of two guard cells in the turgid and flaccid states*	*Stoma closed*
Osmotic potential of cell sap	High	Turgid cells / Flaccid cells	Low
Turgidity	Turgid		Flaccid
Gas exchange and transpiration	Possible		Impossible
Normal rhythm	Open in day	Open stoma / Closed stoma	Closed at night

5.4   Transpiration

Loss of water by transpiration occurs:

(*i*) mainly through open stomata

(*ii*) through waxy cuticle (a small amount)

Functions:

(*i*) provides a means of transporting salts upward in xylem

(*ii*) evaporation cools the leaf heated by the sun (cf. sweating).

Factors raising transpiration rate (opposite conditions lower the rate)

1 High temperature – provides more energy to evaporate water.

2 Low humidity – greater diffusion gradient between air inside leaf spaces and the drier air outside.

3 Open stomata – thousands of pores per leaf (usually open in *sunlight*).

4 Wind – removes water molecules as fast as they arrive outside stomata, thereby maintaining high diffusion rate. Water vapour 'pumped out' due to bending and unbending of leaf. (Severe buffeting by wind actually closes stomata, reducing transpiration.)

Measurement of transpiration rate

(Temperature, humidity, and wind must be recorded.)

1 Weighing – a leaf, or cut shoot, in a test-tube of water covered by oil; or a whole pot plant, the pot and soil sealed off in a polythene bag.

2 Cobalt chloride – blue when anhydrous (dry), turns pink when hydrated (moist). Thus dry blue cobalt chloride paper, sellotaped to upper and lower leaf surfaces, green stems and bark-covered stems turns pink with moisture of transpiration. Timing how long it takes compares rates.

3 Potometer – measures water uptake (not loss) of a cut shoot (a little of the water is used in photosynthesis). Change *one* condition at a time to determine which factor has greatest effect.

Note: light and dark affect opening and closing of stomata. Light may also have a heating effect.

Allow time for plant to adjust to new conditions before taking new measurement of rate.

Never allow air to get into cut end of shoot (air locks form in xylem) – cut shoot under water, and keep the cut wet (see Fig. 5.6).

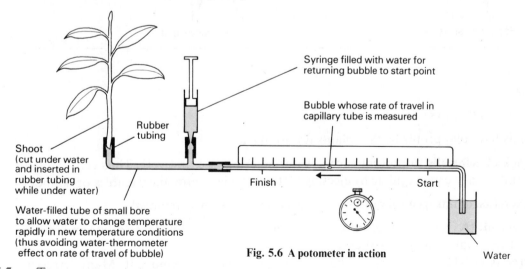

Syringe filled with water for returning bubble to start point

Bubble whose rate of travel in capillary tube is measured

Rubber tubing

Shoot (cut under water and inserted in rubber tubing while under water)

Finish   Start

Water-filled tube of small bore to allow water to change temperature rapidly in new temperature conditions (thus avoiding water-thermometer effect on rate of travel of bubble)

Fig. 5.6 A potometer in action

Water

5.5   Transport of organic food

Flows through **phloem** sieve tube cells in bark (see Table 5.3). Flow rate affected by temperature, available oxygen, poisons – suggests a mechanism involving *living* cells. Mechanism not fully understood.

Flows both *upwards and downwards*. Photosynthesised sugars transported as sucrose (see unit 4.4) from leaves up to stem tips (for growth); to fruits and seeds (for storage as starch); down to root tips (for growth); and to or from storage organs, e.g. tubers (see unit 12.2).

Evidence for pathway:

Ring barking: sugars accumulate where bark ends (due to cutting).

Tracers: radioactive $^{14}CO_2$ supplied to photosynthesising leaf becomes part of sucrose (or other organic molecules), the paths of which can be traced with a Geiger counter.

Table 5.3 Comparison of methods of transport in phloem and xylem

	Phloem (sieve tubes)	*Xylem* (vessels)
Transport	Sugars, amino acids, etc.	Water and salts
Direction	Both *downward* from leaves and *upward* from storage organs, e.g. tubers	Only *upward*
Cells	Cellulose tubes with sieve ends, containing cytoplasm but no nucleus	Woody tubes containing no living matter. Wood is strong and provides support too

Sectioned sieve cell — Strands of cytoplasm; Pores in end wall; Thin cellulose cell wall (not strong); Organic food flows upwards and downwards in solution

Sectioned vessel cell — Thick woody cell wall strengthened further by woody rings — for support of plant; Space free of protoplasm allowing water and salts to flow unhindered upwards

ANIMALS

5.6 WATER UPTAKE AND LOSS IN ANIMALS

Animals have two problems that plants do not have:

1 Lack of cell walls to prevent excess water entering (see unit 2.1). Thus cells liable to burst unless they osmoregulate by ejecting water, e.g. via contractile vacuoles or 'kidneys'.

2 Excretion of nitrogenous wastes which need water for their removal:

(*a*) **ammonia** (NH_3) – very poisonous; needs large quantities of water to dilute and remove it. Fresh-water animals particularly.

(*b*) **urea** ($CO(NH_2)_2$) – less poisonous; needs some water to remove it. Many terrestrial animals, e.g. mammals.

(*c*) **uric acid** – not poisonous, since insoluble; can be removed as a paste. Essential for all animals laying eggs on land to avoid poisoning of embryo, e.g. insects, birds. Very little water wasted.

Like plants, animals have three problems: **obtaining** water, **conserving** what has been obtained and **removing excess** water that has entered. These problems and their solutions differ according to the animal and the habitat in which it lives (see Fig. 5.7).

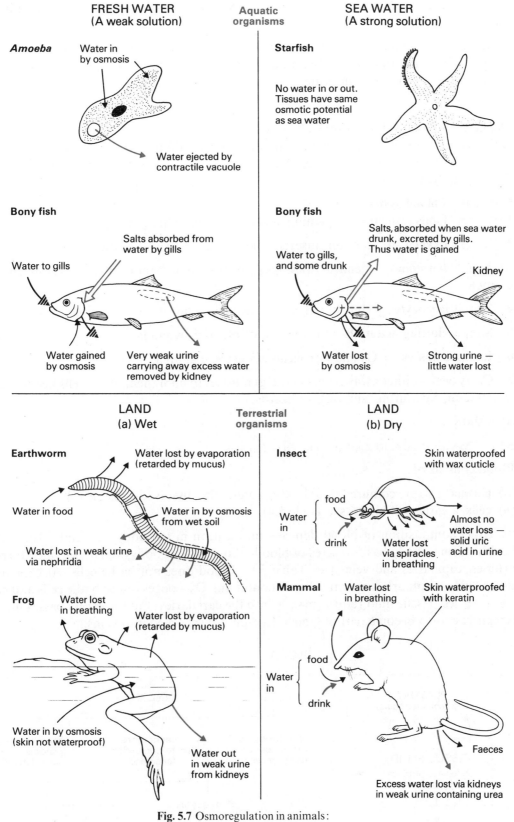

Fig. 5.7 Osmoregulation in animals:
→ problem created by animal's environment
→ corrective measures employed by animal

1 In **fresh water**, water *enters* by osmosis, tending to flood tissues since they have a higher osmotic potential than their external surroundings.

2   In **sea water**, the water inside tissues tends to *leave* by osmosis into the sea since its salty water has a higher osmotic potential than tissues in many cases.

3   In **wet-land** habitats, water still *enters* tissues by osmosis through non-waterproof skin, but there is the hazard of desiccation in the air. Such animals do not drink but can gain some water from food.

4   In **dry-land** habitats, animals must have waterproof skins to prevent desiccation in the air, replacing what they lose in breathing and excreta by *drinking*. Egg-layers excrete uric acid, so little water is lost in urine.

5.7   BLOOD SYSTEMS

The need for blood pumped to cells by a heart
Animals are more active than plants and diffusion would be too slow to supply cells with their needs and remove their wastes. A more *rapid transport system* is necessary to prevent them from dying.

Functions of blood systems
1   Supply **foods** – sugars, fats, amino acids, vitamins, salts, water.

2   Supply **oxygen** – (exception: insects – oxygen direct to cells at tracheoles).

3   Supply **hormones** – chemical 'messages' controlling metabolism and development (see unit 9.8).

4   Supply **leucocytes** – white blood cells for defence against invading organisms.

5   Supply **clotting materials** – to stop loss of blood at wounds.

6   Remove **wastes** – CO_2 and nitrogenous wastes, e.g. urea.

7   Carry **heat** – either away from cells, e.g. muscle, to cool them, or to cells needing to be warmed up, e.g. during 'sunning' of lizards.

MAMMALS

5.8   MAMMAL BLOOD AND OTHER BODY FLUIDS

Blood consists of:

(*a*)   **plasma**, a straw-coloured liquid (90% water, 10% dissolved substances);
(*b*)   **cells**, a variety of kinds (see Table 5.4).

Exact composition of blood depends on location in the body (see unit 5.10) and on health. Human body has 5–6 litres of blood, about 10% of body-weight, pumped through arteries, capillaries and veins (see Table 5.5). Blood does not bathe cells. At capillaries, **tissue fluid** – a colourless nutritive liquid containing O_2 – oozes out to bathe cells and carry away wastes. Tissue fluid returns mainly into the capillaries; but the excess passes into the lymph vessels to become part of **lymph**. Lymph is discharged into veins.

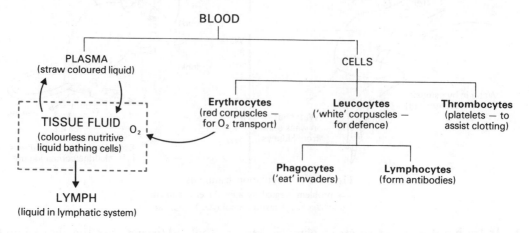

Fig 5.8 Constituents of blood and their functions

Serum is plasma less fibrinogen (protein needed for clotting). Stored by hospitals for transfusions.

Plasma consists of:

1 Water – (90%) solvent for substances listed below; carrier of heat (for temperature regulation).

2 Blood proteins – (7%) e.g. fibrinogen (for blood clotting); antibodies (for defence against pathogens); and albumen (for osmosis, Fig. 5.14).

3 Soluble foods – (1%) e.g. glucose, oil droplets, amino acids (from digestion).

4 Mineral salts – as ions, e.g. Na^+, Cl^-, Ca^{2+}, HCO_3^- (bicarbonate, the main method of transporting CO_2).

5 Wastes – e.g. CO_2, urea.

6 Hormones – in minute traces, e.g. adrenalin and insulin.

7 Gases – small quantities of, e.g. O_2, N_2.

Table 5.4 Blood cells and their functions

Cell structure		No./mm³	Formation	Destruction	Function of cells
Erythrocyte side view	Bi-concave cell with no nucleus. Cytoplasm: mainly red haemoglobin	5 million (more at high altitudes)	In red bone marrow, e.g. of ribs, vertebrae	In liver – by-product: bile pigments Life: 2–3 months	1 Haemoglobin (Hb) combines with O_2 to form unstable oxyhaemoglobin ($Hb.O_2$) at lungs – Passes **oxygen to tissues** 2 O_2 detaches from Hb at capillaries, diffusing into the tissue fluid going to cells (see unit 6.6) $$Hb + O_2 \underset{\text{tissues}}{\overset{\text{lungs}}{\rightleftharpoons}} Hb.O_2$$
Phagocyte	Multi-lobed nucleus in granular cytoplasm, engulfs bacteria	7000 (more during infections)	In red bone marrow		Actively seek and **engulf bacteria** – even squeeze through capillary walls to reach infected tissue. Often die loaded with killed bacteria. In boils this is seen as yellow 'pus'
Lymphocyte	Huge nucleus in little cytoplasm	2–3000 (more during infections)	In lymph nodes		React to proteins of invading organisms by making **'antibodies'**, which kill invaders and make their poisons (toxins) harmless (see unit 16.11)
Thrombocyte	Platelets are fragments of cells	¼ million	In red bone marrow		1 At cut, stick to each other forming **temporary plug** 2 Liberate enzyme thrombokinase to promote **clotting**: (a) prothrombin $\xrightarrow[\text{presence of Ca}^{2+}]{\text{thrombokinase in}}$ thrombin (inactive enzyme) (active enzyme) (b) fibrinogen $\xrightarrow{\text{thrombin}}$ fibrin (soluble protein) (mesh of fibres) (c) fibrin traps blood cells which seal up the blood leak, prevent entry of harmful organisms, and dry to a protective *scab*, allowing healing of the wound beneath it

Notes:

1 Haemoglobin has a greater affinity for carbon monoxide (CO) than O_2 (230 times greater) forming a stable compound, **carboxy-haemoglobin** (Hb . CO) with it. Thus even at small concentrations in the air, CO (which is odourless) tends to be taken up into the blood, preventing O_2 from being carried. This can kill.

2 Haemophiliacs ('bleeders') continue to bleed – perhaps to death – even after minor wounding, e.g. tooth extraction. They have platelets but lack a certain other clotting factor. Effects in males only, who usually die young (see unit 13.10).

5.9 HEART, BLOOD VESSELS AND CIRCULATORY SYSTEM

Table 5.5 Blood vessels and their functions

Arteries	Capillaries	Veins
Carry blood *away* from heart under *high* pressure	Carry blood from artery to vein, very slowly, giving maximum time for diffusion, through a huge surface area	Carry blood *towards* heart under *low* pressure
Carry *oxygenated* blood (except pulmonary artery)		Carry *deoxygenated* blood (except pulmonary vein)

T.S. — Elastic layer — Endothelium — Elastic and muscle layer

(a) Heart refilling; elastic walls squeezing on blood to help it along
(b) Heart pumping; 'pulse' felt as bore expands. Thick walls needed, but no valves

Bore of arteries can be altered by nerve messages to muscle, e.g., more blood to legs and less to guts during exercise.

Endothelium only — Phagocyte emerging between cells of endothelium — 10μm

Tissue fluid leaking out to cells – blood pressure forcing it through

T.S. — L.S. — (a) free flow (b) back-pressure

No pulse: pressure is low at capillaries. Wall has 3 layers as in arteries but is thinner

Valve open — Valve closed

Blood returns partly by muscles of body squeezing veins – hence the need for non-return valves

Portal veins have capillaries at either end, i.e. they carry blood from one organ to another (e.g. hepatic portal vein between small intestine and liver).

The heart

Found between the two lungs inside the chest cavity

Consists of two pumps fused together, each having an *auricle* (= atrium) and a *ventricle*.

The two pumps contract simultaneously according to a heart cycle (Fig. 5.14).

Right one pumps deoxygenated blood to the lungs for oxygenation.

Left one pumps oxygenated blood to the body, which deoxygenates it.

Thus blood passes twice through the heart before going to the body (see Fig. 5.9).
The resulting high blood pressure ensures:

(*a*) speedy supplies to the tissues;
(*b*) squeezing out tissue fluid at capillaries.

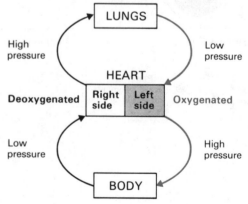

Fig. 5.9 Double circulation of blood through the heart of a mammal

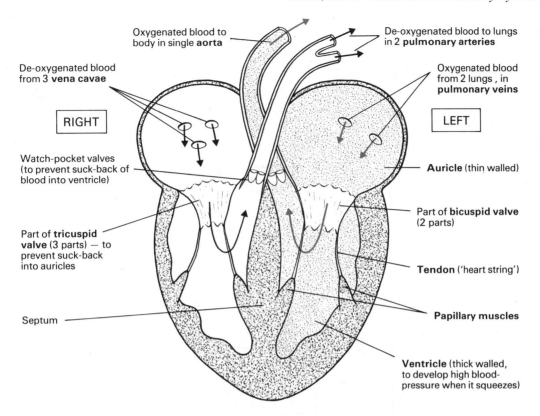

Oxygenated blood to body in single **aorta**

De-oxygenated blood to lungs in 2 **pulmonary arteries**

De-oxygenated blood from 3 **vena cavae**

Oxygenated blood from 2 lungs , in **pulmonary veins**

RIGHT

LEFT

Watch-pocket valves (to prevent suck-back of blood into ventricle)

Auricle (thin walled)

Part of **tricuspid valve** (3 parts) — to prevent suck-back into auricles

Part of **bicuspid valve** (2 parts)

Tendon ('heart string')

Papillary muscles

Septum

Ventricle (thick walled, to develop high blood-pressure when it squeezes)

Fig. 5.10 The mammal heart in section: structure and function

Heart seen from the side during the two stages of contraction (systole)

1. Auricular systole (AS)

2. Ventricular systole (VS)

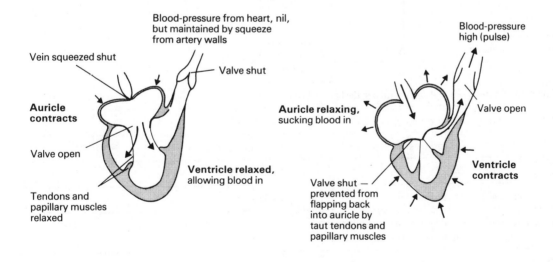

Vein squeezed shut

Blood-pressure from heart, nil, but maintained by squeeze from artery walls

Valve shut

Blood-pressure high (pulse)

Auricle contracts

Auricle relaxing, sucking blood in

Valve open

Valve open

Ventricle relaxed, allowing blood in

Ventricle contracts

Tendons and papillary muscles relaxed

Valve shut — prevented from flapping back into auricle by taut tendons and papillary muscles

3. Diastole

(relaxation of ventricle) follows before the next auricular systole

Duration of heart cycle in man

Diastole

Systoles

0

0.7 sec   0.1 sec

AS

0.6 sec   0.2 sec

VS

0.5 sec   0.3 sec

0.4 sec

Fig. 5.11 The heart cycle of a mammal

5.10   CHANGES IN BLOOD AROUND THE CIRCULATORY SYSTEM

Changes in the composition of blood

As blood passes through the capillaries of organs, it is modified. Blood leaving endocrine glands has gained hormones, while that leaving the kidneys has lost urea and water. Thus *overall* blood composition is kept constant, ensuring that the cells of the body have a constant environment (tissue fluid) to live in.

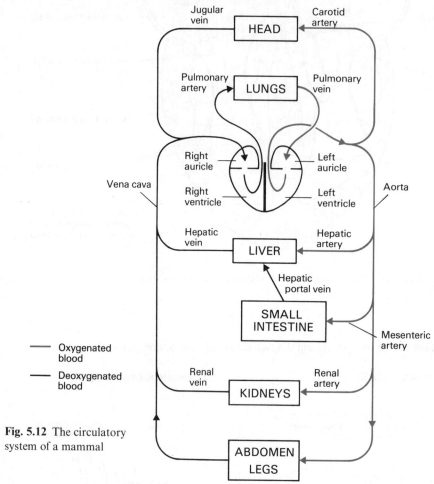

Fig. 5.12 The circulatory system of a mammal

Table 5.6 Changes in blood composition in the human body

Region of body	Blood gains	Blood loses
All tissues	CO_2; nitrogenous wastes	O_2; food; hormones
Lungs	O_2	CO_2; water
Thyroid gland	Thyroxin	Iodine
Small intestine	Food: water, salts, vitamins sugars, amino acids	
Thoracic duct	Fats; lymphocytes; lymph	
Liver	Controlled quantities of glucose and fats; urea	Glucose (for storage as glycogen); excess amino acids; worn out erythrocytes
Kidneys		Urea; water; salts
Spleen	Stores erythrocytes	Worn out erythrocytes
Bones	New erythrocytes and phagocytes	Iron (for haemoglobin) Calcium and phosphate (for bone growth)
Skin	Vitamin D	Heat (by radiation and by evaporation of water in sweat) Salts and urea (in sweat)

5.11   LYMPHATIC SYSTEM

A system of fine tubes ending blindly amongst the tissues, e.g. lacteals in villi of small intestine (see unit 4.18), which join up into ever larger tubes with non-return valves. Along their length are swellings (lymph nodes). The largest tube (thoracic duct) discharges into main vein of left arm.

Functions:

1   Returns excess tissue fluid to blood as lymph.

2   Adds lymphocytes to blood (for defence).

3   Absorbs fats (into lacteals of villi) to discharge them to blood.

4   Filters out bacteria from lymph by means of phagocytes stationary within lymph nodes (see Fig. 5.13).

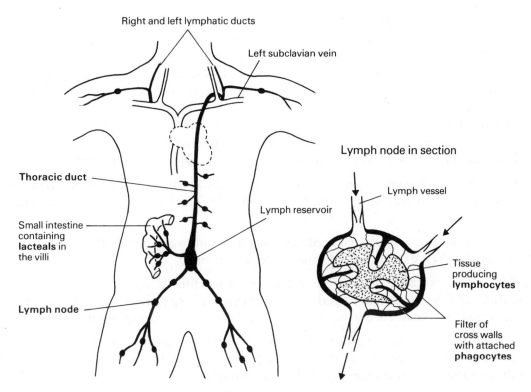

Fig. 5.13 The lymphatic system in man

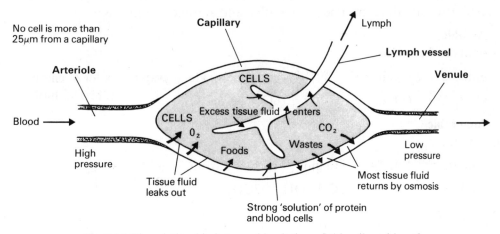

Fig. 5.14 The relationship between blood, tissue fluid, cells and lymph

6 Respiration

6.1   BREATHING, GASEOUS EXCHANGE AND CELLULAR RESPIRATION

Respiration is the sum of processes in organisms that leads to the release of energy from organic molecules, for use in vital functions. *All* organisms respire – plants as well as animals. Thereby they form ATP (see unit 6.9) – energy molecules that power the chemical reactions of metabolism. Depending on the kind of organism, up to *three processes* may be involved:

1   Breathing: *movements*, in animals, that bring a source of O_2 to a surface for gaseous exchange, e.g. chest movements of mammals bring air into lungs; throat movements in fish bring water (containing dissolved O_2) to gills.

2   Gaseous exchange: diffusion, at a moist surface, of O_2 into the organism and of CO_2 outwards.

(*a*) in *single-celled* organisms this exchange surface is the cell membrane (see Fig. 6.8).
(*b*) in *multicellular animals* specialised body parts, e.g. lungs, tracheoles or gills, provide the surface for gaseous exchange. Usually gases are transported rapidly by blood between these surfaces and a second extensive surface area where gaseous exchange occurs between the blood and cells. Only insects pipe air directly to cells and do not use blood for this purpose (see Fig. 6.11).
(*c*) in *multicellular plants* a network of air spaces *between* cells allows for direct gaseous exchange between cells and the air. There is no blood system.
Thus gaseous *exchange* occurs only when organisms respire using oxygen.

3   Cellular respiration (= internal respiration): the chemical reactions occurring within cells that result in the release of energy to form ATP. These reactions can occur under two conditions:

(*a*) anaerobically – no oxygen needed (thus **1** and **2** above unnecessary).
(*b*) aerobically – oxygen needed (thus **2** above essential).

Note: since breathing and gaseous exchange are essentially *physical* processes occurring *outside* cells, they are often lumped together as **external respiration** to distinguish them from the *chemical* processes occurring *within* cells which are **internal respiration**.

Unfortunately the terms above are often used loosely in examinations, e.g. since *Amoeba,* the earthworm and the flowering plant do not make *movements* to gain O_2, strictly speaking they do not *breathe* but they do respire.

6.2   INTERNAL RESPIRATION (AEROBIC AND ANAEROBIC)

Glucose is the main substance respired (other foods can be turned into glucose). The results of respiration are different under anaerobic and aerobic conditions:

1   Aerobic
In plants and animals:

$$\text{glucose} + \text{oxygen} \xrightarrow{\text{enzymes in mitochondria}} \text{carbon dioxide} + \text{water} + \textbf{a lot of energy}$$
$$C_6H_{12}O_6 + 6O_2 \qquad\qquad 6CO_2 + 6H_2O \qquad \text{(2890 kJ/mole)}$$

2   Anaerobic
(*a*) in plants:

$$\text{glucose} \xrightarrow[\text{matrix}]{\text{enzymes in cytoplasmic}} \text{ethanol} + \text{carbon dioxide} + \textbf{a little energy}$$
$$C_6H_{12}O_6 \qquad\qquad 2C_2H_5OH + 2CO_2 \qquad \text{(210 kJ/mole)}$$

(*b*) in animals:

$$\text{glucose} \xrightarrow[\text{matrix}]{\text{enzymes in cytoplasmic}} \text{lactic acid} + \textbf{a little energy}$$
$$C_6H_{12}O_6 \qquad\qquad 2C_3H_6O_3$$

Table 6.1 Comparison of the two stages in respiration

	Anaerobic	*Aerobic*
Oxygen requirement	Nil	Essential
Useful energy from each glucose molecule respired	2 ATP	About 40 ATP
Chemical products	Organic, i.e. still energy-rich, e.g. lactic acid	Inorganic: CO_2 and H_2O, i.e. no energy left
Takes place in	Cytoplasmic matrix (Unit 2.2)	Mitochondria (Unit 2.2)

Note: aerobic and anaerobic respiration are *not* alternatives. Anaerobic reactions are the *first few stages* in a much longer set of reactions made possible under aerobic conditions (Fig. 6.1). Since aerobic respiration has the great advantage over anaerobic of providing about twenty times more energy, not surprisingly most organisms respire aerobically. Only certain bacteria cannot. However, some organisms are forced to respire anaerobically in their environment, e.g. tapeworms (see unit 17.11), or yeast in brewing operations. See Fig. 6.1 for a summary of respiration.

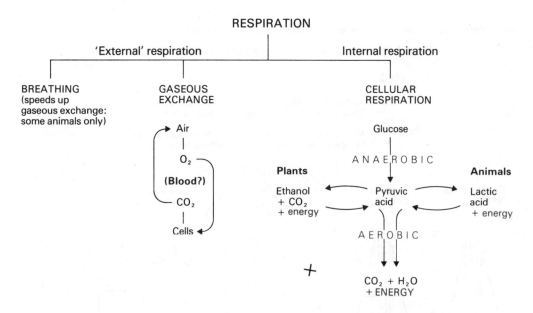

Note: Pyruvic acid (a 3-carbon compound) is common to all three respiration pathways

Fig. 6.1 Respiration: breathing, gaseous exchange and cellular respiration

Examples of anaerobic respiration in aerobic organisms

1 Man

(*a*) at rest, most of the pyruvic acid his cells produce is oxidised to CO_2 and H_2O. The blood contains very little lactic acid.

(*b*) during exercise, blood samples show that the lactic acid level rises at least ten-fold indicating that despite increased breathing and heart rates, oxygen supply to tissues is inadequate. In this relatively anaerobic state man is in **'oxygen debt'**. This debt is 'paid off' by continued rapid aerobic respiration **after** exercise has finished; one fifth of the lactic acid is respired to CO_2 and H_2O. This provides energy to turn the other four-fifths of lactic acid back into glycogen (stored in liver and muscles).

2 Yeast

(a) if aerated, the colony grows very rapidly in nourishing sugared water until all the glucose disappears as CO_2 and H_2O (no use to brewers!).

(b) without air, in similar conditions, the colony grows more slowly, eventually killing itself in the ethanol it produces. This is the basis for *making wine and beer*. The ethanol can be distilled off (as in making *spirits*, e.g. whisky). This will burn, showing it is energy-rich.

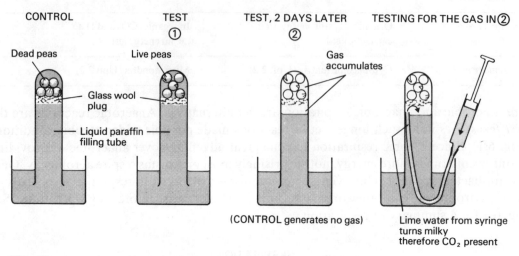

CONTROL   TEST ①   TEST, 2 DAYS LATER ②   TESTING FOR THE GAS IN ②

Dead peas   Live peas   Gas accumulates

Glass wool plug

Liquid paraffin filling tube

(CONTROL generates no gas)

Lime water from syringe turns milky therefore CO_2 present

Note: Mercury can be used instead of liquid paraffin (both lack dissolved O_2)

Fig. 6.2 Demonstration that germinating peas respire anaerobically

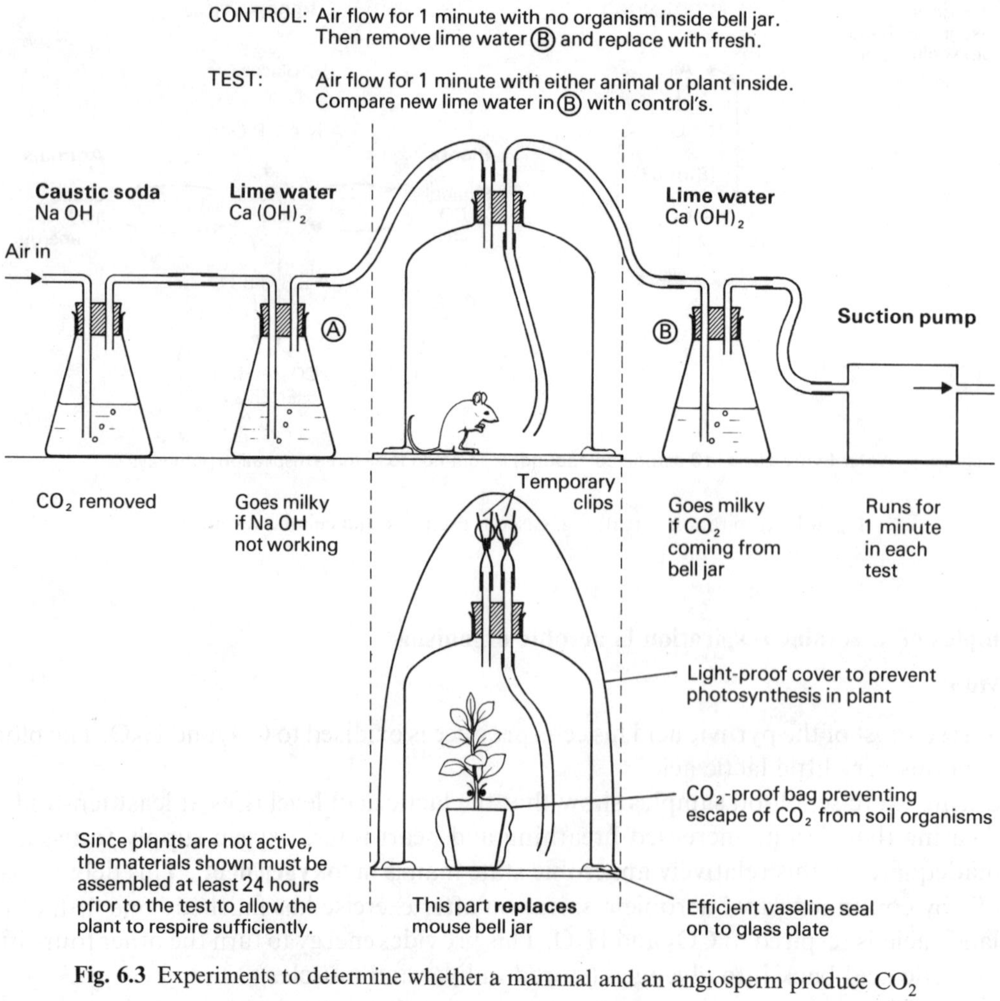

CONTROL: Air flow for 1 minute with no organism inside bell jar. Then remove lime water Ⓑ and replace with fresh.

TEST: Air flow for 1 minute with either animal or plant inside. Compare new lime water in ⒷⒷ with control's.

Caustic soda Na OH   Lime water Ca (OH)₂   Lime water Ca (OH)₂   Suction pump

Air in   Ⓐ   Ⓑ

CO_2 removed   Goes milky if Na OH not working   Goes milky if CO_2 coming from bell jar   Runs for 1 minute in each test

Temporary clips

Light-proof cover to prevent photosynthesis in plant

CO_2-proof bag preventing escape of CO_2 from soil organisms

Since plants are not active, the materials shown must be assembled at least 24 hours prior to the test to allow the plant to respire sufficiently.

This part **replaces** mouse bell jar

Efficient vaseline seal on to glass plate

Fig. 6.3 Experiments to determine whether a mammal and an angiosperm produce CO_2

3   Germinating peas

Half a batch of germinating peas is killed by boiling. Live and dead peas are washed in thymol solution to kill bacteria (which would produce CO_2). Both batches are put in boiling tubes in anaerobic conditions (see Fig. 6.2). Two days later the live peas have produced gas in an anaerobic environment.

Three lines of evidence that organisms are respiring aerobically

1 CO_2 evolved (see Fig. 6.3).

2 O_2 absorbed (see Fig. 6.4).

3   **Heat** evolved. The energy in glucose is not totally converted into useful energy (ATP) during respiration. Some (around 60%) is wasted as heat (see Fig. 6.5). In the experiment shown in Fig. 6.5 both the dead peas (killed by boiling and then cooled for half an hour) and the live ones had been washed in thymol solution to exclude the possibility that bacterial respiration could be causing a rise in temperature. (An animal, e.g. locust could substitute for peas with similar, quicker results).

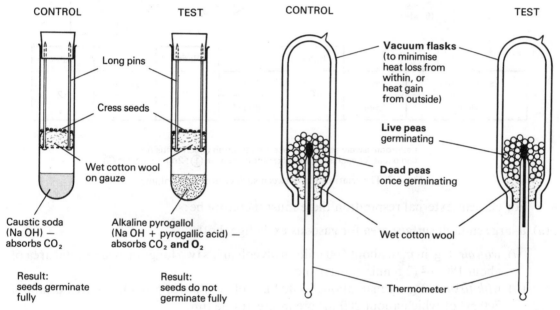

Fig. 6.4 Demonstration that seeds need oxygen to germinate

Fig. 6.5 Demonstration that germinating peas generate heat

The rate of gaseous exchange (i.e. **1** and **2** above) can be used to determine the **rate of respiration** (Fig. 6.6).

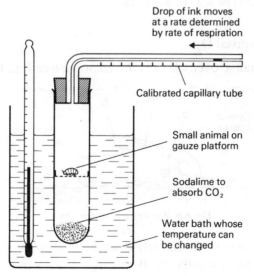

Fig. 6.6 Experiment to determine the rate of respiration, using a respirometer

6.3   EXTERNAL RESPIRATION (GASEOUS EXCHANGE)

Exchange of gases at cells: All cells receive O_2 and lose CO_2 in solution (via water or tissue fluids). Diffusion, a slow process, plays a major part in this (see unit 5.2). Rate of diffusion can be increased by increasing the rate of supply and removal of gases where they are exchanged, e.g. at alveoli and capillaries in man. Hence breathing movements and blood flow.

Gases still have to move (slowly) through the cytoplasm. Thus if a cell were too large (> 1 mm diameter), diffusion of O_2 and CO_2 would not be fast enough to sustain life. Hence cell division is necessary to keep the surface area-to-volume ratio high, i.e. keep the cell small (see Fig. 6.7). Thus the volume of *Amoeba*, say 0.1 mm³, is adequately served by its cell membrane area, say 2.5 mm². But man's volume, say 80 litres, could not be served adequately by his skin surface area, say 1.8 m², *if* it were used for gaseous exchange.

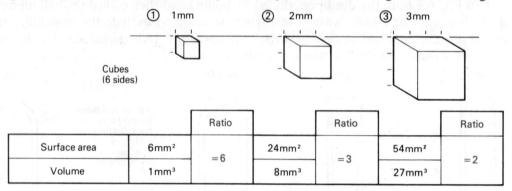

i.e. progressively smaller surface area through which diffusion
can occur for each mm³ of bulk: 6mm²/mm³ in ①; 2mm²/mm³ in ③

Fig. 6.7 The relationship between surface area and volume

For efficient external respiration there must therefore be:

(*a*) a large enough **surface area** for gaseous exchange, both

(*i*) *with air*, e.g. in man about 600 million alveoli in his two lungs provide a total area of about 180 m² (2 tennis courts) and

(*ii*) *with tissues*, e.g. in man about 95 000 km of capillaries provide an area of about 700 m² of which about 200 m² are in use at one time

(*b*) a high enough **rate of supply** of O_2 and removal of CO_2, e.g. in a man exercising: breathing rate goes up 4-fold; volume inhaled per breath, 7-fold; heart rate doubles; volume of blood pumped doubles or trebles (athletes can do better).

6.4   ORGANISMS RESPIRING IN WATER AND AIR

Respiration in water
Water contains < 1% dissolved O_2.

1   **Amoeba:** gaseous exchange over whole *cell membrane* (see Fig. 6.8).

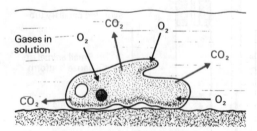

Fig. 6.8 Respiration in *Amoeba*

2   **Bony fish:** gaseous exchange at minutely branched *gill filaments* aided by blood containing erythrocytes flowing in capillaries. Breathing requires use of mouth, pharynx and operculum (see Fig. 6.9).

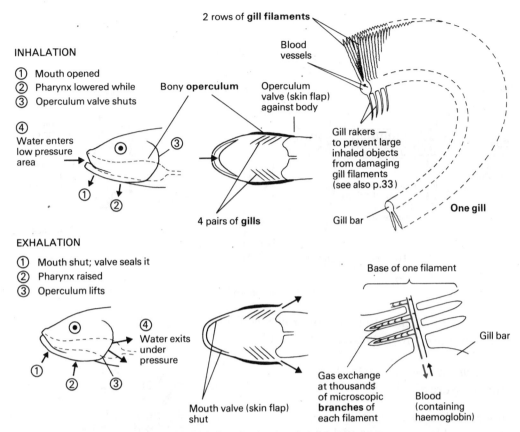

INHALATION

① Mouth opened
② Pharynx lowered while
③ Operculum valve shuts

④
Water enters
low pressure
area

2 rows of **gill filaments**

Blood
vessels

Bony **operculum**

Operculum
valve (skin flap)
against body

Gill rakers —
to prevent large
inhaled objects
from damaging
gill filaments
(see also p.33)

One gill

Gill bar

4 pairs of **gills**

EXHALATION

① Mouth shut; valve seals it
② Pharynx raised
③ Operculum lifts

④
Water exits
under
pressure

Base of one filament

Gill bar

Gas exchange
at thousands
of microscopic
branches of
each filament

Blood
(containing
haemoglobin)

Mouth valve (skin flap)
shut

Fig. 6.9 Respiration in a bony fish

Respiration with wet skins – in air or water

1   Earthworm: gaseous exchange over whole mucus-covered skin aided by blood containing haemoglobin in solution flowing in *skin capillaries*. No breathing movements.

2   Frog: gaseous exchange at mucus-covered skin aided by blood containing erythrocytes flowing in *skin capillaries*. Supplemented by breathing movements of buccal floor ventilating *lungs* and *buccal cavity* (see Fig. 6.10).

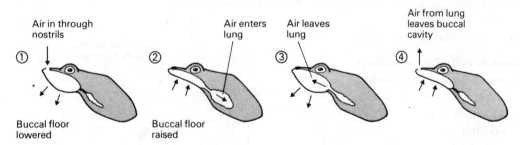

Air in through
nostrils

①

Air enters
lung

②

Air leaves
lung

③

Air from lung
leaves buccal
cavity

④

Buccal floor
lowered

Buccal floor
raised

Fig. 6.10 Breathing in a frog

Respiration in air
Air contains almost 21% O_2.

1   Insect: gaseous exchange at *tracheoles,* thin tubes 1 μm in diameter supplying cells with air *direct* – blood not used for this. Much of the time O_2 and CO_2 just diffuse via *spiracles* and *tracheae* to tracheoles (see Fig. 6.11). Active or strong-flying insects, e.g. bees, and locusts, have air sacs. Abdominal *breathing movements* squash and unsquash these, assisting ventilation of tracheae. Locust group have a 'through system' for air (in through anterior spiracles, out through posterior) – *cf.* birds.

6.5   BIRD RESPIRATION

Gaseous exchange at minute *air passages* (like alveoli open at both ends) since air passes *through*. This happens *twice* for each breath, making gaseous exchange highly efficient –

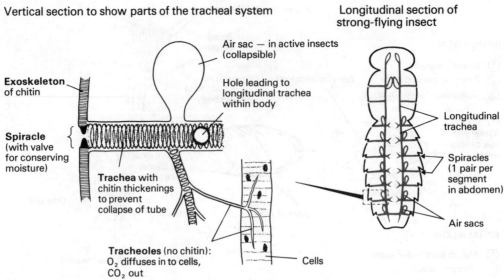

Fig. 6.11 Respiration in an insect

great advantage in generating the power needed for flight. Aided by blood. The four stages of bird respiration are illustrated in Fig. 6.12.

Breathing movements, special valves and tubes ensure air passes:

1 in via trachea to 2 bronchi
2 through 2 lungs (gaseous exchange) to 4 posterior air sacs
3 through 2 lungs (gaseous exchange) to 5 anterior air sacs
4 out via bronchi and trachea.

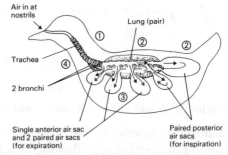

Fig 6.12 Respiration in a bird

Air sacs are not lungs, simply air reservoirs inflated and deflated by body movements to ensure double flow of air through lungs (e.g. in flight, flight-muscles contract next to air sacs and sternum moves in and out). May assist in cooling bird.

6.6   MAMMAL RESPIRATION

Gaseous exchange at millions of tiny air-sacs (*alveoli*), aided by erythrocytes in blood capillaries, in two lungs (see Fig. 6.13).

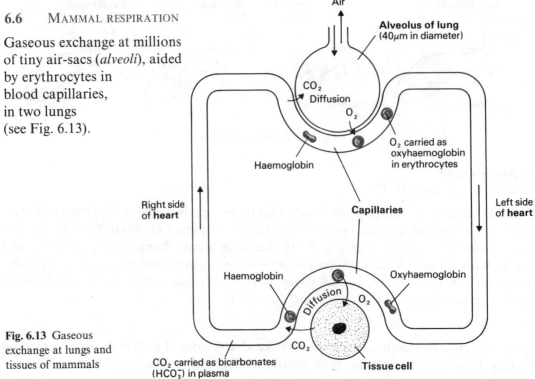

Fig. 6.13 Gaseous exchange at lungs and tissues of mammals

Table 6.2 Breathing movements

	Exhalation	Inhalation
Muscles contracted	Internal intercostals, in *forced* breathing only, e.g. exercise	External intercostals
Ribs	Lowered inwards	Raised outwards
Diaphragm	Relaxes to domed position	Contracts and becomes flatter
Pressure in chest cavity	Raised, therefore air leaves lungs	Lowered, therefore air enters lungs
Vertical section		
Cross section		
	Exhalation	Inhalation

Note: exhalation occurs mainly because lung is elastic, collapsing if allowed to, thus deflating alveoli and bronchioles. Lungs may be made functionless by introducing air between pleural membranes, e.g. medically when treating tuberculosis (TB), or accidentally in a motor crash. A person suffering *asphyxia* (lack of oxygen, e.g. due to drowning or carbon monoxide poisoning) may need *mouth-to-mouth resuscitation*. The rescuer forces the victim's head back (to open the glottis) and pinches the nose. By mouth-to-mouth contact he breathes forcibly into the victim's lungs (= 'the kiss of life'), till breathing is restored. Breathing rate is determined by the CO_2-sensitive part of the brain.

Air breathed

Tidal air: about 0.5 dm³ ($\frac{1}{2}$ litre) – quiet breathing at rest.

Vital capacity: about 3.5 dm³ – volume inhaled or expelled in forced breathing.

Residual air: about 1.5 dm³ – air that cannot be expelled at all (remains in lungs).

Table 6.3 Approximate composition of air inhaled and exhaled (after removal of water vapour)

	Inhaled	Exhaled	Change
Oxygen	21%	17%	20% decrease
Carbon dioxide	0.04%	4%	100-fold increase
Nitrogen	79%	79%	Nil

Air exhaled is also always saturated with water vapour (6%) – a variable loss of water from the body occurs, depending on how moist the inhaled air was.

Respiratory pathway

Air passes to alveoli via nostrils, nasal cavity, trachea, two bronchi with many branches, and millions of bronchioles (see Fig. 6.14). Dust, including bacteria, is 'filtered out' on sticky *mucus* in the nasal cavity as well as in the trachea where *cilia* of lining cells beat the 'sputum' upwards to be swallowed into the acid-bath in the stomach. Heavy *smoking*, especially when young, inactivates ciliated cells making lung infections and the chance of getting lung cancer more likely. Smoking *cannabis* (= 'pot', marijuana, hashish) damages lungs much faster than tobacco and may produce irreversible damage to nervous tissue.

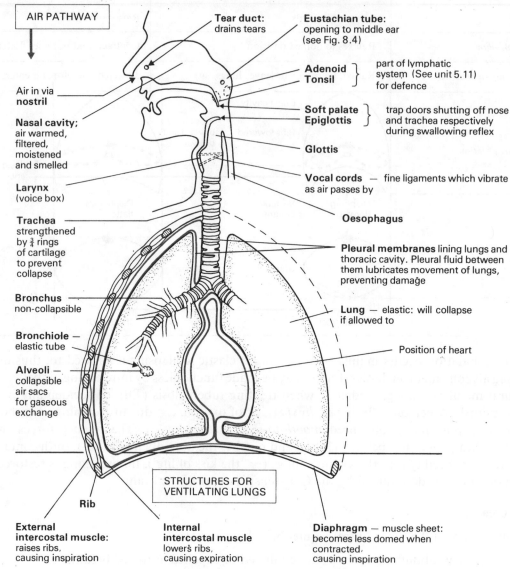

Fig. 6.14 Respiratory pathway in man

6.7 GASEOUS EXCHANGE IN ANGIOSPERMS

Angiosperms are flowering plants. Air diffuses through *stomata* (mostly on leaves; some on green stems) (see unit 4.8) and *lenticels* (on cork-covered roots and stems – see unit 12.3) to *air-spaces* between cells, particularly of cortex and mesophyll (see unit 4.8).

Gaseous exchange: O_2 absorbed and CO_2 released direct from cells to air spaces during **respiration**. However *green cells* in sunlight absorb CO_2 and release O_2 during **photosynthesis** (see unit 4.6) at a rate far greater than the reverse process (due to respiration). In dim light, e.g. dusk or dawn, rates of respiration and photosynthesis can be equal – the **compensation point**. No dead cells, e.g. xylem vessels (the majority in a big tree), respire or photosynthesise.

6.8 USES FOR ENERGY FROM RESPIRATION

Mnemonic: Make tea (**MECH T**).

1 **Mechanical** work, e.g. in contraction of muscles.
2 **Electro-chemical** work, e.g. generating nerve impulses.

3 Chemical work, e.g. synthesising large molecules, such as protein, from amino acids during growth.

4 Heating, e.g. maintaining mammal body temperature.

5 Transporting, e.g. 'active transport' of materials across cell membranes (see unit 5.2).

6.9 ATP (ADENOSINE TRI-PHOSPHATE)

ATP is the 'energy molecule' of cells.

When the terminal phosphate is removed, leaving ADP (adenosine di-phosphate), energy is released for use in any vital function, e.g. movement or growth. The phosphate may be added to ADP again, making ATP, during respiration in mitochondria. The energy for this comes from the bond energy in the sugar that is respired:

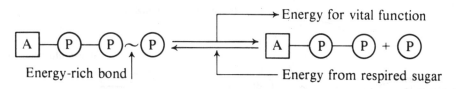

7 Excretion, temperature regulation and homeostasis

7.1 WASTES AND MEANS OF EXCRETION

Excretion is the removal of waste products of metabolism. Accumulation of wastes would lead to death. Examples of excretion:

In **animals**
(*i*) CO_2 (from respiration).
(*ii*) ammonia, urea or uric acid (from protein metabolism – see unit 5.6).

In **green plants:**
(*i*) O_2 (from photosynthesis).
(*ii*) shedding leaves or bark (contain various wastes).

In **all organisms:**
Heat energy (from metabolism – especially respiration, see units 2.2, 7.4). An important waste only in animals, when they move around. Loss of water unfortunately accompanies most forms of excretion. (See question 10, p. 168.)

Mammal excretory organs
1 Lungs: excrete CO_2; lose water vapour.
2 Kidneys: excrete urea; eliminate excess water and salts.
3 Liver: excretes bile pigments (see unit 4.20).
4 Skin: excretes heat, loses water, salts and some urea (in sweat).

7.2 MAMMAL URINARY SYSTEM

Two **kidneys** (see Fig. 7.1) at back of abdominal cavity:

(*a*) **excrete** waste **nitrogen** (from excess protein in diet) as urea.
(*b*) **eliminate** excess **salts** (e.g. NaCl in very salty food).
(*c*) **osmoregulate** to maintain **water** content of blood.

Urine, formed by kidneys, is passed by peristalsis along two **ureters** to bladder (storage); thence via **urethra** to outside (urination) (see Fig. 7.1 Ⓐ).

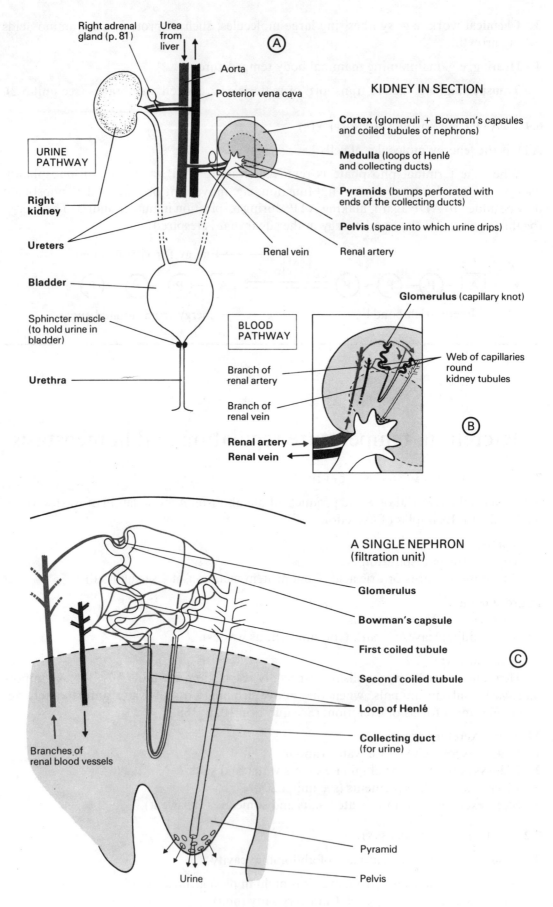

Right adrenal gland (p. 81)

Urea from liver

Ⓐ

Aorta

Posterior vena cava

KIDNEY IN SECTION

Cortex (glomeruli + Bowman's capsules and coiled tubules of nephrons)

Medulla (loops of Henlé and collecting ducts)

Pyramids (bumps perforated with ends of the collecting ducts)

Pelvis (space into which urine drips)

URINE PATHWAY

Right kidney

Ureters

Renal vein   Renal artery

Bladder

Sphincter muscle (to hold urine in bladder)

Urethra

Glomerulus (capillary knot)

Web of capillaries round kidney tubules

BLOOD PATHWAY

Branch of renal artery

Branch of renal vein

Renal artery →
Renal vein ←

Ⓑ

A SINGLE NEPHRON (filtration unit)

Glomerulus

Bowman's capsule

First coiled tubule

Second coiled tubule

Loop of Henlé

Collecting duct (for urine)

Ⓒ

Branches of renal blood vessels

Pyramid

Pelvis

Urine

Fig. 7.1 The mammal urinary system: Ⓐ urine pathway from the kidney; Ⓑ blood pathway in the kidney; Ⓒ a single nephron

Kidney function

1 Blood pathway (see Fig. 7.1 Ⓑ)

Blood containing urea (made in the liver) passes into kidney from aorta via renal artery to about one million **glomeruli** (knots of capillaries); thence via further capillary network to renal vein and posterior vena cava.

2 Nephron (see Fig. 7.1 Ⓒ)

A nephron is a kidney unit receiving tissue fluid and modifying it into urine. Tissue fluid (a filtrate of blood lacking cells and proteins) leaks out from the glomerulus (because of blood pressure) into the cavity of a **Bowman's capsule**. Along the tubules all food and most other useful substances are reabsorbed from the tissue fluid, leaving urine.

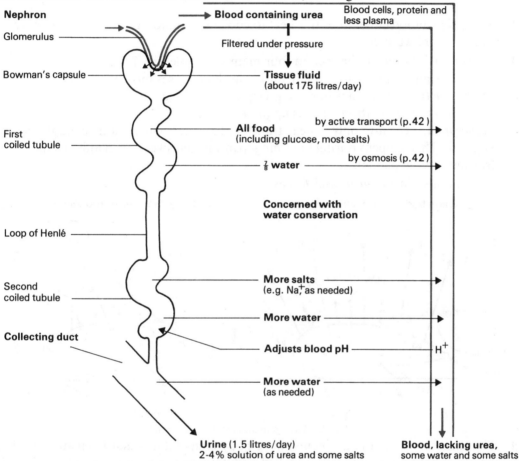

Fig. 7.2 How nephrons make urine in man

Urine in man is a 2–4% solution of urea, some salts, yellow colouring (bile pigments accidentally absorbed in intestine), poisons, drugs and hormones (variously modified). Exact composition varies according to diet, activity and health, e.g. *water loss* exceeds normal 1.5 litres per day if excess water is drunk or extra salts and urea need removing. Level of hormone (ADH) controls this: high levels promote water conservation in kidney – less urine formed.

Water conservation: The **loop of Henlé** makes the tissue fluid surrounding it, salty (by secreting salt from the fluid it receives). This salty solution can osmose water out of the **collecting duct,** but *only* if the hormone ADH (which makes the duct's walls water-permeable) is secreted. ADH is only secreted if water needs to be conserved, e.g. owing to sweating. If excess water is drunk, it passes out in the urine since it is not reabsorbed by the collecting tubule owing to lack of ADH secretion.

7.3   ABNORMAL KIDNEY FUNCTION

Faulty excretion: sugar diabetes – glucose appears in urine. Lack of hormone **insulin** allows high glucose level in blood (see unit 9.8). Consequently tissue fluid is too glucose-rich for first coiled tubule to reabsorb it all into the blood. Therefore glucose is drained, little by little, from the body; can cause coma and death. Remedied by regular insulin injections.

Faulty osmoregulation: water diabetes – large quantities of dilute urine, e.g. 20 litres per day. Lack of hormone **ADH** is cause. Leads to dehydration of body unless large volumes of water drunk.

7.4   BODY TEMPERATURE IN ORGANISMS

Skin and temperature control

1   The *body generates heat* by its metabolism (60% of energy from respiration is wasted as heat) e.g. blood leaving contracting muscles or the liver is warmer than when it entered them.

2   At the *skin*, blood either *loses* this heat to cooler surroundings or *gains* even more if the surroundings are warmer.

3   *Gain or loss of heat* can happen in four main ways (see Fig. 7.3):

(*a*) *radiation* (important in air) – man, at rest in shade, loses most this way.

(*b*) *conduction* (important in water) – e.g. elephants bathing.

(*c*) *convection* (air circulation; speeds up (*a*) and (*b*)).

(*d*) *evaporation* (heat *loss* only – heat transfers to water which gains enough energy to vaporise. This happens during breathing, panting and sweating in animals; and during transpiration in plants).

Some heat is also lost in *urine* and *faeces*.

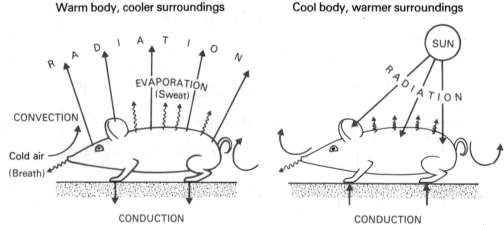
Fig. 7.3 Heat gain and loss by a mammal

4   Thus *most animals* (and all plants) have body **temperatures that fluctuate** with that of their environment. These animals are called poikilotherms or **ectotherms** or 'cold-blooded'.

Birds and mammals have body **temperatures that remain constant** despite the fluctuating environmental temperature. They are called homoiotherms or **endotherms** or 'warm-blooded'.

5   When cold, ectotherms are sluggish (because their enzymes work slowly); they fall easy prey to more active animals. To avoid death they may have to **hibernate** in winter or **aestivate** in summer, e.g. earthworm – curls up into an inactive ball deep in soil.

Endotherms can be constantly active and thus have an advantage over ectotherms; but they need relatively more food to keep up their temperature.

Advantages of endothermy:

Enzymes work continuously at their best temperature. Thus endotherms can remain active in cold; and some live in polar regions.

7.5   MAMMAL TEMPERATURE CONTROL

Mammals have a *thermostat* in the fore-brain (hypothalamus) which monitors blood temperature. Its information causes changes in:

1   Behaviour: e.g. seeking shade or getting wet if it is hot; seeking shelter and huddling into a ball if it is cold (see Fig. 7.4).

2   Skin (physical control):

(*a*) **hair:** traps air – a good insulator. Amount of insulation can be varied by raising or lowering hair using erector muscles.

(*b*) **fat:** also a good insulator. Whales (in very cold water) have thick 'blubber' but camels have no fat except in hump. Mammals prepare for winter cold by laying down more fat.

(*c*) **capillaries and shunts:** skin 'flushes' with blood flowing to surface capillaries (*vaso-dilation*) which radiate heat when mammal is hot. Skin goes pale if cold since blood is diverted from surface capillaries (*vaso-constriction*) often by going through a 'shunt' deeper down.

(*d*) **sweat glands:** secrete sweat (salty water containing some urea). Water evaporates, removing excess heat.

3   Metabolic control:

(*a*) **shivering:** involuntary contractions of muscles generate heat.

(*b*) **liver:** metabolises faster owing to increased thyroxin secretion (see unit 4.20).

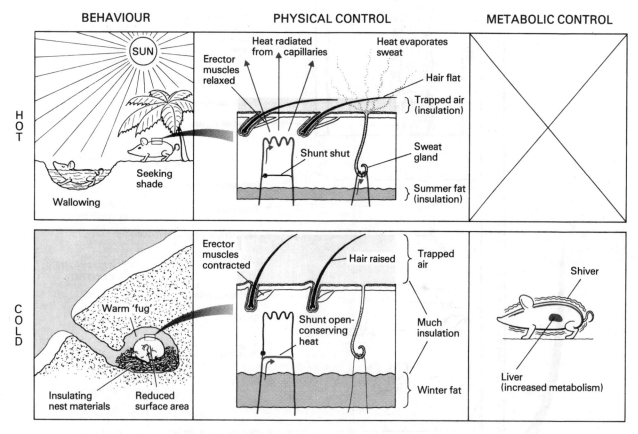

Fig. 7.4 Three ways of maintaining constant body temperature

Temperature control in other organisms

1   Ectotherms: attempt to keep a constant temperature by moving to warm or cold places as the situation demands. Do not use skin or metabolic means as mammals do.

2   Angiosperms: cannot move; perennate if temperature becomes impossible. If hot they *transpire* more (water evaporation) or *wilt* reducing area of leaves gaining heat from sun.

7.6   HOMEOSTASIS

Homeostasis is the maintenance of a constant environment immediately around cells. For unicellular organisms this is the water they inhabit and their only means of homeostasis is to move (if they can) to a suitable area. The immediate environment of cells in a multicellular animal is the tissue fluid. In mammals the composition of this is kept very constant by a variety of organs, each of which controls particular factors in the blood (the source of tissue fluid).

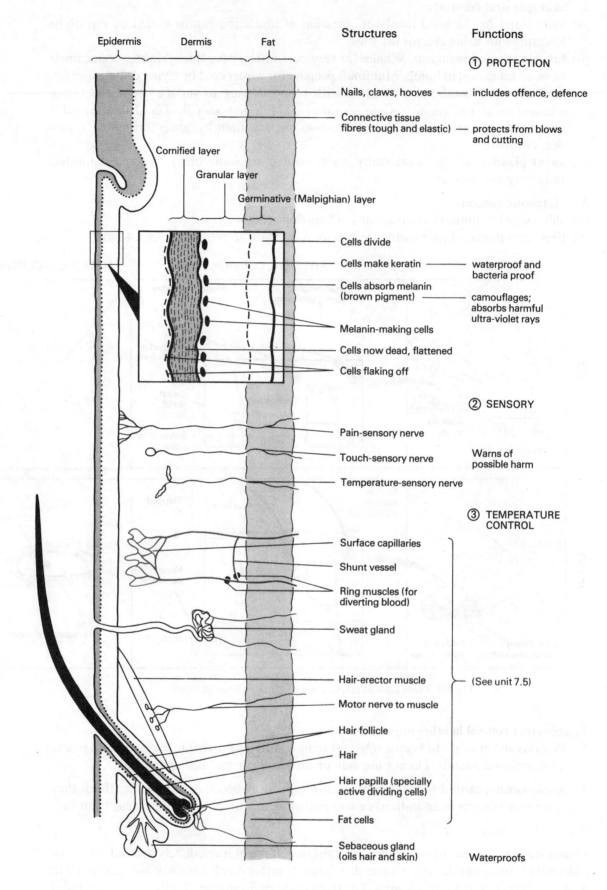

Fig. 7.5 The structure and functions of mammal skin

Table 7.1 Organs concerned with homeostasis in man

Organs concerned	Factors controlled in blood	Healthy blood levels in man
Liver and islet tissue of pancreas (Unit 4.15)	Glucose	1 g/l
Skin, liver (Fig. 7.4)	Temperature	36.8°C (under tongue)
Kidneys (Unit 7.2)	Osmoregulation (water) pH (acidity/alkalinity) Urea (nitrogen waste)	90% pH 7.4 0.3 g/l
Lungs (Unit 6.6)	Carbon dioxide (carbon waste) Oxygen	550 cm^3/l (at rest, deoxygenated) 193 cm^3/l (at rest, oxygenated)

Note: blood does of course vary in composition according to where it is in the body (see unit 5.10), but overall the levels of factors affecting the vital functions of cells are kept within narrow limits.

7.7   SKIN FUNCTIONS

1   Sensory: sensitive nerve endings give warning of harm – pain, touch, heat or cold.

2   Protection: skin acts as barrier between the internal environment of cells (tissue fluid) and the external environment (anything from climate, air or water to bacteria or predators).

Skin *resists:*

(a) **puncture** – (from slashes, blows or friction) by being tough and hair-padded;
(b) **desiccation** – (drying of body) by the waterproof protein keratin, aided by oils;
(c) **entry of pathogens** – (viruses, bacteria, etc.);
(d) **damage from ultra violet light** – ('sunburn'; skin cancer) by suntanning, i.e. producing more pigment when in sunshine.

Skin *assists* predators and prey by providing:

(e) **weapons** from modified skin – (claws, hooves) for attacking or defending;
(f) **camouflage** – by special distribution of pigment in three ways:

　　(i) *blending:* similar colour to background, e.g. khaki colour of lion.
　　(ii) *countershading:* pale belly is darkened by shadow; dark back is made paler by sun. Therefore from the side the animal looks 'flat'; difficult to see, e.g. deer.
　　(iii) *disruptive:* regular outline broken up by stripes or blotches to blend with light and shade amongst vegetation, e.g. leopard.

3   Synthesis: certain oils in the skin are changed to *vitamin D* (see unit 4.5) when subjected to ultra violet light.

4   Excretion: some *urea* is lost in sweat.

5   Temperature control is dealt with in unit 7.5.

8 Sensitivity

8.1   SENSITIVITY IN PLANTS AND ANIMALS

Organisms must be aware of their surroundings and respond to them, where necessary, to keep alive. Plants must seek light; animals, food. Organisms respond to various **stimuli**. Plants respond to light, gravity, touch, water (see units 9.12, 9.13) and animals respond to these as well as temperature, chemicals in air (smells) or water (tastes) and sound. Plants and animals show fundamental differences both in the complexity of their sensory areas and in the way they respond to stimuli (see unit 9).

Table 8.1 Comparison of sensitivity and response in animals and plants

Multicellular animals	*Multicellular plants*
1 **Special sense cells** or organs (which usually do nothing else – e.g. eyes which only see)	No *special* sense organs, e.g. shoot tips sense light
2 **Nerves** relay messages from sensory areas	No nerves
3 **Brain** (present in most) 'computes a decision', sent to muscles	No brain
4 **Muscles** which can move the whole body towards or away from the stimulus	No muscles: cannot move the whole body

8.2 MAMMAL SENSE ORGANS

Sense organs *sense*, but sensations are interpreted (*perceived*) by the brain, e.g. eyes may work perfectly but if the optic nerve or the visual centre of the brain is damaged, the person is blind.

Sense organs sense stimuli in both the external and internal environments:

External
(*a*) *Skin* – touch, heat, cold, pressure (extremes of which can cause pain) (see unit 7.7).
(*b*) *Nose* – air-borne chemicals (smells – including the 'taste' of food).
(*c*) *Tongue* – chemicals causing perception of bitter, sweet, salt and sour tastes.
(*d*) *Ear* – sound (high frequency pressure changes); changes of body position.
(*e*) *Eye* – light (as light or dark, colour, and the form of objects).

Internal (often concerned with homeostasis, see unit 7.6). Examples:
(*a*) *Thermostat* in hypothalamus of brain (see unit 7.5).
(*b*) *Breathing centre* (CO_2-sensitive) in medulla oblongata of brain (see unit 6.6).

There are many others, e.g. *spindle organs* (sensing tension) in muscles. These assist muscle co-ordination.

8.3 THE EYE

1 The **eyeball** is tough (sclera) and transparent in front (cornea); kept in shape by pressure from tissue fluid (exuded from *ciliary body* capillaries) (see Fig. 8.1).

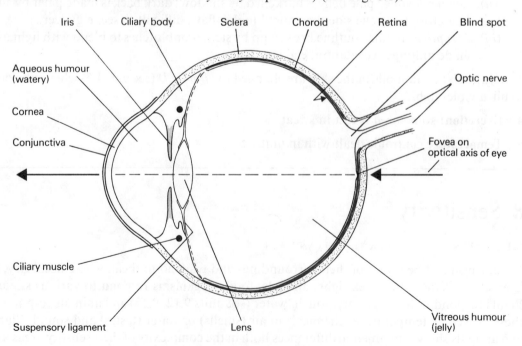

Fig. 8.1 Horizontal section through the left eye of man

2 It is **protected** within a bony socket (*orbit*) and by **three reflexes:**

(*a*) *weep reflex: dust and irritants* sensed by the **conjunctiva** cause an increase in tears and blinking to wash them away;

(*b*) *iris reflex: strong light* on the *retina* causes a narrowing of the pupil to prevent damage to the light-sensitive cells;

(*c*) *blinking reflex:* seen *objects* which may hit the head cause the eyelids to close.

3 The **retina** contains nerve cells linked with two kinds of **light-sensitive** cell:

(*a*) *rods:* see in black and white, in dim light;

(*b*) *cones:* see in colour, in brighter light.

The *fovea* has cones only, very close together: colour vision only and in great detail. Image is only in complete focus at this spot.

The *blind spot* has only nerve cells (gathering into the *optic nerve*): no vision.

4 The **choroid:**

(*a*) Black pigment cells prevent internal reflection of light.

(*b*) Capillaries nourish the retina with tissue fluid.

Focusing

Cornea responsible for most (at least 70%) of the converging of light rays.

Lens makes the final adjustment, i.e. *accommodates*.

1 **Far-focusing: lens pulled thin** by strain on suspensory ligaments exerted by sclera under pressure from tissue fluid.

2 **Near-focusing:** strain on suspensory ligaments relieved by contraction of ciliary muscle, so **lens collapses fat** due to its elasticity.

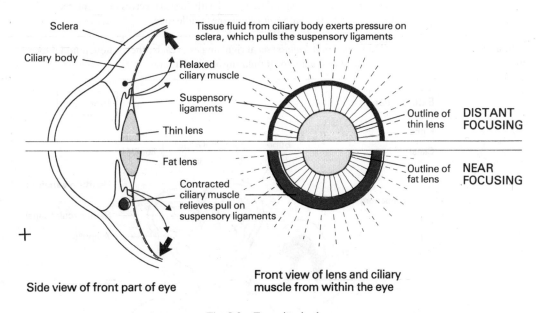

Fig. 8.2 Focusing in the eye

8.4 ABNORMALITIES IN FOCUSING

In normal young human eyes, cornea has a focusing power of 43 dioptres (D); lens has 16D.

1 In old people, *lens becomes less elastic* (collapsible), power falling to 1D. This **presbyopia** is corrected by wearing bifocal lenses or reading glasses (they give extra power).

2 Long sight **(hypermetropia)** ⎫
3 Short sight **(myopia)** ⎬ the problems and solutions are shown in Fig. 8.3
⎭

THE PROBLEMS

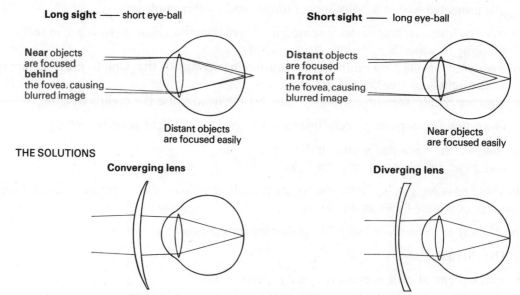

Fig. 8.3   Long sight and short sight and their correction

8.5   THE EAR

Table 8.2   Functions and parts of the ear

Functions	Parts
Hearing	Outer: ear *pinna* and *canal* for sound-gathering
	Middle: *ear-drum* vibrates; *3 ossicles* transmit vibrations; together they amplify the sound at *oval window*
	Inner: (*a*) *cochlea* (a 3-part spiral tube filled with liquid) receives the amplified sound waves which stimulate *hair cells* in the middle tube
Detecting change in position	Inner: (*b*) *3 semicircular canals* (set at right angles to each other) whose liquid moves inside *ampullae* (swellings), so stimulating *hair cells* there

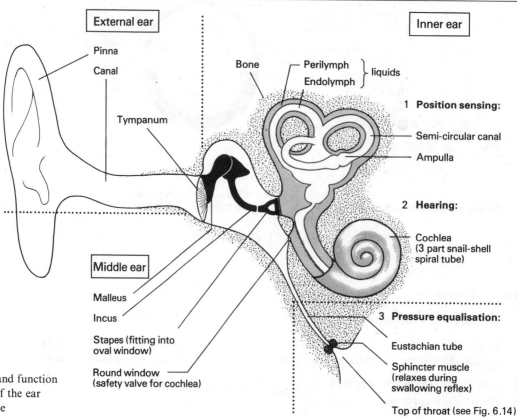

Fig. 8.4 Structure and function of the three parts of the ear and Eustachian tube

Messages from both sets of hair cells go via the *auditory nerve* to the brain: the *cerebrum* interprets sounds received and the cerebellum contributes to sense of balance (see unit 9.7 and Fig. 8.4).

Hearing

Man can hear sound *frequencies* of 20–20 000 Hertz.

Volume can be amplified up to 22 times; area of tympanum (ear-drum) is 22 times the area of the base of stapes. Muscles acting on ossicles can also diminish their movements during loud noise, preventing ear damage.

Stapes vibrates in sympathy with tympanum; thus air-borne sound waves are changed into water-borne sound waves in perilymph. These waves cause movement of a membrane on which hair-cells sit. Their hairs, embedded in a jelly shelf, are pulled or crushed as the cells rise or fall on the membrane, sending impulses along the auditory nerve. This sound-sensing part of the cochlea is called the organ of Corti (see Fig. 8.5).

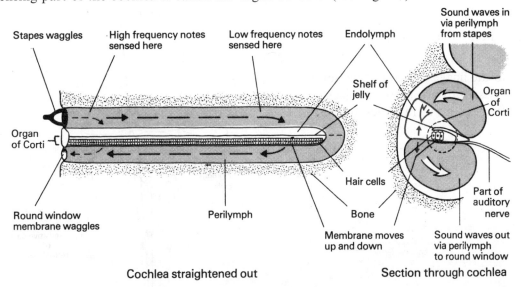

Fig. 8.5   How sounds are sensed in the cochlea

Detecting change in position

Inside the ampulla are hair cells capped by a cone of jelly (cupula) which can move like a swing-door. Head movement in the same plane as one of the canals causes the canal to move, but not the endolymph within it; this lags behind due to inertia. The static endolymph thus swings the cupula, distorting hairs of the hair-cells, which send impulses to the brain (see Fig. 8.6). According to which of the 6 semicircular canals (in 2 ears) are stimulated, the brain can 'compute' how to keep balance. Eye information assists in this.

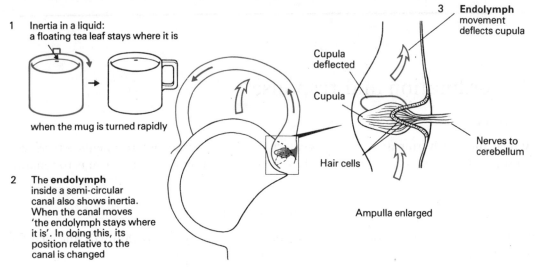

Fig. 8.6   Detection of change in position by an ampulla

8.6   INSECT ANTENNAE AND EYES

The whole insect exoskeleton has variety of sensory cells (especially touch-bristles).

Antennae (depending on species) may have:

(*a*) touch-bristles (possibly also sensitive to sound).
(*b*) taste or smell (chemical sense) pegs or pits.

Eyes (see Fig. 17.16)

1   Compound eye: up to thousands of light-sensing units (*ommatidia*) side by side. An ommatidium gathers light from a small angle and focuses it by two lenses into the central part called the *rhabdom*. The rhabdom consists of light-sensitive 'hairs' projecting from the inner edges of eight long cells arranged in a circle below the crystalline cone. Pigment cells around these cells prevent light travelling on to other ommatidia (see Fig. 8.7).

Differences from mammal eye:

(*a*) fixed focus.
(*b*) mosaic image (not very precise).
(*c*) very sensitive to moving objects.
(*d*) often can see ultra-violet light.

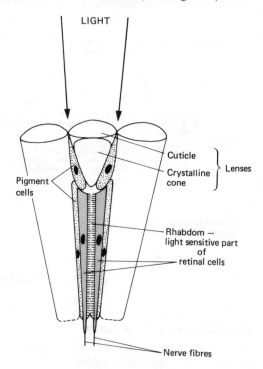

Fig. 8.7   Vertical section through an insect ommatidium

Both mammals and insects have colour-seeing (man and bee) and colour-blind (bull and stick-insect) species.

2   Simple eye: an arrangement similar to a single ommatidium.

---

9 Co-ordination and response

9.1   INFORMATION, MESSAGES AND ACTION

1   Information both from an organism's external and its internal environments is received by sensory cells (see unit 8.1). Often this has to be acted upon if the organism is to remain alive.

2   Messages of two types result from the information:

(*a*) *chemical* – hormones, transported in solution, relatively slowly (animals and plants);
(*b*) *electrical* – along nerves, relatively quickly (animals only).

This accounts for the different rates at which plants and animals react.

3 Action resulting from the message:

(*a*) in *plants* (which have no muscles or obvious glands like the liver, as have animals) is usually by:

   (*i*) *special growth*, e.g. tropisms, flowering, or
   (*ii*) *inhibiting growth*, e.g. dormancy of seed, leaf shedding;

(*b*) in *animals* action is by:

   (*i*) *movement* (muscles), or
   (*ii*) *secretion* (glands).

Growth, although still controlled by hormones, as in plants, is a response only to the rate at which food can be built up into protoplasm.

Co-ordination of actions

Each response to a stimulus, unless co-ordinated with others, would lead to chaos. Thus feeding on bread includes muscle co-ordination to get the bread into the mouth (and not the ear) and to cause chewing, swallowing and peristalsis, as well as co-ordination of secretion of saliva, mucus and pancreatic juice (at the right times).

9.2   MAMMAL NERVOUS SYSTEM

Composed of *neurons* (nerve cells). Neurons are bundled up into *nerves* in the *peripheral nervous system (PNS)*. Nerves link sensory cells and action (effector) cells with the *central nervous system (CNS)* – the brain and spinal cord (see Figs. 9.1a, 9.1b).

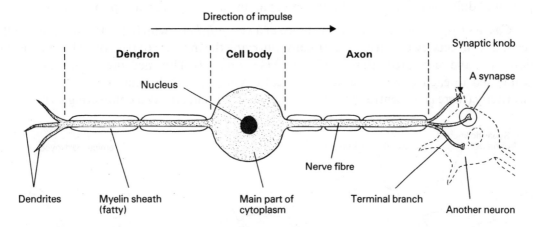

Fig. 9.1a A generalised neuron

As far as function is concerned there are *four types of neuron*:

1 Sensory: may connect with sensory cells, e.g. in retina of eye, or have sensory ends themselves, e.g. touch receptors in skin. Have long dendrons, short axons; carry 'messages' about the environment *to* the CNS.

2 Relay: always act as links between neurons, e.g. sensory neurons and either motor neurons or pyramidal neurons. Thus allow a large number of cross-connections, as in a switch-board.

3 Pyramidal: connect with relay neurons and other pyramidal neurons which have a vast network of cell processes (up to 50 000), each a possible inter-connection. This allows the 'computer' function of the brain.

4   Motor: always link with relay neurons and with muscle or gland cells, to which they carry 'messages' *from* the CNS, calling for action; have short dendrons, long axons.

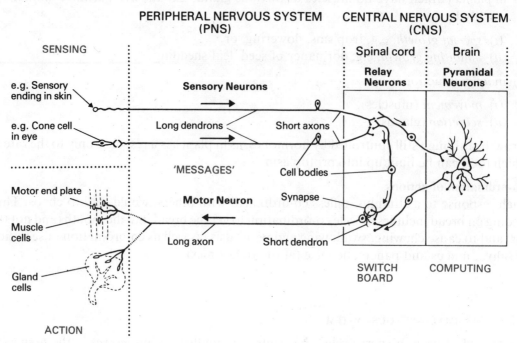

Fig. 9.1b Four different kinds of neuron and their functions in the body

9.3   NERVOUS IMPULSES

Neuron 'messages' (impulses) are *identical* from neuron to neuron. *Electro-chemical* in nature, they require flow of Na^+ ions into neuron and K^+ out, giving about 100 millivolts potential difference at cell membrane only, passing along neuron at up to 120 m/s.

Cause secretion of a chemical substance at a *synaptic knob* which, for less than one millisecond 'connects' two neurons electrically, allowing the impulse to pass on. The chemical is destroyed and re-created after each impulse (see Fig. 9.2). Thus neurons are not physically connected to each other (as in an electrical circuit) and each neuron generates its own electricity (there is no central battery). Each synapse is effectively a connecting switch.

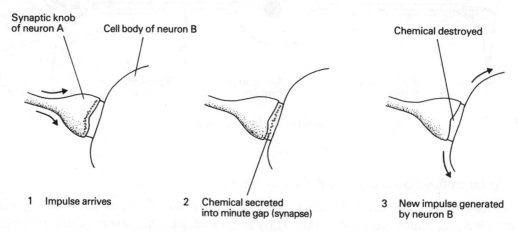

Fig. 9.2 Passing a 'message' at a synapse

9.4   TYPES OF NERVOUS SYSTEM

1   Nerve net (coelenterates, e.g. *Hydra*). No nerves; each neuron passes its message to a number of others, so the message 'spreads' in all directions (see unit 17.6).

2   Central nervous system (higher animals). Neurons are grouped into nerves both receiving and sending messages and are linked to a nerve cord. Nerve cord acts as:

(*a*) local 'decision-maker' (reflex actions);

(*b*) 'switch-board' for passing messages on to brain for higher decisions (intelligent actions).

Animals with small brains rely mostly on automatic reactions (instinct). Those with larger brains have more scope for working out solutions (intelligence).

9.5 REFLEX, CONDITIONED REFLEX AND INTELLIGENT ACTION

Reflex action: an automatic rapid, *unlearned* response to a stimulus which has a high survival value. It is a reaction to sensory information of an *urgent* nature (e.g. withdrawing hand from flame; righting oneself when overbalancing; swallowing) which could mean the difference between survival and death (see also unit 8.3 – eye).

A maximum of *five* kinds of cell (*reflex arc*) take part in the action (see Fig. 9.3).

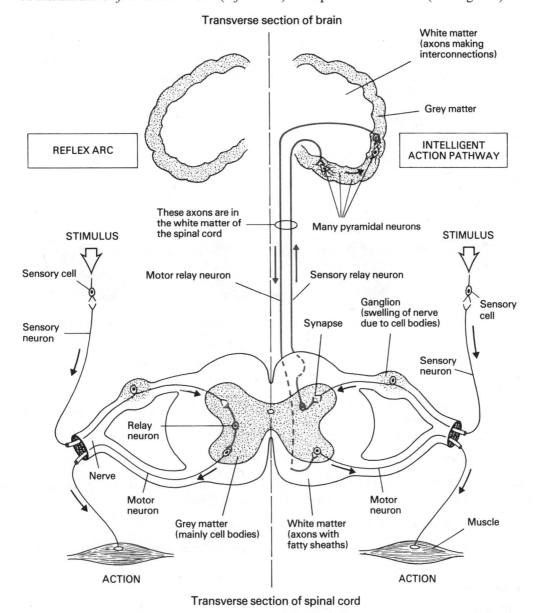

Fig. 9.3 Comparison of reflex and intelligent action pathways

Conditioned reflex action: a *learned* reflex, i.e. the brain is involved. During the training period an inappropriate stimulus is substituted for the appropriate one, as Pavlov discovered with dogs (see Table 9.1).

Conditioned reflexes can be 'unlearned' too, if the reaction is not rewarded. Many skills, e.g. feeding oneself, writing, riding a bicycle, are conditioned reflexes learned by hard practice (training).

Table 9.1 Pavlov's experiment – conditioned reflex in dogs

	Stimulus	*Reaction*
Reflex action	Smell of food	Saliva flows
Training period	Bell rung when food given	Saliva flows
Conditioned reflex	Bell rung (inappropriate)	Saliva still flows

Intelligent action: sensory information goes to the brain before action is taken (see Fig. 9.3). All the little delays in transmission of messages at thousands of synapses in the brain add up to make reaction time slower than in reflex actions.

9.6   INSTINCTIVE BEHAVIOUR

Instinctive behaviour: a series of reflex actions, the completion of one being the signal for starting the next. Often a highly complex 'behaviour pattern', any disruption of which leads to total failure and a recommencement of the sequence of actions, e.g. provision of food for a hunting-wasp's larvae (see Fig. 9.4).

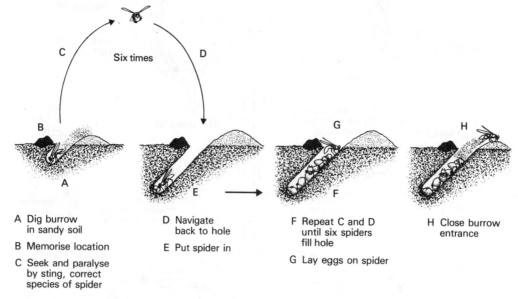

Six times

A Dig burrow in sandy soil
B Memorise location
C Seek and paralyse by sting, correct species of spider

D Navigate back to hole
E Put spider in

F Repeat C and D until six spiders fill hole
G Lay eggs on spider

H Close burrow entrance

If at stage E, spiders are removed by forceps, wasp continues to bring more spiders, eventually giving up and starting at A again, elsewhere.

Fig. 9.4 Instinctive behaviour of a hunting wasp in providing food for its larvae

9.7   THE BRAIN

Expanded front part of nerve cord; but grey matter is outside the white. In primitive vertebrates, brain has three main parts: fore-, mid- and hind-.

In most mammals same three parts are easily seen.

In man, fore-part (cerebrum) is so vast that it covers mid-brain and part of hind-brain too (see Fig. 9.5).

1   Fore-brain

(*a*) **olfactory lobes** (in front) – sense of smell.

(*b*) **cerebrum** (upper part) – centre for memory, aesthetic and moral sense, hearing, vision, speech and muscular action, other than in the viscera (guts).

(*c*) **hypothalamus** (lower part) – receptors for control of internal environment (homeostasis), e.g. temperature, water content of blood. An outgrowth of it is the **pituitary** (the 'master' endocrine gland, see unit 9.8).

2   Mid-brain

Optic lobes (upper part) – simple auditory and visual (pupil) reflexes.

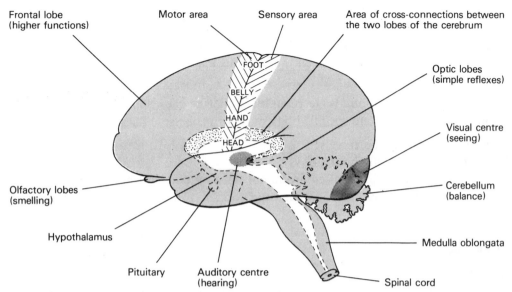

Fig. 9.5 Functional areas of the human brain. (Fore-brain shown overlying mid-brain and hind-brain in section)

3 Hind-brain

(*a*) **cerebellum** (large upper outgrowth) – balance, co-ordination of muscle action.

(*b*) **medulla oblongata** (brain-stem, merging with spinal cord behind) – control of many vital 'automatic' actions, e.g. breathing, heart rate, constriction of arteries to direct blood to specific regions of the body etc.

Summary of brain functions: receives all sensory information and 'processes' it (see Fig. 9.6) either:

(*a*) immediately – reflex action (as in spinal cord), or

(*b*) more slowly – *storing* it as 'memory'
- using past memory to compare with the new, and *calculating*
- *co-ordinating* memories from other brain centres
- reaching a *'decision'*
- passing out *'orders'* via neurons and hormones (from the pituitary).

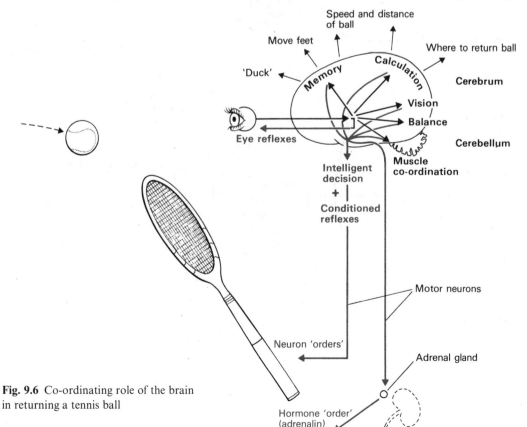

Fig. 9.6 Co-ordinating role of the brain in returning a tennis ball

9.8   ENDOCRINE SYSTEM

A variety of endocrine (ductless) glands discharging their products, hormones, in minute quantities directly into the blood. The pituitary is the 'master gland' controlling the rest (see Fig. 9.7).

Hormones are organic compounds (secreted by endocrine glands in minute quantities into the blood) which affect certain specific body parts or processes. These 'messages':

(*a*) arrive at the speed blood travels;
(*b*) have long-lasting effects (hours, days);
(*c*) control factors in the internal environment needing constant adjustment, e.g. blood sugar level; or processes needing integrated control over a long period, e.g. growth or sexual development.

Glands and their hormones

1   Pituitary

(*a*) **Tropic hormones:** stimulate other endocrine glands, e.g. TSH (thyroid stimulating hormone).
(*b*) **Growth hormone:** promotes growth of muscle, bone (protein synthesis). Deficiency results in a dwarf; excess – a giant.
(*c*) **Antidiuretic hormone** (ADH): water conservation in kidney. Deficiency causes *water diabetes* (see unit 7.3).
(*d*) Secretes many other hormones, including *oxytocin* (ensures contraction of uterus during birth and milk ejection during suckling) and *prolactin* (milk synthesis).

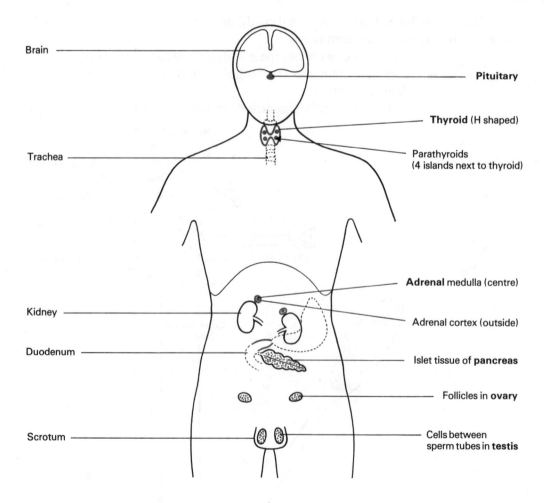

Fig. 9.7 The endocrine system in humans

2 Thyroid

Thyroxin: affects energy release at mitochondria (see unit 2.2) in all cells, raising metabolic rate. Deficiency causes sluggishness, puffy skin; excess produces over-active person with 'pop-eyes'. Deficiency in baby causes *cretinism* – mental and physical retardation (see also mongolism, unit 16.10, and goitre, unit 4.3).

3 Parathyroids

Separate glands next to the thyroid secreting *parathormone* (promotes Ca^{2+} release from bones to blood).

4 Islet tissue of the pancreas

Insulin: causes absorption of glucose from blood into cells, e.g. by liver and muscles to store it as *glycogen*. Deficiency causes *sugar diabetes (diabetes mellitus* – see unit 7.3).

5 Adrenals

Adrenalin (the 'fight or flight hormone'): raises blood glucose level (from glycogen breakdown in liver); increases heart and breathing rates; diverts blood from guts to limb muscles. Adrenalin comes from the adrenal **medulla** which is nerve-stimulated.

The adrenal **cortex** (hormone-stimulated) secretes other hormones including *aldosterone* (Na^+ conservation in kidney) and *cortisol* (promotes protein breakdown).

6 Ovaries and testes

Produce **sex-hormones**, e.g. oestrogen and testosterone respectively, which promote changes in body proportions, development of gametes and hair, and changes in behaviour and voice, at *puberty* (see Fig. 9.8). (For oestrous cycle, see unit 12.18.)

7 Duodenum (HCl-sensitive cells)

Secretin: causes secretion of pancreatic juice when acid contents of stomach reach duodenum.

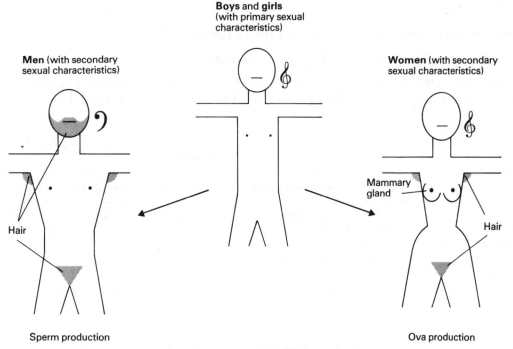

Fig. 9.8 Changes at puberty in humans

9.9 NERVOUS AND HORMONAL SYSTEMS COMPARED

Both achieve co-ordination by *antagonistic action*, e.g. biceps/triceps control of forearm position (see unit 10.4), and insulin/adrenalin control of blood sugar (see unit 4.20).

Table 9.2 Comparison of nervous and endocrine systems

	Nervous system	*Endocrine system*
Speed of 'message'	Fast	Slow
Duration of effect	Short	Long
Precision of 'message'	To a very precise area	A more general effect
Reaction required	Immediate	Long-term

Both systems are *linked to each other,* e.g. hypothalamus (nervous) stimulates pituitary (hormonal); nerves stimulate adrenal medulla; adrenalin stimulates the heart, just as certain nerves do.

9.10 FEED-BACK

Feed-back is the means by which a hormone adjusts its own output by affecting the endocrine glands that cause its secretion. Very important in oestrous cycle (see unit 12.18). If faulty, can cause metabolic disease, e.g. goitre (see summary diagram).

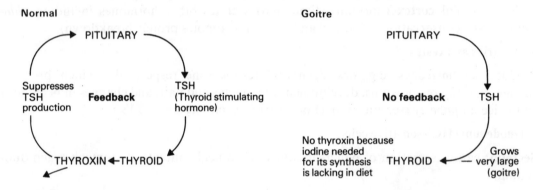

9.11 TAXIS

There are three main simple responses to simple stimuli:

    1 taxis,   **2** tropism,   **3** photoperiodism.

Taxis: movement of an organism bodily towards or away from a stimulus. Applies to many invertebrate animals, unicells and even sperm. For examples see Table 9.3.

Table 9.3 Examples of taxes

Stimulus (and response prefix)	*Responses*	
	Positive (+ = towards stimulus)	*Negative* (− = away from stimulus)
Light (photo-)	Fly, having escaped swatting, flies towards window	Woodlouse seeks darkness
Water (hydro-)	Woodlouse seeks humid area	
Gravity (geo-)	Fly maggots burrow to pupate	
Chemicals (chemo-)	*Amoeba* follows chemicals diffusing from prey	Earthworms rise from soil dosed with formalin
Contact (thigmo-)	Woodlice huddle together	

Thus woodlice can be described as negatively phototaxic and positively hydrotaxic.

9.12   TROPISMS

Tropism: growth-movement of a plant towards or away from a stimulus. Usually controlled by hormones. For examples see Table 9.4.

Mechanism: auxin (hormone) is made at root and shoot tips (which are sensitive). It diffuses back to region of cell elongation (Fig. 9.9) and here it affects the rate at which cells swell by osmosis (vacuolate). Under normal conditions, equal distribution of auxin gives even growth. With a one-sided stimulus, distribution becomes unequal giving unequal growth. Roots and shoots behave differently to an increase in auxin concentration (see Fig. 9.9).

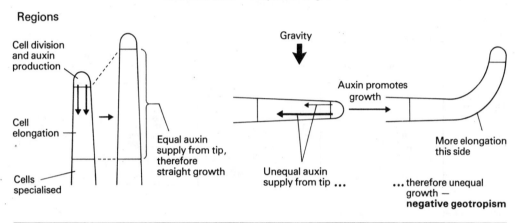

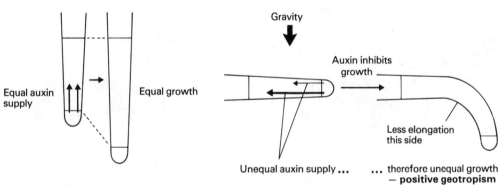

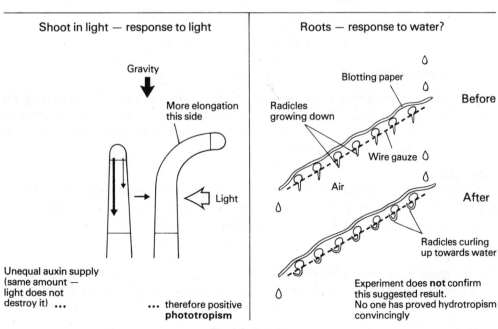

Fig. 9.9 Tropisms

Thus the auxin theory explains geotropism and phototropism and is backed by evidence (see Fig. 9.10). No satisfactory evidence for hydrotropism and its mechanism exists.

Table 9.4 Examples of tropisms

Stimulus	Main shoot response	Main root response	Notes
Light	+ Phototropic	Neutral usually	(Lateral roots and shoots do not behave in this way)
Gravity	− Geotropic	+ Geotropic	
Water	Neutral	? + Hydrotropic	Mechanism unknown

1   Oat coleoptiles are positively phototropic:

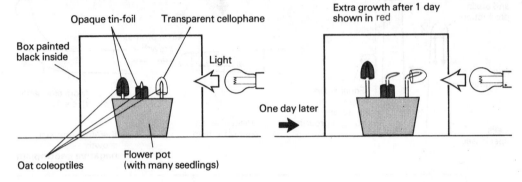

2   A bean tap-root is positively geotropic:

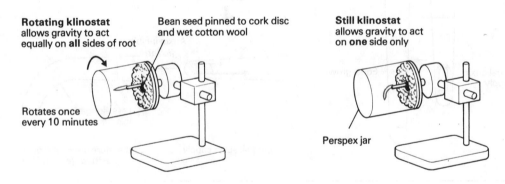

Resulting growth after 1 day shown in red

Fig. 9.10 Two demonstrations of tropisms

9.13   PHOTOPERIODISM

Photoperiodism: an organism's response to *length of day* (or night) by initiating an important event in the life cycle. This event (e.g. migration of birds, emergence of some insects from pupae, or flowering in most angiosperms) is usually linked with reproduction, ensuring that it occurs in the right season.

1   Angiosperms

Length of night is 'measured' by the leaves, within which is a blue pigment, *phytochrome*, which reacts differently to day and night. This acts as the 'clock' to start synthesis of a flowering-hormone (*florigen*). Florigen starts flower formation.

2   Mammals

Many *mammals* have a breeding season, e.g. deer, lions (but not man). Day-length probably influences the pituitary gland via the eyes and brain. The pituitary secretes hormones influencing the testes and ovaries to grow and produce gametes. After breeding, the testes and ovaries become small again.

10 Support and locomotion

10.1   PRINCIPLES OF SUPPORT

Organisms are supported ultimately by their environment (water, land or air).

Plants transmit their weight to it via *cell walls*, e.g. in angiosperms, *turgor pressure* (on cellulose cell walls) (see unit 5.3) and *xylem* (strength of wood-substance) (see unit 5.5) keep the plant in shape by providing mutual *support*.

Animals, since they lack cell walls, have cells specially designed to secrete substances, e.g. chitin, chalk, bone minerals and protein fibres, to provide a *skeleton*. Since most animals move, skeleton is used both for *support and locomotion*.

10.2   SKELETONS USED IN WATER, LAND AND AIR

The environment has a strong influence on **skeleton design** (see below).

Aquatic	*Terrestrial*	*Aerial*
(*a*) Great *support* from water (organism 'made lighter' by mass of water it displaces)	*Negligible support* from air (since volume of air displaced has small mass)	
(*b*) Therefore *weaker skeleton* (sharks manage on cartilage) and massive animals (e.g. whales and giant squids) possible	Therefore *strong skeleton* essential because full weight of body acts through the small areas where limbs are attached to body. Also prevents internal organs crushing each other as they sag downwards	
(*c*) *Streamlining* and *buoyancy* important in saving energy when moving through water (dense medium)	*Foot design* important for efficient movement on, e.g. sand (camel), rock (mountain goat), trees (leopard)	*Streamlining* and *wing design* important for sufficient lift and speed

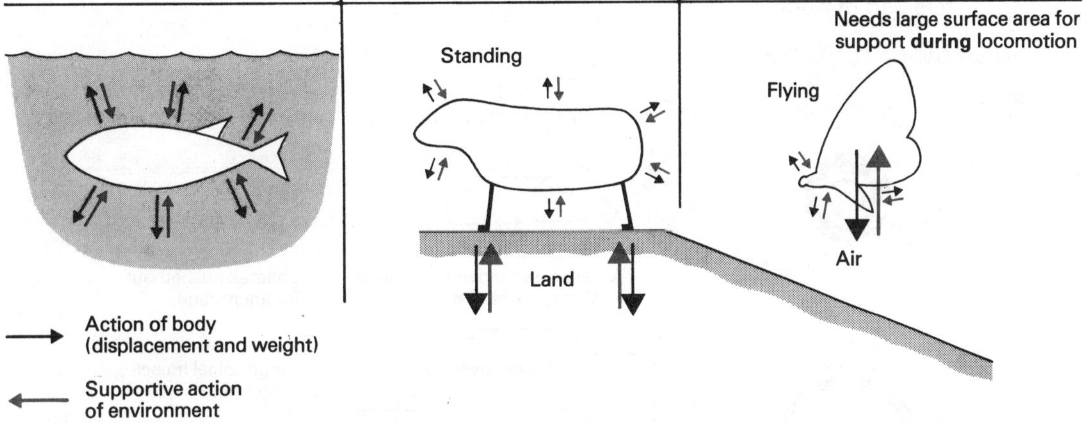

Fig. 10.1 The influence of environment on skeleton design

Various types of vertebrate locomotion
Fish: swimming (see unit 17.20).
Frog: crawling, leaping (see unit 17.22).
Bird: flying (see unit 17.23).

10.3   EXO-, ENDO- AND HYDROSTATIC SKELETONS

1   **Exoskeleton** (on outside): used by all arthropods (see unit 10.6); made of chitin, with protein or chalk to make it harder; has to be shed (ecdysis) from time to time to allow growth of body within a new one before it hardens. Acts as skin also.

2   **Endoskeleton** (inside); used by all vertebrates (see unit 10.7); made of bone and cartilage linked up with connective tissue; grows with the rest of the body.

3   **Hydrostatic** (water inside a cavity): used by annelids (see unit 10.5); its fluid nature allows animal to change shape easily, e.g. in burrowing (see Fig. 10.2), withdrawing into

shells, etc. (Liquid food acts as 'skeleton' for muscles of peristalsis (see unit 4.18) in intestine of mammals in a similar way.)

10.4   PRINCIPLES OF MOVEMENT

1   Muscle can only *contract* (pull) – cannot push. To be lengthened again it must (*a*) relax, (*b*) be pulled back into shape – by another muscle, its antagonist, e.g. biceps and triceps (see Fig. 10.7). Thus muscles work in *antagonistic pairs*.

2   Nerve impulses are essential to make muscles *contract* (except heart). The antagonistic muscles are kept *relaxed* by impulses too (reflex inhibition).

3   Skeleton transmits the contraction force of muscle to the environment e.g. water, land, air (or food in gut).

4   Load-bearing surface in contact with the environment must get purchase on it if locomotion is to result, e.g. fish tail on water, bird wing on air, hooves on ground or claws on trees.

10.5   HYDROSTATIC SKELETON AND EARTHWORM MOVEMENT

Earthworm is adapted to moving in *tunnels* and spaces in the soil (mucus lubricates) (see Fig. 10.2). Solid skeleton is a disadvantage for this. Watery 'skeleton' within a segmented body-cavity (coelome) is incompressible, but can be forced hydraulically into different shapes by muscle action:

(*a*)   when **circular muscles** contract, coelomic fluid is forced into long thin shape which *extends* the segments, and relaxes the longitudinal muscles.

(*b*)   when **longitudinal muscles** contract, fluid is forced into short fat shape which *shortens* segments, and relaxes the circular muscles. Purchase on soil is obtained by pushing out pegs (**chaetae** – eight per segment) where segments are short and fat.

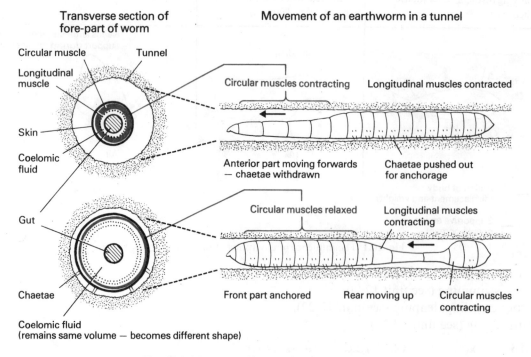

Fig. 10.2 Movement of an earthworm in a tunnel

10.6   EXOSKELETON AND INSECT MOVEMENT

(*a*) **Walking** (see Fig. 10.3)
A system of tubular levers (of hard chitin).
Antagonistic muscles are inside these tubes.
Levers pivot at peg-in-socket joints, sealed by flexible chitin.
Claws or foot-pads provide adhesion to surfaces.

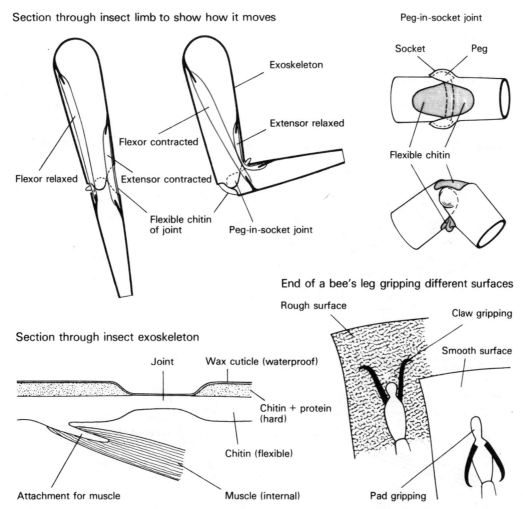

Section through insect limb to show how it moves

Exoskeleton

Extensor relaxed

Flexor contracted

Flexor relaxed   Extensor contracted

Flexible chitin of joint   Peg-in-socket joint

Peg-in-socket joint

Socket   Peg

Flexible chitin

End of a bee's leg gripping different surfaces

Rough surface

Claw gripping

Smooth surface

Section through insect exoskeleton

Joint   Wax cuticle (waterproof)

Chitin + protein (hard)

Chitin (flexible)

Attachment for muscle   Muscle (internal)   Pad gripping

Fig. 10.3 Insect exoskeleton showing parts used for walking

(*b*) **Flight** (see Fig. 10.4)

Wing is a thin plate of chitin, strengthened by veins.

On down-stroke it is horizontal (for maximum lift) (see unit 17.23).

On up-stroke, special muscles rotate it vertically (for minimum air-resistance).

Flight muscles are either:

    (*i*) *direct* (large wings, slow beat), e.g. butterfly, or
    (*ii*) *indirect* (small wings, fast beat), e.g. fly.

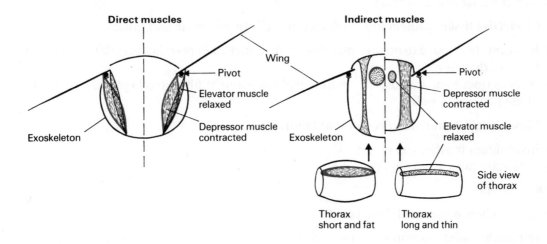

Direct muscles   **Indirect muscles**

Wing

Pivot   Pivot

Elevator muscle relaxed   Depressor muscle contracted

Depressor muscle contracted   Elevator muscle relaxed

Exoskeleton   Exoskeleton   Side view of thorax

Thorax short and fat   Thorax long and thin

Fig. 10.4 Cross-section of insect thorax showing action of flight muscles

10.7   ENDOSKELETON AND MAMMAL MOVEMENT (TISSUES)

Mammal skeletal and muscle tissues:

1   Bone: hard spicules of calcium phosphate, secreted in layers by bone cells, and inelastic protein fibres (see Fig. 10.5).

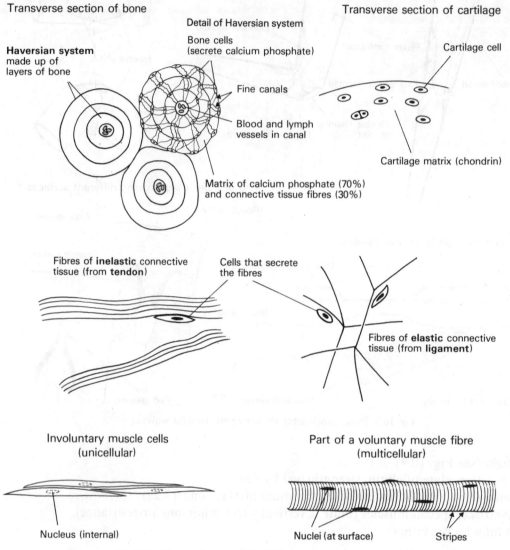

Fig. 10.5 Tissues for support and locomotion in a mammal

2   Cartilage: rubbery protein (chondrin) secreted by cells. Cushions the ends of long bones and vertebrae (shock-absorber).

3   Connective tissue: protein fibres secreted by cells to join bone and muscle.

(*a*) **ligaments** (join bone to bone) – mainly *elastic* branched fibres (elastin) taking the strain from all directions.

(*b*) **tendons** (join bone to muscle) – mainly *inelastic* straight fibres (collagen) taking strain along one line of pull.

4   Muscle: cells containing protein that contracts

(*a*) involuntary muscle, e.g. in gut.
(*b*) voluntary muscle, e.g. in arm.

10.8   JOINTS

Joints are where bones are linked (see Fig. 10.6).

1   Immovable joints (sutures): wavy interlocking edges of bone are held together by collagen, e.g. bones of cranium.

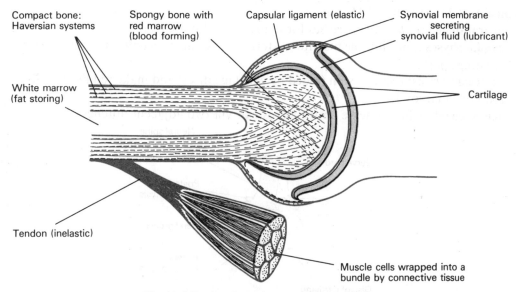

Fig. 10.6 Section through mammal synovial joint

2 Movable joints (synovial joints): bones have cartilage ends; these move on each other, lubricated by synovial fluid secreted by synovial membrane within joint capsule. Types:

(*a*) *Ball-and-socket*, e.g. at shoulder, hip – rotation in two planes of space (see Fig. 10.11).
(*b*) *Hinge*, e.g. at elbow (see Fig. 10.7) and knee – movement in one plane only (like door).
(*c*) *Slipping*, e.g. at wrist and ankle – limited rocking movement.

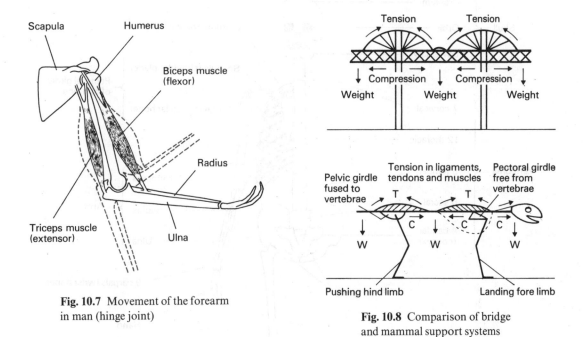

Fig. 10.7 Movement of the forearm in man (hinge joint)

Fig. 10.8 Comparison of bridge and mammal support systems

10.9 MAMMAL SKELETON

1 Skull: cranium protects brain; houses all major sense organs; jaws for chewing.

2 Vertebral column: protects nerve cord; acts as anchorage for four limbs via limb girdles and for ribs. Also a flexible, segmented rod from which internal organs are slung.

Overall, acts as a double cantilever bridge in a quadruped, e.g. dog (see Fig. 10.8).

However, limbs are not static, so *pushing* hind limbs need *firm* attachment via pelvic girdle to vertebrae; but *shock-absorbing* front limbs require an *elastically* attached pectoral girdle.

Typical vertebra (see Fig. 10.9) has:

(*a*) **neural spine** and *lateral processes* for ligament and muscle attachment;

(*b*) **zygapophyses** (anterior one fits into posterior one of next vertebra) to prevent vertebrae twisting apart;

(*c*) **centrum** to resist compression (aided by cartilage discs) and make red blood cells (in its red bone marrow);

(*d*) **neural canal** to house nerve cord (nerves exit via two adjacent notches).

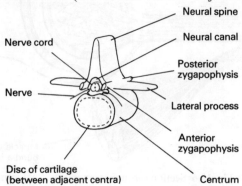

Fig. 10.9 A generalised vertebra (with nearby structures shown in red)

Specialisation of vertebrae

The five types of vertebrae (see Fig. 10.10) have special functions, e.g. thoracic ones have ribs, caudal ones aid balancing (not in man – fused and functionless: the coccyx).

Atlas is first cervical vertebra; supports cranium, allowing nodding i.e. 'yes' movement.

Axis is second; has peg fitting inside atlas which allows swivelling, i.e. 'no' movement.

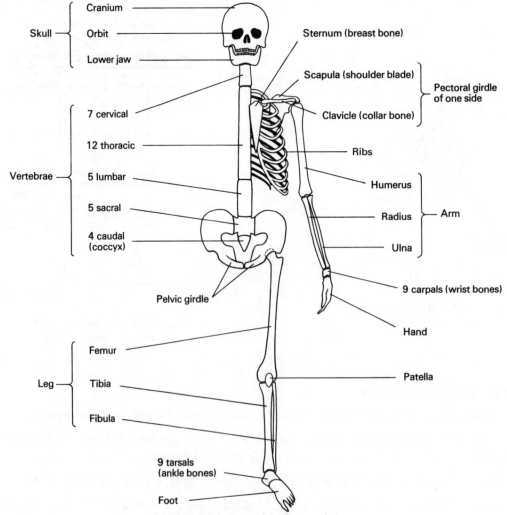

Fig. 10.10 Main parts of the human skeleton

3 Limbs: built on exactly the same plan (see Fig. 10.11) – one upper bone, two lower, and same number of bones in wrist and hand as in ankle and foot (not so in all mammals).

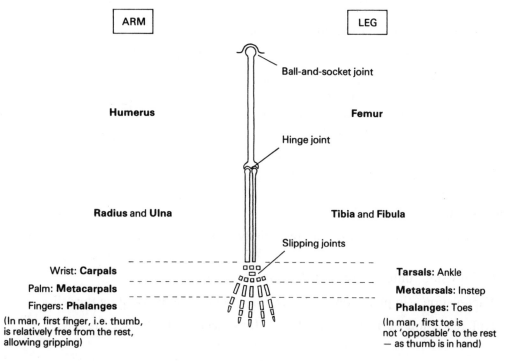

Fig. 10.11 Comparison of bones and joints of human arm and leg

4 Limb girdles:

(*a*) **pectoral girdle** attached loosely to vertebral column to allow shock of landing to be absorbed (muscles link *scapula* to thoracic vertebrae: *clavicle* links to vertebrae via sternum and ribs).

(*b*) **pelvic girdle** fused very firmly to sacral vertebrae to allow thrust of back legs to be transmitted efficiently up the vertebral column. Made of three fused bones on each side, welded into a hoop.

10.10 INSECT AND MAMMAL SKELETONS COMPARED

Functions of mammal skeletons

1 Support: of body off ground; of internal organs, preventing crushing.

2 Shape: important adaptations, e.g. man's hand, bat's wing, porpoise's streamline and flippers.

3 Locomotion: system of levers.

4 Protection: cranium protects brain; ribs protect heart and lungs.

5 Breathing: role of ribs (see unit 6.6).

6 Making blood cells: in red bone marrow, e.g. of ribs, vertebrae (see Fig. 10.6).

7 Sound conduction: three ossicles in middle ear (see unit 8.5).

Functions of insect skeletons

1–5 above (but with different examples). *Note:* the tracheal system is chitin and is continuous with the exoskeleton.

6 Skin function, e.g. providing camouflage, barrier to bacteria.

11 Growth

11.1 GROWTH IN PLANTS AND ANIMALS

Growth: increase in size or weight of an organism.

Plants and animals grow differently, resulting in shapes suited to their type of nutrition:

1 Green plants grow at their tips giving a branching shape with a large surface area for absorption of nutrients (necessary when anchored), and of sunlight energy.

2 Animals' bodies grow into a compact shape, except for their limbs (needed for food-seeking).

Processes involved in growth

1 Formation of more protoplasm (especially proteins – formed at ribosomes: see units 2.2, 2.3).

2 Cell division (mitosis – see unit 13.12).

3 Vacuolation – in plants only; absorption of much water, swelling the cell.

4 Differentiation – cells become different for special purposes (see Fig. 11.1).

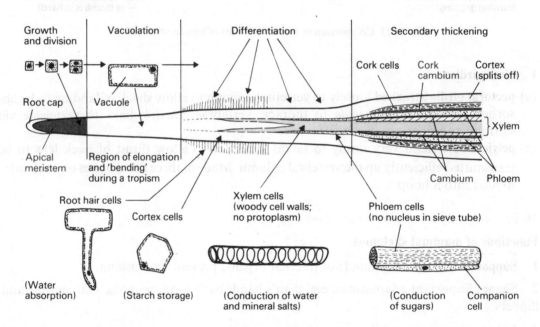

Fig. 11.1 Longitudinal section through a root showing regions of cell division (in red) and subsequent stages in growth

In a similar way, animal cells divide (but do not form vacuoles) and differentiate into cheek cells, muscle cells, neurons and blood cells etc.

All four processes are controlled by hormones (see units 9.8: pituitary, 9.12: auxin).

11.2 GROWTH IN ANGIOSPERMS (PRIMARY)

Primary growth: growth mainly in length (see Fig. 11.1) occurring during first season. Results from cell division at root and shoot tips (apical meristems).

11.3 SECONDARY THICKENING

Secondary growth: growth mainly in thickness (see Fig. 11.2) occurring during second and subsequent seasons. Results from cell division of the cambium and cork cambium (forming new vascular tissue and cork respectively) in both roots and shoots.

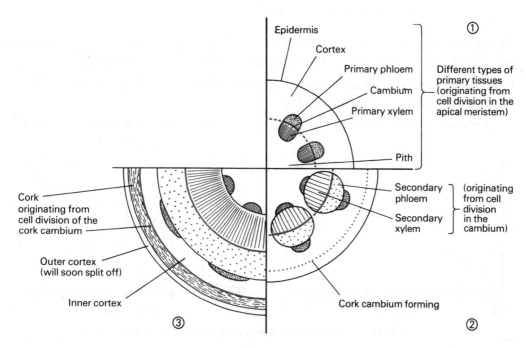

Fig. 11.2 Three stages in secondary thickening – stem shown in cross section

1 In spring the *cambium* grows into a complete ring and begins to divide.

2 The new cells differentiate into *secondary xylem* (wood) *and phloem*. Cork cambium forms in the cortex.

3 *Cork cambium* divides to form cork cells. These waterproof the expanding stem except at **lenticels** (pores for gaseous exchange, formed of loose cells).

4 In autumn, cell division slows down and denser wood with smaller cells is formed. In spring and summer rapid division resumes forming less dense wood. The successive rings of dense and less dense wood are **'annual rings'**. Phloem lacks these rings – older cells are crushed and only the newly formed ones function.

11.4 FACTORS AFFECTING GROWTH

A Plants

1 Genes: responsible for tall and dwarf varieties of pea plants, the different shapes of runner bean, gooseberry bush and beetroot; and the faster growth of pine trees compared with oak. These factors are *inherited*.

2 Climate: *warmth* promotes respiration (source of energy for growth); *sunlight* promotes photosynthesis (source of materials for growth).

3 Nutrients: good supply of mineral salts (e.g. from fertilisers) promotes growth; adequate water essential.

4 Hormones: auxin (and others) promote vacuolation and cell division; tropisms (see unit 9.12).

B Animals

1 Genes: inherited factors – as important as in plants.

2 Climate: temperature affects ectotherms (see unit 7.4) but not endotherms (e.g. mammals) – warmth speeds growth.

3 Nutrients: quantity and quality (a balanced diet, see unit 4.21) of food.

4 Hormones: affect feeding and moulting behaviour in insects; rate of growth in mammals, e.g. growth hormone (see unit 9.8).

11.5 ANIMAL GROWTH PATTERNS

1 Discontinuous: e.g. in insects, animal increases in mass within an *exoskeleton* until it no longer fits, then this is shed (ecdysis) for a larger one formed beneath the old one.

2 Continuous: e.g. in mammals, animal increases gradually in both mass and size, its *endoskeleton* growing all the time (see Fig. 11.3).

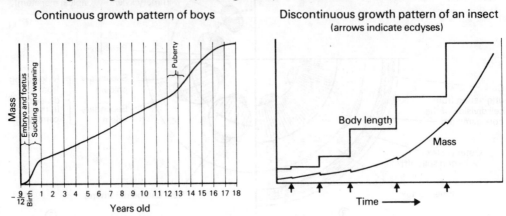

Fig. 11.3 Graphs of continuous and discontinuous growth

11.6 SEEDS (STRUCTURE AND GERMINATION)

Seeds are embryo plants enclosed by the testa (seed coat); found only in *gymnosperms* and *angiosperms*; developed from the ovule (see unit 12.11) after fertilisation. When dormant are dehydrated (about 10% water).

Factors needed for germination (see Fig. 11.4)

1 Water: to hydrate protoplasm, mobilise enzymes, hydrolyse stored food (e.g. starch to sugars).

2 Warmth: to enable enzymes to work.

3 Oxygen: for aerobic respiration to supply energy for growth.

Some seeds require *light*, others dark, for germination; most are indifferent.

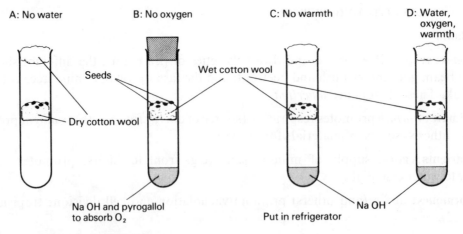

Fig. 11.4 Experiment to determine the conditions necessary for seed germination

Seed structure

All seeds have an embryo consisting of *radicle* (root) and *plumule* (shoot) joined to one or more *cotyledons* (first seed leaves) within the testa. Cotyledons may either not absorb the endosperm (food store) until germination (**endospermic** seeds, e.g. maize (monocot), castor oil (dicot)), or they may be fat with endosperm which has been totally absorbed before the seed was shed (**non-endospermic** seeds, e.g. pea, beans see unit 12.11). *Testa* (seed coat) bears a hilum (attachment scar where seed linked with the fruit) and a micropyle (pore for water entry during germination) (see Fig. 11.5).

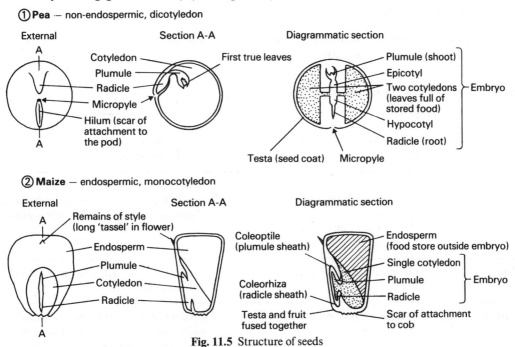

Fig. 11.5 Structure of seeds

Types of germination

1 Hypogeal: cotyledons remain *below ground* (because epicotyl grows rapidly).

2 Epigeal: cotyledons are pushed *above ground* and photosynthesise (because hypocotyl grows rapidly) (see Fig. 11.6).

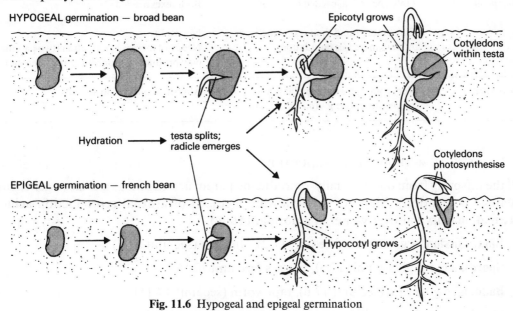

Fig. 11.6 Hypogeal and epigeal germination

11.7 GROWTH MEASUREMENT AND ITS DIFFICULTIES

1 Length or height – all organisms. A crude method: volume would be better.

2 Live mass – terrestrial animals. Difficult for:
 (*a*) plants: roots are broken off, or soil remains attached to them.
 (*b*) aquatic organisms: how much does one dry them before weighing?

3 Dry mass – all organisms, but they have to be killed (and dried in an oven at 110°C). Avoids errors of hydration, e.g. Did the animal drink or urinate before it was weighed? Were the plant cells fully turgid on weighing?

12 Reproduction

12.1 ASEXUAL AND SEXUAL REPRODUCTION COMPARED

No individual organism is immortal; reproduction avoids extinction. Most organisms reproduce sexually, many asexually as well.

Table 12.1 Comparison of asexual and sexual reproduction

	Asexual	Sexual
Parents	One	Two (unless parent is hermaphrodite)
Method	Mitosis forms either: (a) reproductive bodies, e.g. spores, tubers, or (b) replicas of adult by outgrowth, e.g. runners	Meiosis forms gametes (sperm and ova) which fuse to form zygotes (at fertilisation) Zygote grows by mitosis into new organism
Offspring	Genetically identical to parent	Not identical – half its genes are maternal, half paternal
Advantage	Maintains a good strain exactly	Produces new varieties which, if 'better', enable survival and in the long-term their evolution (see unit 14.4)
Disadvantage	Species liable to be wiped out, e.g. by disease, if no resistant varieties	Excellent individuals, e.g. prize milk-cow, cannot give identical offspring
Other points	Only one arrival needed to colonise a new area Often more rapid than sexual methods Always increases population	Both sexes needed Not rapid Need not increase population (two parents may produce only one offspring, then die)
Occurrence	Very common amongst plants and *simple* animals, e.g. *Amoeba, Hydra*	Almost all plants and animals

12.2 ASEXUAL METHODS OF REPRODUCTION

All the offspring from one asexually-reproducing parent are known as a **clone** (a genetically identical population), Many of the following methods of asexual reproduction achieve **perennation** (survival over winter in a dormant state).

1 **Binary fission,** e.g. bacteria (see unit 17.2), *Amoeba* (see unit 17.4).

2 **Spores,** e.g. fungi (see unit 17.5), mosses (see unit 17.8).

3 **Budding,** e.g. *Hydra* (see unit 17.6), tapeworm (see unit 17.11).

4 **Identical twinning,** e.g. in humans, a single zygote may develop into two babies.

5 **Parthenogenesis** ('virgin birth'), e.g. aphids (greenfly) do not have to mate to produce young; drone bees (see unit 17.18) are also produced in this way.

6 **Vegetative propagation** by outgrowths of new plantlets usually from *stems* (see Fig. 12.1) but sometimes from *leaves*, e.g. *Bryophyllum*.

Bulb: a disc-shaped stem bearing roots and:

(a) *buds* – for new growth in spring, surrounded by
(b) *fleshy leaf-bases* of last year's foliage – swollen with food for buds when they grow, and
(c) *brown, papery leaf-bases* – last year's leaf-bases, now totally exhausted of food.

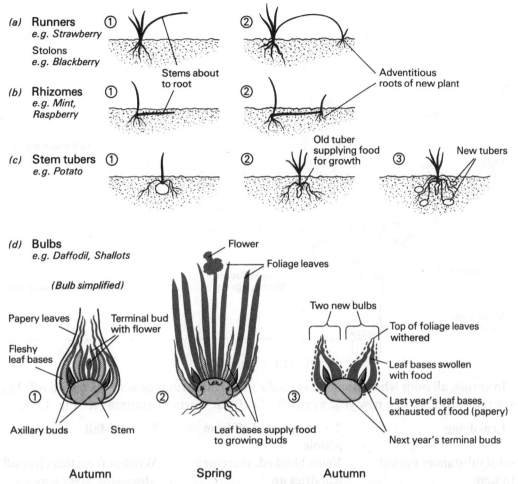

Fig. 12.1 Asexual reproduction: vegetative propagation

In the daffodil, the terminal bud usually flowers and dies. The lateral (axillary) buds form new bulbs, thus *reproducing asexually*. They also *perennate*, dying in their second season i.e. after flowering.

Potato tuber: an underground *stem*-tip swollen with food (especially starch) received from the parent plant, which dies down. Each tuber is a potential new plant (thus *asexual reproduction*) and allows *perennation*. New shoots and adventitious roots arise from 'eyes' (see Fig. 12.2).

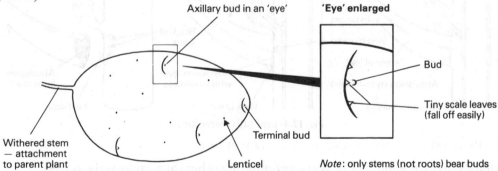

Fig. 12.2 A potato tuber

12.3   WINTER TWIG

Many trees also perennate by shedding leaves in autumn, protecting new late summer growth inside *buds* ('compressed stems') (see Fig. 12.3). These consist of protective scale leaves (leathery) around unexpanded foliage leaves spaced at very short internodes. If they also contain flower buds, growth ends there after flowering, leaving a *scar* where the *inflorescence* withered and fell off. Otherwise *terminal* and *lateral* buds continue growth, unless they are dormant. *Dormant* buds lie in reserve, only growing if other buds die.

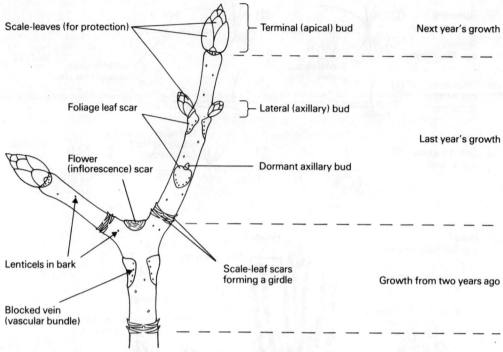

Fig. 12.3 A winter twig

In spring, all buds which burst leave *girdle scars* where rings of scale leaves fall off, These mark the beginning of a new year's growth. *Leaf scars* form in autumn (see Fig. 12.4).

1 Leaf dying	2 Stem sealed off from petiole	3 Leaf-fall
Useful substances passed into stem. Wastes, e.g. tannins received by leaf for excretion. New layer of dividing cells (abscission layer) arises.	Veins blocked, therefore leaf dries up. Abscission layer forms cork cells on stem-side; loosely packed cells (line of weakness) on leaf-side.	Wind or frost tears leaf off at abscission layer leaving leaf scar.

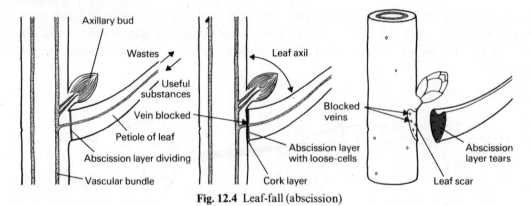

Fig. 12.4 Leaf-fall (abscission)

12.4 PERENNIAL, BIENNIAL AND ANNUAL SEED-PLANTS

Perennials: live for a number of years, perennating other than exclusively as seed.

(a) *deciduous perennials:* shed leaves all at once usually when water supply becomes short, e.g. in winter. Advantages:

  (i) avoids transpiration losses which might kill (plant cannot absorb frozen water);
  (ii) avoids uprooting in autumn gales (leaves offer great wind-resistance).

(b) *evergreen perennials:* shed leaves little by little throughout the year:

  (i) either leaves are designed to reduce transpiration (see unit 5.4), e.g. by thick cuticles, woody leaves and fewer (often sunken) stomata, e.g. holly, pine, or (*ii*) most of the leaves die down, thus reducing transpiration, e.g. iris, grasses.

Biennials: live for two years, dying down to perennating organs at end of year 1 and flowering in year 2 to perennate as seed, e.g. carrot, onion (most root-crops and bulbs) (see Fig. 12.5).

Annuals: complete their life cycle in one year, perennating as seed only, e.g. pea, poppy.

Ephemerals: complete their life cycle in less than one season, thus allowing a number of generations in one year, e.g. groundsel, and desert species causing 'flowering of the desert' – plants germinate, grow and form new seed all in the few weeks of a rare wet spell.

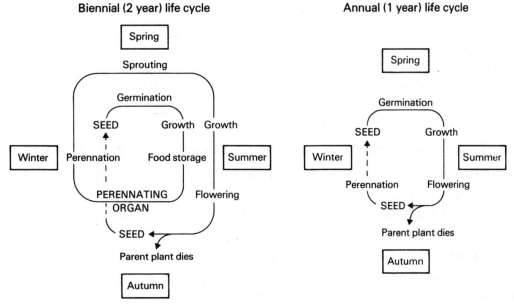

Fig. 12.5 Life cycles of biennials and annuals

12.5 GRAFTING AND CUTTING

(Artificial methods of vegetative propagation)

Grafting: growth together of a vigorous root (**stock**) with a stem (**scion**) bearing large fruit or flowers to give the benefits of both (see Fig. 12.6).

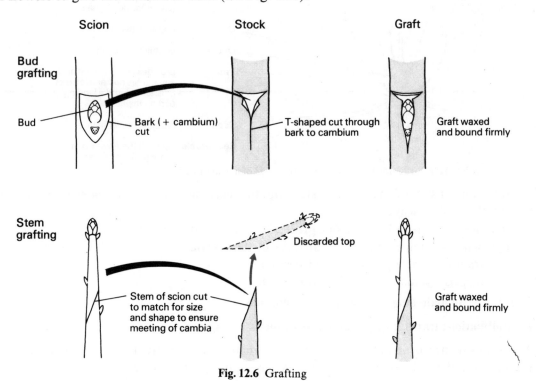

Fig. 12.6 Grafting

Grafting method requires:

(*a*) that cambiums (see unit 11.3) of stock and scion must meet (to grow together);
(*b*) firm binding at junction (to prevent joining tissue tearing);
(*c*) autumn grafting (to minimise death from excessive transpiration);
(*d*) waterproofing wound with tape or wax (minimises infection and desiccation);
(*e*) compatible species (lemon will not graft onto an apple).

Note: Neither stock nor scion are altered *genetically* by grafting, e.g. '*suckers*' from the garden rose 'Masquerade' are stems arising from the *stock*; they will only give wild briar roses, not 'Masquerade', if allowed to flower.

Grafting is used extensively in producing apples, pears, citrus fruit and roses.

Cutting: cutting a short length of young stem at a node and immersing the cut end in aerated damp soil (e.g. sandy peat mix) to form roots. Most leaves are detached to lessen transpiration. Dipping cut end in hormone powder (artificial auxin) assists rooting. Cutting is used extensively to produce ornamental plants and unique new varieties produced by selective breeding. Essential for propagating seedless oranges and grapes.

12.6   SEXUAL REPRODUCTION IN PLANTS

1   Bacteria, *Spirogyra* and *Mucor* reproduce by conjugation (see unit 17.2, 17.3, 17.5).

2   Moss and fern reproduce by sperm swimming in water (see unit 17.8).

3   Angiosperms (flowering plants) avoid the need for water for male gametes to swim in to ovum by enclosing them inside a pollen tube which liberates them near the ovum – hence they are the dominant plants on dry land.

12.7   FLOWERS

The organ of sexual reproduction is the **flower** (see Fig. 12.7). It is usually bi-sexual (hermaphrodite) but sometimes unisexual, e.g. holly.

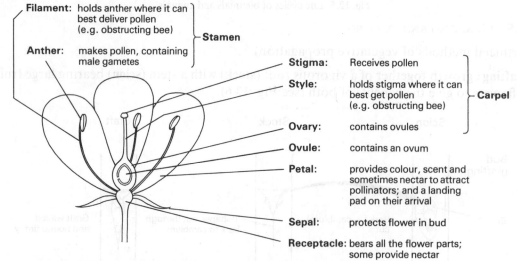

Filament: holds anther where it can best deliver pollen (e.g. obstructing bee) ⎱ **Stamen**
Anther: makes pollen, containing male gametes ⎰

Stigma: Receives pollen
Style: holds stigma where it can best get pollen (e.g. obstructing bee) ⎱ **Carpel**
Ovary: contains ovules
Ovule: contains an ovum
Petal: provides colour, scent and sometimes nectar to attract pollinators; and a landing pad on their arrival
Sepal: protects flower in bud
Receptacle: bears all the flower parts; some provide nectar

Fig. 12.7 Structure and functions of the parts of a generalised insect-pollinated flower

A flower consists of an expanded stem-tip, the **receptacle,** on which is borne four whorls (rings) of modified leaves:

(*i*) *sepals* – almost leaf-like but protective forming the **calyx**;
(*ii*) *petals* – often coloured and attractive: the **corolla**;
(*iii*) *stamens* – male parts: the **androecium**;
(*iv*) *carpels* – female parts: the **gynoecium**.

There are **two main stages in sexual reproduction:**

1   **Pollination:** transfer of pollen from stamens to stigmas.

2   **Fertilisation:** fusion of male with female gametes inside the ovule. This results from the growth of pollen tubes from the pollen on the stigmas to the ovules.

12.8   Wind and insect pollination

Table 12.2   Comparison of flowers adapted for wind or insect pollination

		Wind pollination	*Insect pollination*
1	*Petals*	**Not attractive:** usually green, unscented; no nectar **Small:** leaving stamens and carpels exposed	**Attractive:** coloured, scented, often with nectaries **Large:** protect stamens and carpels inside
2	*Stamens*	Long filaments and large mobile anthers **exposed to wind**	Stiff filaments and anthers **obstruct visiting insects**
3	*Pollen*	**Large quantities** (enormous chances against it all reaching stigmas) Small, dry, light (easily wind-borne)	**Small quantities** (more certain 'delivery service') Rougher, sometimes sticky (to catch on insect 'hairs')
4	*Stigmas*	**Large, exposed** to wind (to catch passing pollen)	**Small, unexposed,** sticky with stiff style (to obstruct insects)
	Examples	Plantain, grasses, hazel, oak	Buttercup, dead-nettle, horse-chestnut, cherry

Variations: certain flowers, which appear to be designed for insect pollination, in fact use other methods. For example:

(*a*) *peas* **self-pollinate** when still in the bud stage.

(*b*) *dandelions* develop seed from ovules without fertilisation, i.e. asexually.

12.9   Self- and cross-pollination

Self-pollination: transfer of pollen from any stamen to any stigma on the same *plant* (not necessarily the same flower). Results in fewer varieties of offspring than cross-pollination. Frequent in cereal crops, grasses.

Cross-pollination: transfer of pollen of one plant to the stigmas of another plant of the same *species*. Thus rose pollen landing on an apple stigma will not germinate there. Results in a great variety of offspring. Since this is biologically desirable many plants have developed means of improving the chances of cross-pollination.

12.10   Adaptations for cross-pollination

1   Protandry: stamens ripen first (i.e. androcium), so little pollen is left when the stigma becomes receptive to pollen, e.g. deadnettle (see Fig. 12.8 Ⓐ).

2   Protogyny: carpels ripen first (i.e. gynaecium), so pollination and fertilisation by other plants is achieved before the stamens shed their pollen, e.g. plantain (see Fig. 12.8 Ⓑ).

Note: comparable mechanisms to ensure cross-fertilisation occur in hermaphrodite animals, e.g. *Hydra* (see unit 17.6), earthworm (see unit 17.7).

3   Incompatibility: chemicals in the stigma prevent germination of the plant's own pollen (same mechanism as that which prevents other species' pollen germinating), e.g *Primula*.

4   Unisexual plants: impossible to self-pollinate, e.g. holly.

Note: unisexual *flowers,* both on the same plant, *can* allow self-pollination, e.g. hazel, oak.

12.11   Fertilisation and its consequences

1   Compatible pollen on the stigma germinates, forming a pollen tube containing three nuclei; the *pollen tube nucleus* directs growth to the micropyle of the ovule, liberating the *two male nuclei* into it (see Fig. 12.9).

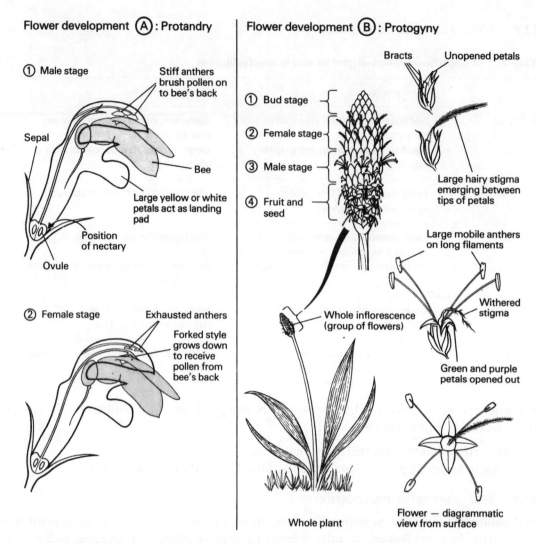

Fig. 12.8 Ⓐ Features of an insect-pollinated flower illustrated by the deadnettle (seen in section) Ⓑ Features of a wind-pollinated flower illustrated by the narrow-leaved plantain

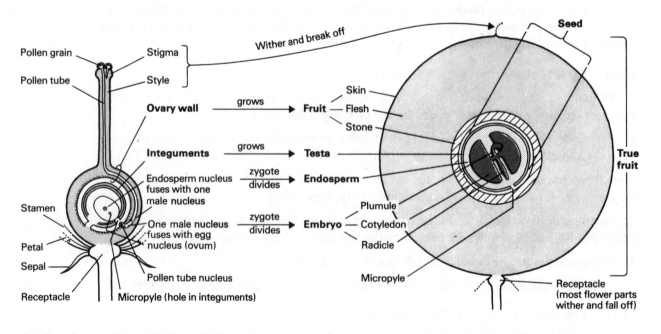

Section of a carpel just prior to fertilisation

Section of a developing fruit and seed

Fig. 12.9 Fertilisation and its results (based on the cherry)

2 Angiosperms are unique in having a *double fertilisation*:

(*a*) one male nucleus + ovum → *embryo zygote*.
   This grows into the embryo: plumule (shoot), radicle (root) and one or two cotyledons (seed leaves for absorbing food for embryo).

(*b*) one male nucleus + endosperm nucleus → *endosperm zygote*.
   This grows into the *endosperm* (food-store for the embryo) by absorbing food from the parent plant.
   If cotyledons absorb endosperm *after* germination an endospermic seed results, e.g. maize; if *before* germination, a non-endospermic one, e.g. pea, bean (see unit 11.6).

3 The integuments grow and harden into the *testa* (seed coat) still with its micropyle (for water entry at germination).

4 The ovary wall grows into the *fruit* (for dispersal of seed).

5 Most of the other flower parts drop off, i.e. sepals, petals, stamens, stigma and style.

12.12 FRUITS

Functions

1 Protects developing seed; in stone-fruits, e.g. peach, protects seed from being eaten by animal.

2 Disperses seed (see below).

Classification of fruits

True fruits: derived mainly from the ovary (i.e. as described in unit 12.11).
False fruits: derived mainly from the *receptacle* which grows fleshy.
Succulent fruits: juicy, often coloured to attract animals.
Dry fruits: non-juicy. To disperse their seed they are either:

(*a*) *dehiscent*: split open, or
(*b*) *indehiscent*: do not split, therefore must rot or be broken open.

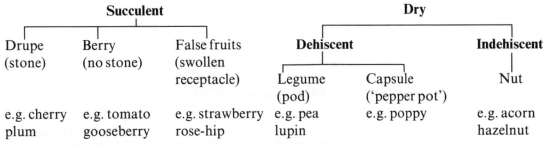

For illustrations see Fig. 12.10.

12.13 DISPERSAL OF SEEDS BY FRUITS (see Fig. 12.10)

1 By animals: hooks may cling to mammals' fur, e.g. burr of cleavers.
Succulent fruits may be passed through the gut, depositing seeds, in a dose of manure (faeces), e.g. tomato, or stone is discarded with seed inside, e.g. plum.

2 By wind: fruits have a large surface area to catch wind. Sycamore has a **'wing'** to allow a slow descent away from the tree; dandelion has a **'parachute'** of hairs to allow blowing far away.

3 By 'explosion': as dry fruits dry, strains building up are suddenly released as the fruits split, scattering seeds, e.g. lupin.

4 By water: air or oils make fruits buoyant, e.g. water lilies, coconuts and mangroves.

Dispersal of seed *avoids overcrowding* (a hazard of some methods of asexual reproduction, e.g. by runners); *aids colonisation* of new areas.

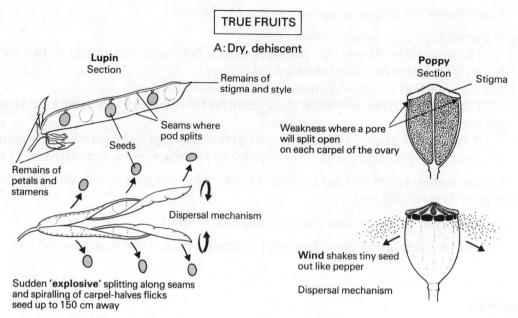

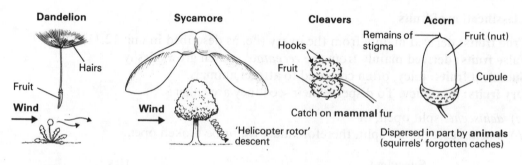

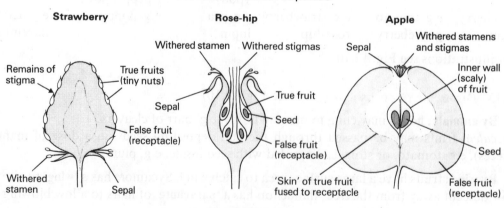

Fig. 12.10 Fruits

12.14 SEXUAL REPRODUCTION IN MAMMALS

The sexual organs of man and woman are shown in Fig. 12.11.

Sequence of events in the sexual process in man

1   Development of secondary sexual characteristics at **puberty** (12–14 years old) (see unit 9.8) making reproduction possible.

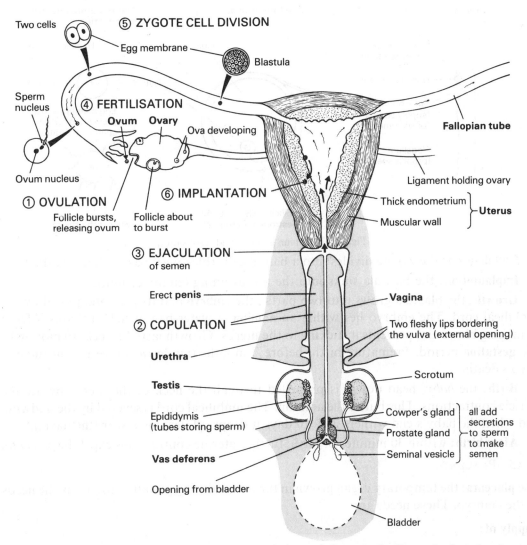

Fig. 12.11 Human male and female sex organs at copulation and the events leading to implantation (see unit 12.14)

2 Gamete production

Table 12.3 Comparison of gamete production in humans

	Male	*Female*
Gonads	Two **testes**, kept outside the body in a sac (scrotum), produce sperm	Two **ovaries**, kept within the body cavity attached to a ligament, produce ova
Gametes	Many millions of **sperm** formed continuously throughout life after puberty (see Fig. 12.12)	Many thousands of potential **ova** formed before birth, but only about 400 will be shed between puberty and menopause (about 45 years old: end of reproduction)
Gamete release	About **200 million** sperm are ejaculated into female by *reflex action* of the penis during copulation. They pass via vas deferens and urethra, picking up nutritive secretions from glands to form *semen*.	Usually only **one** ovum is shed *automatically* per month (Unit 12.18) from the ovary and wafted into the oviduct (Fallopian tube), the only place where it can be fertilised. Once in the uterus the ovum is lost.

3 Copulation: the erect penis transfers sperm during ejaculation from the testes of the male to the end of the vagina of the female.

4 Fertilisation: any sperm that manages to swim into an oviduct containing an ovum has a chance of fertilising it. One sperm only enters the ovum and the two nuclei fuse, forming the zygote cell.

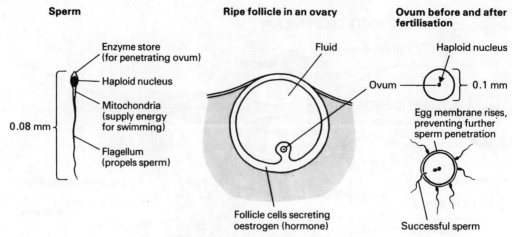

Fig. 12.12 Human gametes and fertilisation

5   Cell division: the zygote divides into a ball of cells (blastula); passes down oviduct.

6   Implantation: the blastula sinks into the uterus lining (endometrium).

7   Growth: the blastula grows into two parts – the **embryo** and its **placenta,** joined by the umbilical cord. The embryo lies within an **amnion,** a water-bag, which cushions it from damaging blows and prevents it sticking to the uterus. Growth lasts 40 weeks (9 months) – the **gestation** period. Premature birth, before 7 months (*miscarriage*), results in the embryo's death.

8   Birth: the *baby*, head down, is propelled through the neck of the uterus by uterine muscle contractions. This bursts the amnion. The umbilical cord is severed by the midwife, and when the baby's end withers in 5–10 days it drops off, leaving a scar (the navel).

9   After-birth: within 30 minutes of birth, further uterine contractions expel the *placenta*.

12.15 PLACENTA

The placenta: the temporary organ grown in the uterus during gestation to supply the needs of the embryo. These needs are:

Supply of:

(*a*) *food* – soluble nutrients, e.g. amino acids, glucose.
(*b*) *oxygen* – for respiration.

Removal of:

(*a*) *carbon dioxide*.
(*b*) *urea* and other wastes.

Transfer of these substances occurs at the end of the umbilical cord, at capillaries within villi. These villi lie in small spaces containing maternal blood (see Fig. 12.13). The embryo's blood does *not* mix with its mother's blood.

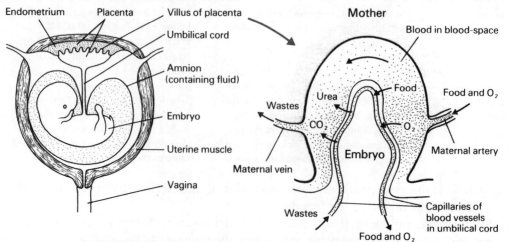

Fig. 12.13 Placenta–relationship between mother and embryo

12.16 PARENTAL CARE

1 Suckling: baby mammals are toothless and need easily digestible food. Milk supplies all the water, sugar (lactose), protein (caseinogen), fats, salts and vitamins for growth (except possibly vitamins A and D in humans).

2 Protection: often in the nest or 'home'; by mother's aggressive behaviour and by her body warmth (many young are hairless).

3 Education: young learn by parents' example, particularly carnivores – hunting techniques.

12.17 BREEDING SUCCESS IN VERTEBRATES COMPARED

Breeding success is measured as the number of adults developed from the number of eggs originally shed. Success improves with internal fertilisation, parental care of eggs and young and adoption of a nest. Table 12.4 excludes exceptions to the rule, e.g. stickleback amongst fish (see unit 17.21):

Table 12.4 Comparison of breeding success of mammals and other vertebrates

	Fish	*Amphibia*	*Reptiles*	*Birds*	*Mammals*
Fertilisation	External	External	Internal	Internal	Internal
Number of eggs laid by oviparous groups	Very many (thousands)	Many (hundreds)	Few (on land)	Few (in nest)	Do not lay eggs (i.e. are viviparous)
Development	In water	In water	In eggs with chalky shells		In uterus
Food from	Little yolk	Some yolk	Much yolk	Much yolk	Placenta
Parental care	Rare	Rare	Of eggs in some groups	Of eggs and young	Highly developed

12.18 MENSTRUAL CYCLE

Menstrual cycles: periods of approximately 28 days during which a reproductive woman alternately ovulates and menstruates.

Ovulation: shedding of an ovum when a follicle in the ovary bursts (see Fig. 12.11). Copulation within 3 days of ovulation could lead to fertilisation, so the uterus lining (endometrium) is prepared for implantation (see Fig. 12.14).

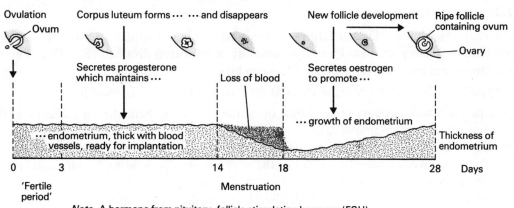

Fig. 12.14 The menstrual cycle

Menstruation: shedding of most of the endometrium 14 days after ovulation, when fertilisation or implantation are unsuccessful. This occurs over 4 days as a loss of up to 500 cm³ of blood and tissue through the vagina.

(For other mammal breeding cycles see unit 9.13.)

12.19 CONTRACEPTION

Contraception: the prevention of fertilisation and implantation.

1 Restricting copulation to the *'safe period'*, i.e. outside the 'fertile period', is **unreliable**. Ovulation is sometimes irregular; sperm may survive 48 hours in woman.

2 **Reliable methods** (see Fig. 12.15) include:

(*a*) *temporary* methods allowing sensible spacing of a family.

(*b*) *permanent* methods, when desired family size has been reached. Removal of testes (castration) or ovaries achieves the same result but is undesirable since a person's 'nature' is changed owing to lack of sex hormones from these organs.

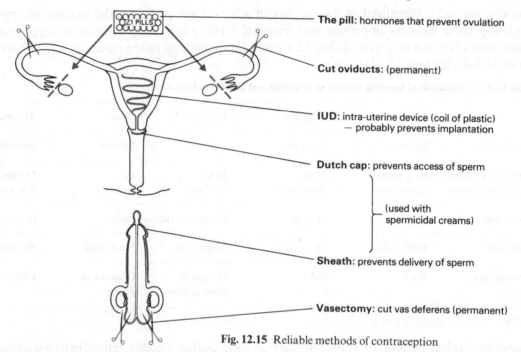

The pill: hormones that prevent ovulation

Cut oviducts: (permanent)

IUD: intra-uterine device (coil of plastic) — probably prevents implantation

Dutch cap: prevents access of sperm

(used with spermicidal creams)

Sheath: prevents delivery of sperm

Vasectomy: cut vas deferens (permanent)

Fig. 12.15 Reliable methods of contraception

Practice of contraception world-wide is essential if humans are to avoid destruction of their environment by pollution (see unit 16.6), erosion, and social problems. A stable or falling birth-rate has been achieved in a number of industrialised nations already; developing nations lag behind in effective contraception.

12.20 VENEREAL DISEASES

Venereal diseases (V.D.) are those transmitted when copulation occurs in sexual reproduction. They are also known as sexually transmitted diseases (S.T.D.). The two best known are caused by bacteria and so can be cured by antibiotics:

1 **Syphilis:** this disease occurs in three stages; by the third it is incurable;

(*a*) a painless *sore* appears at the point of contact, e.g. the penis tip or the cervix (thus the woman is often unaware of her infection) within 90 days; this disappears;

(*b*) four to eight weeks later skin *rashes* may appear or patches of hair may fall out;

(*c*) after some weeks, infection reaches the *nervous system*, leading to paralysis, idiocy, blindness, etc.

Unborn babies can be infected via the placenta; they may suffer abnormalities or be born dead.

2 **Gonorrhoea:** within two to eight days a yellowish discharge of mucus may appear from penis or vagina. In both sexes there may be permanent *problems with urination*; and both may become sexually *sterile* (through blocking of the vas deferens or the oviducts with scar tissue where there has been infection).

A third V.D. is caused by a virus, *Herpes*, and is thus incurable. The sores which appear on the genitals are very painful.

13 Genes, chromosomes and heredity

13.1 THE NUCLEUS, CHROMOSOMES AND GENES

The **nucleus** normally contains long threads of DNA (see unit 2.3) which are not visible under the light microscope.

Before cell division each DNA thread spiralises, with protein, into a compact 'sausage' called a **chromosome** which, when stained, is visible under the microscope (see Fig. 13.1). Chromosomes are present in **homologous pairs,** both members being of identical length (and gene number). One chromosome of the pair came from the male parent, the other from the female parent, when their gametes fused together to form a zygote. Sections of the DNA strands are **genes**, each determining the synthesis of an enzyme (see unit 2.4).

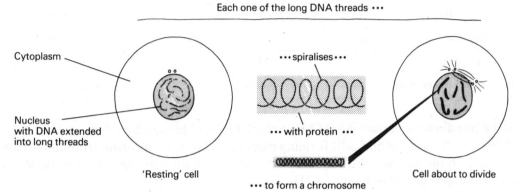

Fig. 13.1 Chromosome formation within the nucleus of a cell

13.2 GENES AND CHARACTERISTICS

Groups of enzymes from different *genes* co-operate in determining **characteristics.** The *environment* also helps to determine characteristics, e.g. a well-fed youngster is more likely to develop into a larger adult than his starved identical twin; some alpine plants grown in exposed, windy situations develop much hairier leaves than if they grow in sheltered crevices. The gene make-up of an organism is called its **genotype**. The interaction of its genotype with its particular environmental circumstances results in its **phenotype**, i.e. its observable or measurable characteristics. Examples of these are black curly hair, blood group, and hairiness of leaves.

To simplify the above, consider an unfastened pearl necklace. The pearls are genes; the necklace a chromosome. A similar necklace would be its homologous partner (see Fig. 13.2). Genes at an identical position (locus) on two homologous chromosomes, between them determine a characteristic.

Diagram of chromosomes	a B Pair 1		C_1 Pair 2
	aa Homozygous	Bb Heterozygous	C_1C_2 Heterozygous
Genotype			
Status of these genes	Recessive	B : dominant b : recessive	C_1 and C_2 are co-dominant
Phenotype	a	B	C_1/C_2 (both)

Fig. 13.2 Genetical terms illustrated with reference to two homologous pairs of chromosomes

Dominant genes (symbolised by capital letters) always express themselves as a characteristic.

Recessive genes (symbolised by small letters) only express themselves when the partner is also recessive.

Thus genotype **AA** or **Aa** will be expressed as an **A** phenotype and genotype **aa** is the only way of producing the **a** phenotype. Organisms with two identical genes at a locus (**AA** or **aa** genotypes) are said to be **homozygous**; those with alternative genes at the locus (**Aa**) are called **heterozygous**.

The alternative genes (**A** and **a**) are called **alleles**.

13.3 HUMAN BLOOD GROUPS: CO-DOMINANCE

Unfortunately things are not always as simple as this. Certain alleles are **co-dominant**: both alleles express themselves, e.g. in the determination of human blood groups (Table 13.1).

Table 13.1   Genetics of blood groups A, B and O in humans

Gene status		Blood Groups (i.e. phenotypes)	Genotypes
O^a	(dominant)	A	$O^a O^a$ or O^a o
O^b	(dominant)	B	$O^b O^b$ or O^b o
o	(recessive)	O	oo
O^a and O^b are **co-dominant**		AB	$O^a O^b$

In **blood transfusion** a person should only receive blood of his *own* blood group to avoid the possibility of 'foreign' blood cells forming clots in his body. Clots result from the person's antibodies (in the plasma) reacting with the antigens on the 'foreign' blood cells, causing them to clump together (see unit 16.11).

13.4 MENDEL'S EXPERIMENTS

Genetics (the study of heredity) was only put on a firm basis in 1865 thanks to *Gregor Mendel*, an Austrian abbot, who published his research on inheritance in peas. Despite his total lack of knowledge of the nucleus and its chromosomes and the ways in which they divide, his conclusions remain valid today.

His materials: *Pisum sativum,* the garden pea. This:

(a) normally *self-pollinates* (and self-fertilises) when the flower is still unopened. To *cross-pollinate* plants, Mendel had to remove the unripe anthers of strain **A** flowers and dust their stigmas with pollen from strain **B** using an artist's paint-brush. Interference by insects was avoided by enclosing their flowers in muslin bags.

(b) has *strongly contrasting phenotypes*, e.g. pea plants are either tall (180–150 cm) or dwarf (20–45 cm); the seeds are either round or wrinkled.

His methods: As parents (**P₁**, or first parental generation) he chose two contrasting 'pure lines' which 'bred true', i.e. were homozygous. These he mated by cross-pollination. The offspring (**F₁**, or first filial generation) were allowed to self-pollinate. This gave the **F₂**, or second filial generation.

Results from one such experiment:

P₁   Tall × Dwarf

F₁   All Tall

Conclusion 1: factor for Tall is dominant to factor for Dwarf.

F₂   Ratio of 3 Tall : Dwarf

Conclusion 2: factor for Dwarf was not lost (as it seemed to have been in the **F₁**). This suggested that 'factors' were particles of hereditary material which remained unaltered as they were handed on at each generation.

We now know that 'factors' are genes, and that the material is DNA in chromosomes.

Mendel had to make five assumptions about gametes before coming to further conclusions, all of which happen to be true. Put in modern terms these were:

1 Gametes carry genes.

2 They carry only *one* gene of the two determining a characteristic.

3 The two members of a gene pair separate and go into different gametes when these are being formed (see **2**); and the two possible types of gamete are formed in *equal numbers*.

4 Each kind of male gamete, e.g. ⋀⋀Ⓐ and ⋀⋀ⓐ from an adult of **Aa** genotype has an *equal chance* of fusing with each of the female kinds of gamete e.g. Ⓐ and ⓐ. Thus resultant combinations **AA, Aa, aA** and **aa** are all as likely as each other (see Table 13.2).

5 Male and female gametes contribute *equally* to the genotype of the offspring.

Although these assumptions fitted in with Mendel's experimental results some could only be finally proved when the details, of e.g. meiosis and fertilisation, had been studied (see unit 13.14).

Table 13.2 Summary of a Mendelian experiment using modern genetical terms

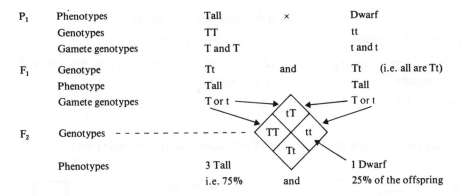

P_1	Phenotypes	Tall	×	Dwarf
	Genotypes	TT		tt
	Gamete genotypes	T and T		t and t
F_1	Genotype	Tt	and	Tt (i.e. all are Tt)
	Phenotype	Tall		Tall
	Gamete genotypes	T or t →		← T or t
F_2	Genotypes	TT / tT / tt / Tt		
	Phenotypes	3 Tall i.e. 75%	and	1 Dwarf 25% of the offspring

13.5 HINTS ON TACKLING GENETIC PROBLEMS

When numerical problems are set as questions in genetics it is essential that the eight lines of terms relating to the P_1, F_1, and F_2 on the left of Table 13.2 be set out first before the data in the question is inserted in the appropriate places. By reasoning, the rest of the 'form' you have thus created can be filled in. It is vital to remember that gametes are **haploid** (have *one* set of genes) and organisms are **diploid** (have *two* sets of genes). The diamond checkerboard giving the F_2 genotypes is called a Punnett square (after a great geneticist).

13.6 BACK-CROSS TEST

Back-cross test: distinguishes between organisms of dominant phenotype but different genotype.

Table 13.3

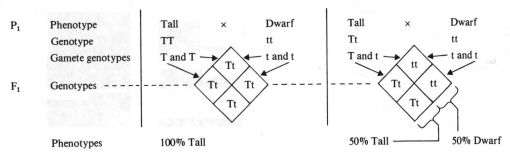

P_1	Phenotype	Tall	×	Dwarf		Tall	×	Dwarf
	Genotype	TT		tt		Tt		tt
	Gamete genotypes	T and T →		← t and t		T and t →		← t and t
F_1	Genotypes	Tt / Tt / Tt				Tt / tt / Tt		
	Phenotypes	100% Tall				50% Tall ———— 50% Dwarf		

In Table 13.2, the F_2 shows that both **TT** (homozygous dominant) offspring and **Tt** (heterozygous) offspring have the Tall phenotype. If both kinds are crossed with a homozygous recessive **tt** they can readily be distinguished; only the heterozygous organisms will give recessive phenotype offspring (50%) (see Table 13.3 on page 111).

13.7   RATIOS OF PHENOTYPES

Tables 13.2 and 13.3 state certain ratios of offspring: 75:25 and 50:50. These are only *expected* ratios relying on Mendel's assumptions **3–5** in unit 13.4 The ratios *obtained* in a breeding experiment are rarely identical with those expected. Thus Mendel obtained 787 Tall:277 Dwarf in the F_2 of the experiment explained in Table 13.2, a ratio of 2.84:1. Likewise a coin tossed 1000 times is *expected* to give 500 'heads' and 500 'tails' – but rarely does so. Scientists apply a 'test of significance' to ratios obtained to see whether they are near enough to the expected ratios to be regarded as the same. For example, is 26:24 near enough to 25:25 to be regarded as 50% of each?

Note: You are not expected to know the 'test of significance'. But if you were given a ratio of, say, 505:499 offspring in a numerical example, you must first *explain why* you assume this is a 50:50 ratio before proceeding.

13.8   VARIATION IN POPULATIONS

Continuous variation

E.g. human height and intelligence

1   A complete *range* of types, e.g. from giants to dwarfs in humans.

2   Phenotype controlled by

(*a*) *many pairs* of alleles

(*b*) environment (may play a major part).

Discontinuous variation

E.g. height of pea plants

1   Sharply *contrasting* types, e.g. tall and dwarf pea plants.

2   Phenotype controlled by

(*a*) a *single pair* of alleles

(*b*) environment (plays little part).

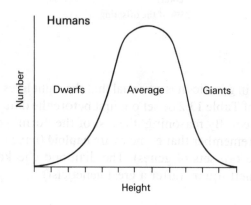 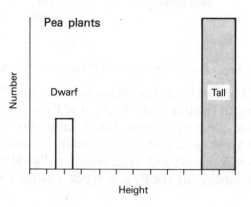

Fig. 13.3 Continuous and discontinuous variation in populations

Table 13.4

Genes for	Environment
Pituitary function (growth hormone) (Unit 9.8)	Disease
Bone metabolism	Diet (e.g. Ca²⁺ protein content)
Ability to make Vitamin D (Unit 4.5)	Sunshine

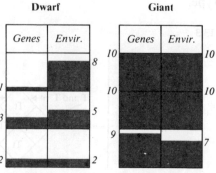

Total: 21 units   Total: 56 units

Examples: factors contributing to the variation in human height include those in Table 13.4. For simplicity, imagine these to be the *only* six factors influencing height. Imagine that each can contribute ten units towards height. Stature could then be accounted for by adding together all the contributions from all six sources – as shown for the dwarf and the giant on the right. (This is *one* hypothesis accounting for continuous variation.)

Variation is *inheritable* only if it is due to genes. Effects caused by the environment are *not inheritable* (see unit 14.3, 'Notes on the above' no. **4**).

13.9 SEX DETERMINATION IN MAMMALS

Males possess two unlike sex chromosomes called **X** and **Y** after the sex-determining genes they contain. The **Y** (male) is dominant to **X**.

Females possess two similar sex chromosomes, *both* **X**. By this means (see Fig. 13.4) males 'determine' the sex of offspring.

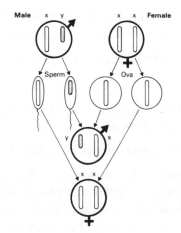

Fig. 13.4 Sex determination

13.10 SEX LINKAGE

Sex linkage: the appearance of certain characteristics in one sex and not the other (in mammals appear in the male).

The **Y** chromosome, being shorter than the **X**, lacks a number of genes present on the longer chromosome. In a male (**XY**) therefore, these genes are present singly and not in pairs, as in the female (**XX**). All these 'single' genes are derived from the mother (on the **X**) and express themselves, even if recessive. Examples: red/green colour blindness and haemophilia. In haemophilia blood fails to clot; so trivial cuts and tooth extractions can be lethal through bleeding. Nowadays, injections of the clotting factor that they lack (Factor VIII) can help haemophiliacs to lead near-normal lives.

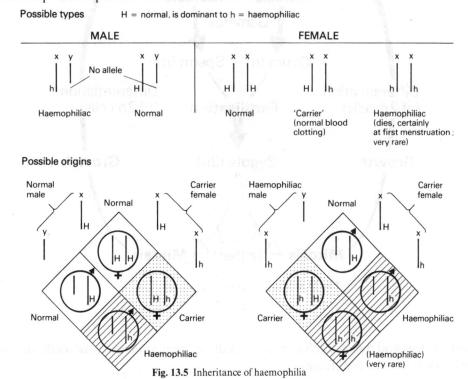

Fig. 13.5 Inheritance of haemophilia

13.11 MUTATION

Mutation: an inheritable change in a cell, e.g. the alteration of a gene to a new one (**M→m**).

Cause: cosmic, ultra violet and X-rays and certain chemicals, e.g. LSD or mustard gas, are mutagenic agents (induce mutations).

Effect: These change DNA, resulting in the manufacture of 'new' proteins in the cell (see unit 2.3) which may be useless to it. Thus most mutations are harmful to the cell (usually lethal).

Cells surviving mutation have little effect on the *organism* unless they divide frequently (e.g. causing leukaemia, skin cancers).

Mutations in cells that produce gametes can affect *evolution* (see unit 14.3).

13.12 MITOSIS AND MEIOSIS IN THE LIFE CYCLE

1 Most organisms start from a *zygote* cell containing chromosomes in pairs, i.e. the double or *diploid* number (2n).

2 The zygote divides by *mitosis* to form new cells during *growth*.

3 These cells, in a multicellular organism *differentiate* (see unit 11.2) into cells as different as neurons and phagocytes. This happens because although all the cells possess identical genes (see unit 13.14), they use different combinations of them according to their location in the body. For example, muscle cells do not use their hair-colour genes.

4 Certain cells in sex organs divide by *meiosis* to form *gametes*. These contain the single-set or *haploid* (monoploid) number of chromosomes (n).

5 At *fertilisation*, gametes fuse to form a zygote (n + n → 2n). Meiosis thus ensures that the chromosome number does not double at each new generation (which it would if gametes were 2n, i.e.2n + 2n → 4n).

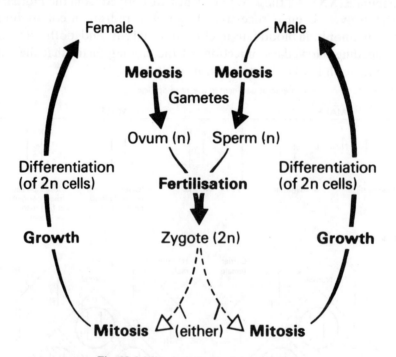

Fig. 13.6 Mitosis and meiosis in a life cycle

Both mitosis and meiosis achieve their results by similar *mechanical* methods, but their *chromosome behaviour* is different.

13.13 MECHANISM FOR SEPARATING CHROMOSOMES (SIMILARITY)

The names used to describe the six stages in the process are for convenience only – the process is actually continuous (see Fig. 13.7).

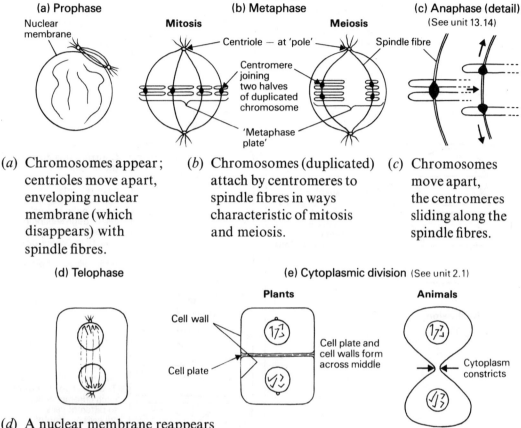

(*a*) Chromosomes appear; centrioles move apart, enveloping nuclear membrane (which disappears) with spindle fibres.

(*b*) Chromosomes (duplicated) attach by centromeres to spindle fibres in ways characteristic of mitosis and meiosis.

(*c*) Chromosomes move apart, the centromeres sliding along the spindle fibres.

(*d*) A nuclear membrane reappears around each group of chromosomes (which have reached the poles).

Fig. 13.7 Separating chromosomes

(*f*) *Interphase* ('resting stage'): chromatids disappear as DNA threads uncoil; these:

   (*i*) synthesise proteins (see unit 2.3) for growth, and
   (*ii*) duplicate themselves just prior to the next cell division.

13.14 CHROMOSOME BEHAVIOUR (DIFFERENCES)

Table 13.5 Summary comparison of mitosis and meiosis

	Mitosis	*Meiosis*
Number of cell divisions	1	2
Resulting cells are	Diploid, identical	Haploid, not identical
Purpose	Growth, replacement (e.g. of skin, blood cells)	Gamete formation
Occurrence in	Growth areas (Unit 11.1)	Gonads e.g. testes, ovaries; anthers, ovules (Units 12.7, 12.14)

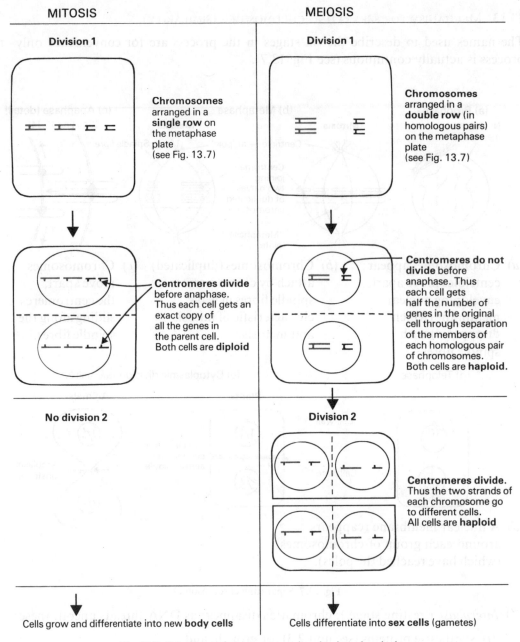

Fig. 13.8 Behaviour of chromosomes in mitosis and meiosis

13.15 NUCLEIC ACIDS AND THE GENETIC CODE

Nucleic acids

Elements: C, H, O, N, P.
Examples: **RNA** (ribose nucleic acid).
              DNA (deoxy-ribose nucleic acid).
Units: 4 organic bases + sugar + phosphate.
Functions: DNA carries genetic information from generation to generation in chromo-somes (see unit 2.2).
              RNA is involved in protein formation in the cell at ribosomes (see unit 2.3).

The 'genetic code' – and translation of its 'message' (see Fig. 13.9 on page 117).

1   There are **four 'letters'** in the 'alphabet', each determined by one of the four bases (**A**denine, **G**uanine, **C**ytosine and **T**hymine) in DNA.

2   The **'words'** are always three lettered (triplets) and made up from any combination of the four possible letters, read *one* way, e.g. **AGT** and **TGA** are different.

3 The **'vocabulary'** is thus $4 \times 4 \times 4 = 64$ possible words.

4 The **'sentence'** of words making up the information of a gene is 'copied' into messenger-RNA and sent to the ribosomes (see Fig. 2.3).

5 At the ribosome, transfer-RNA molecules arrive with an amino acid attached to each.

6 Each transfer-RNA molecule can attach to only one type of amino acid at one end and to only one triplet word on the messenger-RNA at the other (see Fig. 13.9).

7 Thus indirectly the coded 'sentence' of the gene is 'translated' at the ribosome into a special sequence of amino acids, which joins up into a protein.

8 Since different genes have different sequences of the code words, each of the proteins formed will also be different.

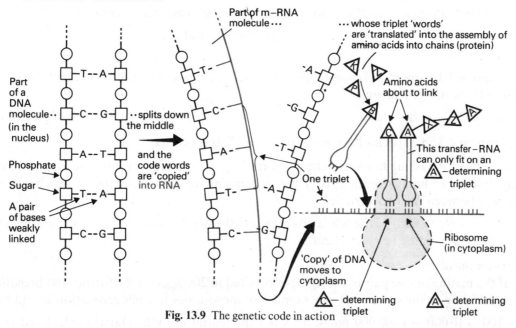

Fig. 13.9 The genetic code in action

14 Evolution

14.1 ORGANIC EVOLUTION – DIFFERENT THEORIES

Organic evolution is the change in a population of a species over a large number of generations that results in the formation of new species (see unit 3.1). The change implies 'advance' (improvement), i.e. better adaptation to the environment.

Three main views of this idea exist:

1 Neo-Darwinian: species are modified by inheritance of small changes in the *genotype* (see unit 3.2) which have passed the test of *natural selection*.

2 Lamarckian: species are modified by inheritance of changes in the *phenotype* acquired by *'use or disuse'* of body parts (see unit 14.5).

3 Biblical: species do not change ('immutability of the species'). They were created once and for all, as described in *Genesis* (see unit 14.5).

14.2 CHARLES DARWIN (1809–82)

As naturalist on *HMS Beagle* (1831–36), Darwin collected much evidence around the world of 'modification of species by descent' (which challenged biblical views).

In 1839 Darwin read *An essay on population* by Reverend Malthus which suggested that though the human population was growing exponentially (see unit 16.5), the food supply for it was not and starvation would result. This provided Darwin with the idea that in similar circumstances in nature the fittest organisms would survive.

Darwin failed to understand the mechanism of inheritance through ignorance of Mendel's work, published in 1865 (see unit 13.4) and despite his own genetical experiments. **Neo-Darwinians** (evolutionists who understand modern genetics) have added strength to Darwin's theory by pointing to:

(*i*) the 'particulate' (and not 'blending') nature of inheritance in accounting for the variety of types in a species.

(*ii*) the ultimate origin of these new types from mutations.

14.3   SUMMARY OF THE NEO-DARWINIAN THEORY

Observation 1 All organisms could, theoretically, increase in numbers exponentially, i.e. **organisms produce more offspring than could possibly survive.**

Observation 2 Populations of organisms, in fact, remain reasonably constant.

Deduction 1 Organisms must have to **struggle for survival** against factors that check their increase in numbers.

Observation 3 In any population there is a variety of types. Much of this variation is inherited by future generations.

Deduction 2 Those best adapted to their environment will survive, i.e. **survival of the fittest.**

Observation 4 Some species have more than one distinct variety.

Observation 5 Anything hindering the interbreeding of two varieties will tend to accentuate their differences because each variety will accumulate mutations, many of which will be different between the two varieties.

Deduction 3 New species arise when **divergence of the two varieties** is sufficiently extreme to prevent interbreeding between them.

Notes on the above

1   If the mating of one pair of mosquitoes resulted in 200 eggs (and a further 100 breeding pairs breeding at the same rate), the number of mosquitoes in each generation would be:

$1 \rightarrow 100 \rightarrow 10\,000 \rightarrow 1\,000\,000$ pairs. This is exponential growth. Darwin calculated that one pair of elephants (a slow-breeding species) could originate 19 million elephants in 750 years.

2   Neither mosquitoes nor elephants achieve their breeding potential. Mosquitoes in the tropics can achieve their life cycle in less than a week; fossil elephants 25 million years old have been found.

3   The 'factors that check increase in numbers' are the biotic and abiotic factors of the environment (see unit 15.1) e.g. predation, disease and competition (especially for food): or inclement weather. There is no literal 'struggle' (except in some animals competing for mates). Organisms simply undergo the survival tests set by their environment (**natural selection**) and large numbers perish.

4   *Variety* in a population arises by:

(*a*) *recombination* of genes (mother and father are different);

(*b*) *meiosis* (the way chromosomes end up in the gametes shuffles the genes);

(*c*) *mutation* (the origin of 'new' genes, see unit 13.11);

(*d*) *environmental* influences other than mutagenic agents.

Only (*a*)–(*c*) are inheritable and can have any effect on evolution.

5   An ***adaptation*** is a solution to a biological problem. The great majority of adaptations are *inherited*. Only mammals (and particularly man) have much scope for altering the destiny laid down in their genes, by reasoning out a solution instead of having the solution ready-made.

Chameleons adapt themselves to different backgrounds by changing colour because they have *inherited* the capacity to do so. Pale peppered moths (see unit 14.4) cannot camouflage themselves on black bark because they have not inherited that ability. Man has inherited intelligence enough to reason out ways of camouflaging soldiers. Those that pass the environment's tests of survival are the 'fittest' and can breed to pass on their genes; those 'unfit' die sooner and their genes are not so well represented in the next generation.

6 The herring gull and lesser black-backed gull (see Fig. 14.1) illustrate this. Something similar occurs with great tits and certain frogs. These species all have varieties that in certain places cannot breed (i.e. are *two* species), yet elsewhere they can and thus are *one* species.

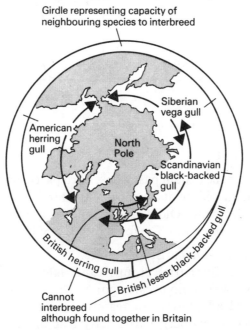

Fig. 14.1 Gulls: two species or one?

7 Darwin studied the **finches of the Galapagos Islands** (1000 kilometres west of South America). They had similar plumage to mainland species and were poor fliers. Those on the various islands, miles apart, were special to each one. On certain islands there was more than one species, each with a different beak shape adapted to a different diet (seeds, insects, cactus flowers etc.). Darwin speculated that these finches, blown perhaps by storm from the mainland, had from a few species evolved into many. The sea around each island had isolated the various populations, and each had accumulated its own inheritable variations to meet the special challenges of its own island.

Factors hindering interbreeding, i.e. **breeding barriers,** may be:
(*a*) **spatial** – the sea surrounding New Zealand for 1600 kilometres in every direction very effectively isolates her varieties of organisms;
(*b*) **temporal** – varieties of the same species in northern and southern hemispheres tend to be in a breeding condition at different times;
(*c*) **physical** – dogs are all one species but dachshunds and great danes have problems in mating;
(*d*) **genetical** – a male donkey mated to a mare can give a mule: mules are sterile because horse and donkey chromosomes will not pair up properly at meiosis, so they produce ineffective gametes.

8 Darwin recognised that evolution is a *branching* process. Modern types of ape, e.g. gorillas, did *not* give rise to man, but both man and gorilla are likely to have had common ancestors in the distant past (see Fig. 14.2).

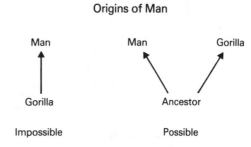

Fig. 14.2

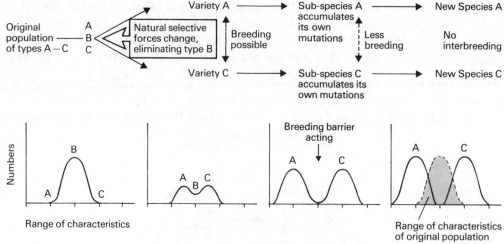

Fig. 14.3 Summary of the processes of evolution

14.4   EVIDENCE FOR EVOLUTION

1   Fossils: organisms from the distant past whose hard parts and sometimes impressions of soft parts are preserved in sedimentary rocks. Are rarely found since dead organisms usually disintegrate by decaying. Oldest fossils known are blue-green algae (similar to bacteria) from 1600 million years ago. The fossil record (see Fig. 14.4) clearly indicates that:

(a) the variety of life today did *not* arise all at once.

(b) first life was aquatic. Terrestrial groups came later (fern-like plants, insects and amphibia arose about 400 million years ago).

(c) groups with improved adaptations increase in importance while those less efficient decline (or even become extinct). Particularly true of improvements in methods of reproduction. Thus ferns, dependent on water for fertilisation (see unit 17.8), gave way to conifers whose gametes are enclosed in a pollen tube and thus need no water to swim in. Similarly, amphibia gave way to reptiles as the dominant land group (see unit 12.17). Fossils of pollinating insects and of insect-pollinated flowers are of approximately the same age. These 'coincidences' can be explained in evolutionary terms.

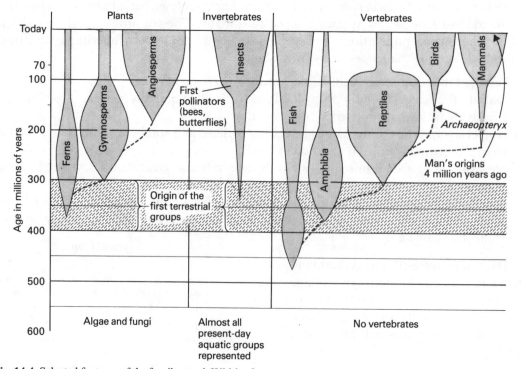

Fig. 14.4 Selected features of the fossil record. Width of areas representing groups named above relates to increase or decrease in abundance

2 Comparative anatomy

(a) *'Link organisms'*, so intermediate in structure between recognised groups that they are hard to place in either, suggest a means of transition. Examples: *Archaeopteryx*, a fossil was lizard-like but feathered, suggesting a reptile to bird transition. Modern cycads (primitive gymnosperms) have *swimming* gametes inside their pollen tubes, suggesting the intermediate stage between fern and conifer methods of fertilisation. Molluscs are unsegmented; annelids segmented. Yet *Neopilina*, a modern limpet-like mollusc, apparently very similar to very ancient fossils, has some annelid structures segmentally arranged in its body. This suggests an annelid to mollusc link (see also **3**(b) below).

(b) The *pentadactyl limb* of vertebrates has a common structure: five fingers, wrist bones and two lower and one upper long bones. Yet the purposes to which they are put are very different in bats, men and whales. Their limbs are thought by evolutionists to have been 'modified by descent' i.e. they are *homologous:* same origin, but different purposes. Wings of bats and butterflies have the same purpose but different structural origins and are *analogous* (see Fig. 14.5).

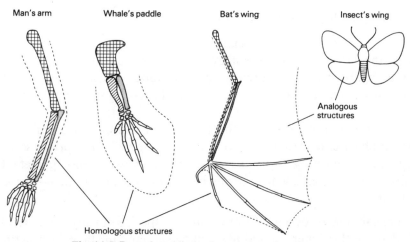

Fig. 14.5 Pentadactyl limbs: homology and analogy

3 Embryos and larvae

(a) Despite very different adult forms, early embryos of *all* vertebrates are very similar, e.g. with gill pouches in the neck region.

(b) Larvae of marine annelids and molluscs are very similar.

Evolutionists claim that, up to a point, each individual organism's development follows its embryonic evolutionary history, and so points to groups from which it has been derived.

4 Classification

Taxonomists (see unit 3.1) often have great difficulty in deciding where one species ends and another begins. This is explicable if one accepts that species are continuously changing into new species. Even Linnaeus believed that species were 'not immutable'.

5 Geographical distribution

Fossil marsupials are found world-wide but decline in numbers soon after fossil placental mammals appeared. Australia, with its abundant marsupials, separated from mainland Asia before placentals appeared. Evolutionists suggest that such a wide range of types of marsupial exists in Australia alone because they were able to evolve in the absence of the more efficient placentals (which had their origins outside Australia).

6 Direct evidence of change in species

(a) *Resistance:* bacteria become drug-resistant (e.g. to penicillin); insects become insecticide-resistant (e.g. to DDT); and rats resistant to rodenticides (e.g. Warfarin).

(b) *Selective breeding* has produced radically new strains of plants, e.g. rice and maize, and of animals, e.g. dogs and horses (see unit 14.6). What man can do, so can nature.

(*c*) *Industrial melanism* in the peppered moth, *Biston betularia*. Paleness results from the genotype **pp**. A mutation to **P** causes blackness (melanism). Black moths survive predation from birds better than pale ones on sooty, lichen-free tree trunks. Pale ones survive better than black on lichen-covered (unpolluted) trunks. From 1850–1900 the proportion of blacks rose to up to 98% in polluted woods to the north-east of our main industrial towns (the prevailing winds in Britain are south-westerly).

Evolutionists argue that the accumulation of many such useful mutations over much longer periods of time lead to evolution of new species.

14.5   OTHER THEORIES OF EVOLUTION

1   Lamarck suggested that ancestors of giraffes (with short necks) achieved longer necks by striving to reach up to foliage of trees. This change, he said, was passed on to offspring. Conversely humans achieved their vestigial tail (coccyx) by failing to use it enough. Weissmann prevented mice from using their tails for one hundred generations by cutting their tails off at birth but the one-hundred-and-first generation had tails as long as the first.

The theory of use and disuse is *wrong:* organisms inherit genotypes, not phenotypes.

2   Biblical views (added to by theologians)

(*a*) The variety of organisms was specially created, all at once – Bishop Usher in Victorian times put the date at 4004 BC. Fossil evidence disproves this.

(*b*) Man was regarded as the supreme creation, quite separate from and 'lord' over all animals. Now, even the Roman Catholic encyclical of 1951 recognises the animal origin of man.

(*c*) The 'Creation' was regarded as the product of a grand 'Design' by a 'Designer'. Science emphasises that *chance* events largely shape biological progress. Mutations and meiosis; the first meeting of your parents, and which two of their gametes fused to form your first cell – all events with a strong element of chance in them – these have shaped your destiny.

If the biblical view of design of organisms for special purposes is correct, it is indeed surprising that the 'Designer' should have made so many mistakes (extinction) or created half-way houses such as *Archaeopteryx*.

A very few Christians ('fundamentalists') today believe the account of the origin of species exactly as it appears in the book of *Genesis* in the bible. However, the neo-Darwinian theory is still only a theory and requires further evidence to convince some people.

14.6   ARTIFICIAL SELECTION

(Selective breeding by man)

(*a*) **Plants:** by cross-breeding strains with desirable characteristics, increasing the mutation rate in stamens using radioactive materials, and by vegetative propagation of new strains thus obtained, man has produced:

  (*i*) disease-resistant crops, e.g. strawberries resistant to viruses;
  (*ii*) high-yielding crops, e.g. rice plants that do not blow over in wind, so spoiling the rice grains: they also grow fast enough to allow two or three crops per year instead of one;
  (*iii*) nutritious crops, e.g. maize strains containing all the essential amino acids, so helping to fight kwashiorkor (see unit 4.21).

(*b*) **Animals:** by cross-breeding strains and breeding from interesting mutants, man has produced:

  (*i*) dogs as different as bull-dogs, dachshunds, St Bernards and Afghan hounds;
  (*ii*) horses such as Shetlands, shires, race-horses and mules;
  (*iii*) cattle for milk (Jerseys), for beef (Herefords) and resistant to trypanosome diseases in Africa (Zebu × Brahmin).

15 Ecology

15.1 THE BIOSPHERE – (ITS LIMITS AND ORGANISATION)

Ecology is the scientific study of organisms in relation to their environment.

Environment: the influences acting upon organisms. Two kinds:

(*a*) **biotic:** other organisms such as predators, competitors, parasites.
(*b*) **abiotic:** non-living influences, such as climate, soil and water currents.

Habitat: the particular type of locality in an environment in which an organism lives, e.g. amongst weeds in a pond (stickleback) or at low tide mark on exposed rocky shores (mussels).

Usually every species of organism exists as a **population** in its environment and not just as a single individual. Together, all the populations of all the species interact to form a **community** within their ecosystem. The role each species plays in the community is its **niche,** e.g. an earthworm's niche is to affect soil fertility by its activities (see unit 15.8) and provide food for shrews, moles and some birds.

Ecosystem: any area in which organisms interact both with each other *and* with their abiotic environment, to form a self-sustaining unit (see Fig. 15.1).

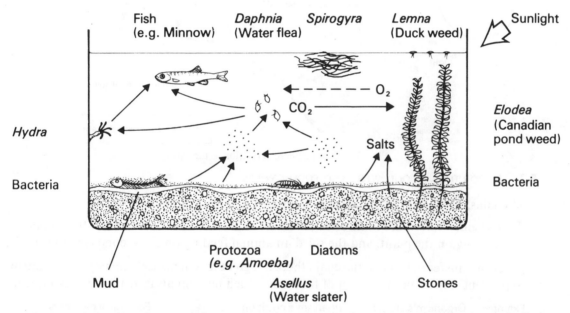

Fig. 15.1 Interrelationships of representative pond organisms of an aquarium ecosystem (arrows represent feeding)

Examples: ponds, jungle, ocean or even a puddle. Ecosystems are not actually distinct, they interact with others. Thus dragonfly nymphs in a pond emerge as flying predators which catch their insect prey over both pond and meadow, so linking both these ecosystems. Even ecosystems in the UK and Africa are linked – by the same swallows feeding on insects in both areas according to the time of year.

Biosphere: (the earth's surface that harbours life) a very thin layer of soil and the oceans, lakes, rivers and air (see Fig. 15.2). The biosphere is the sum of all the world's ecosystems and is isolated from any others that may exist in space. However, other celestial bodies influence it:

(*a*) life depends on solar energy (from the sun);
(*b*) other radiations from various sources cause mutations;
(*c*) gravitational fields of sun and moon cause tides;
(*d*) at least 200 tonnes of cosmic dust arrive on earth daily.

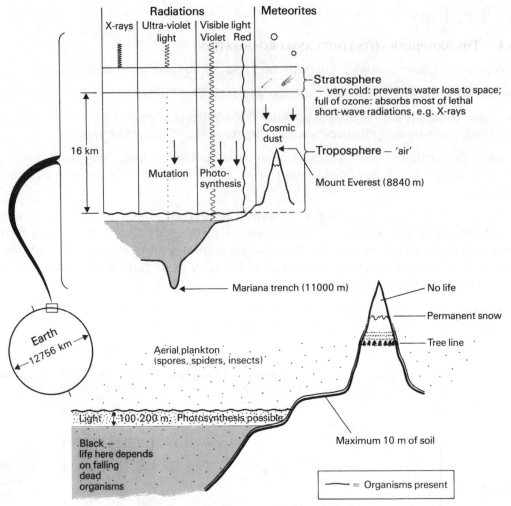

Fig. 15.2 The biosphere in relation to the earth

15.2   FOOD CHAINS, FOOD WEBS AND FOOD CYCLES

Food chains, webs and cycles are units composing an ecosystem.

1   Food chain: a minimum of three organisms, the first always a green plant, the second an animal feeding on the plant, and the third an animal feeding on the second (see Fig. 15.3).

At each transfer of food up the chain there is a great loss in mass **(biomass)** – anything up to 90 per cent. This is because a lot of food consumed by animals is lost due to respiration,

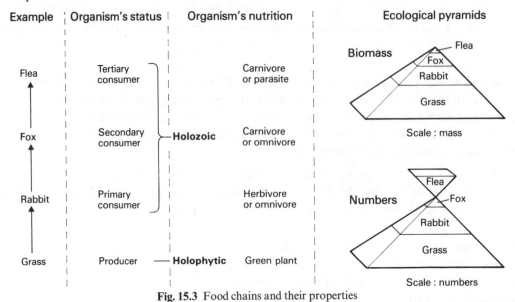

Fig. 15.3 Food chains and their properties

excretion and indigestibility (faeces), and never reaches the next member of the chain. Thus food chains can be expressed quantitatively as **pyramids of numbers** or, more usefully to farmers and game-wardens, as **pyramids of biomass** (see Fig. 15.3). Such considerations of quantity (of organisms) explain why:

(*a*) the number of species in a food chain rarely exceeds five;

(*b*) the biomass of each species is limited by the capacity of producers (green plants) to produce food.

2 Food web: a number of interlinked food chains. In an ecosystem that includes foxes and rabbits, the diet of consumers is usually more varied than a food chain suggests. Foxes eat beetles, voles, chickens and pheasants as well as rabbits, and rabbits eat a great variety of green plants (see Fig. 15.4).

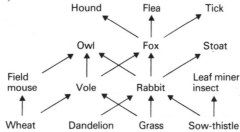

Fig. 15.4 Food web: a number of interrelated food chains

3 Food cycles: food chains with decomposers added. Decomposers decay dead organisms and excreta (organic matter), releasing mineral salts and CO_2 (inorganic matter) – which producers need and could not otherwise obtain (see unit 16.2). Food cycles can be expressed in more detail as element cycles (see units 15.6, 15.7).

4 Energy chain: the passage of energy from the sun along a food chain and on to decomposers. Energy is *not* cycled (Fig. 15.5). It is progressively lost along the chain, e.g. as heat from respiration.

The units making up the biosphere may be summarised as in Fig. 15.6.

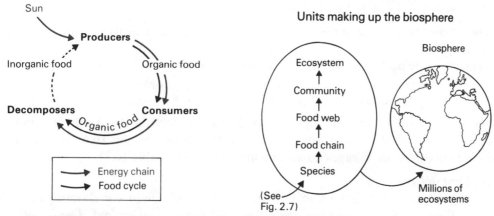

Fig. 15.5 The energy chain in a food cycle   Fig. 15.6 Units making up the biosphere

15.3   FEEDING RELATIONSHIPS BETWEEN SPECIES

1 Predation: a *predator* is usually larger than its prey, an organism it kills for food, e.g. fox kills rabbit; seal kills penguin. *Note:* Both organisms are animals, never plants.

2 Parasitism: a *parasite* is an organism living on or in another organism called its *host*, from which it derives its food usually without killing it.

Examples: mosquito, green-fly (ecto-parasites); tapeworm (see unit 17.11), trypanosome (endo-parasites).

3 Symbiosis: a *symbiont* and its partner (also a *symbiont*) live in close association mutually assisting each other, e.g. nitrogen-fixing bacteria supply nitrates they have made to legumes, which supply carbohydrates in return (see unit 16.3); or bees gain nectar and pollen from plants which in return get pollinated (see unit 17.18).

4   Competition: occurs between two organisms (*competitors*) both attempting to obtain a commodity which is in short supply in the environment.
Examples: plants compete for light, birds for nesting sites, stags for hinds, foxes for voles. The planting density for crops is determined so as to minimise competition between individual plants. Weeds are successful competitors of crops.

5   Commensalism: a loose relationship between two organisms in which the *commensal* (smaller) benefits by feeding on scraps of food wasted by the *host* (larger) – who is neither harmed nor helped, e.g. sparrows feed on man's discarded bread. Commensals have alternative food, so relationship is not obligatory.

Table 15.1   Summary comparison of feeding relationships between organisms
($+$ = benefits, $-$ = harmed, $\bigcirc$ = unaffected)

	Organisms		Size relationship
	A	B	
Predation	Predator $+$	Prey $-$	A > B
Parasitism	Parasite $+$	Host $-$	A < B
Symbiosis	Symbiont $+$	Symbiont $+$	Any
Competition	Competitor $-$	Competitor $-$	Any
Commensalism	Commensal $+$	Host $\bigcirc$	A > B

15.4   STABLE AND UNSTABLE ECOSYSTEMS

Stable ecosystem: the numbers of organisms fluctuate about a mean, e.g. due to winter and summer. Has main (dominant) plant species which cannot be out-competed in its environment, e.g. oaks in mature oakwood.

Unstable ecosystem: large changes in numbers of most species due to a changing environment. Examples:
(*a*)   *succession* – one dominant group of species out-competes another group, *e.g.*:

> **pond**   **marsh**   **oakwood**
> (with *Elodea, Spirogyra, Daphnia*) $\xrightarrow{\text{silting}}$ (with bullrush, *Iris*) $\xrightarrow{\text{drying}}$ (with oaks)

(*b*)   *pollution or disease* – may disrupt the food web by causing the death of important organisms, e.g. sooty smoke from industry kills lichens (see unit 16.6); or Dutch-elm disease kills elms; or sewage causes eutrophication (see Table 16.2).

Causes of instability
If any member of a food chain is removed, it affects the whole chain, e.g. shooting foxes kills their fleas, allows rabbits to increase and grass will become over-grazed. *Thus an effect on one is an effect on all.*

In simple ecosystems (few food chains), e.g. the terrestrial Arctic or man's monocultures on farms, any effect on one species can easily affect the rest. Complex ecosystems are more stable, e.g. tropical forest, owing to a great variety of alternative foods.

15.5   SOIL COMPONENTS

Soil: the layer of earth that harbours life. Consists of·
1 Rock particles
2 air
3 water
4 mineral salts
5 humus
6 organisms.

Table 15.2 Comparison of sandy soil and clay soil

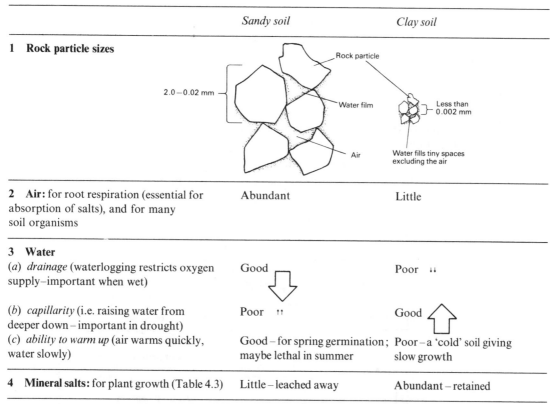

	Sandy soil	*Clay soil*
1 Rock particle sizes	(diagram)	(diagram)
2 Air: for root respiration (essential for absorption of salts), and for many soil organisms	Abundant	Little
3 Water		
(*a*) *drainage* (waterlogging restricts oxygen supply–important when wet)	Good	Poor
(*b*) *capillarity* (i.e. raising water from deeper down – important in drought)	Poor	Good
(*c*) *ability to warm up* (air warms quickly, water slowly)	Good – for spring germination; maybe lethal in summer	Poor – a 'cold' soil giving slow growth
4 Mineral salts: for plant growth (Table 4.3)	Little – leached away	Abundant – retained

Thus a **silty soil,** with its particle size intermediate between sand and clay (0.02–0.002 mm) 'averages out' their properties, giving near-ideal conditions for plant growth.

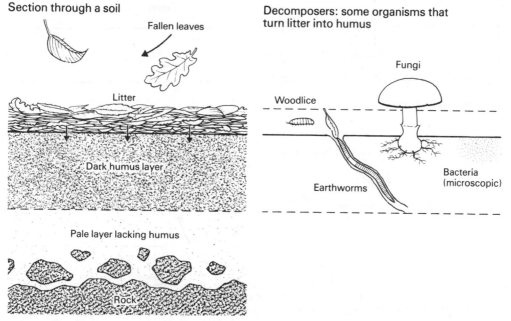

Fig. 15.7 Structure of soil and the effects of decomposers in incorporating humus

5 Humus – dead organic matter in soil. Mostly decomposing *litter* (fallen leaves) *or manure.* Improves soil by: (*a*) providing mineral salts from decay; (*b*) providing air spaces (improves clay); (*c*) retaining moisture (improves sand); (*d*) improving crumb structure (prevents soil from being blown away); (*e*) encouraging earthworms (see unit 15.8).

6 Organisms: assist circulation of elements. **Decomposers** in soil are particularly important, turning dead organic matter (unusable by green plants) into inorganic food for them, e.g. salts and CO_2. **Bacteria** have special roles in the circulation of nitrogen and carbon in nature (see Fig. 15.8). Roots of **green plants** bind soil, preventing erosion.

15.6 NITROGEN CYCLE

Green plants need nitrates for protein synthesis.

Nitrates are available to green plants from four sources:

(*a*) man-made fertilisers;

(*b*) lightning – causes a little nitrate to fall in rain;

(*c*) nitrogen-fixing bacteria – the only organisms capable of converting nitrogen gas into compounds;

(*d*) nitrifying bacteria – oxidise ammonium compounds to nitrites and then nitrates, if there is air for them to use.

Nitrates are turned into nitrogen by de-nitrifying bacteria if the soil lacks air, as in waterlogged conditions. Nitrogen gas is useless to green plants.

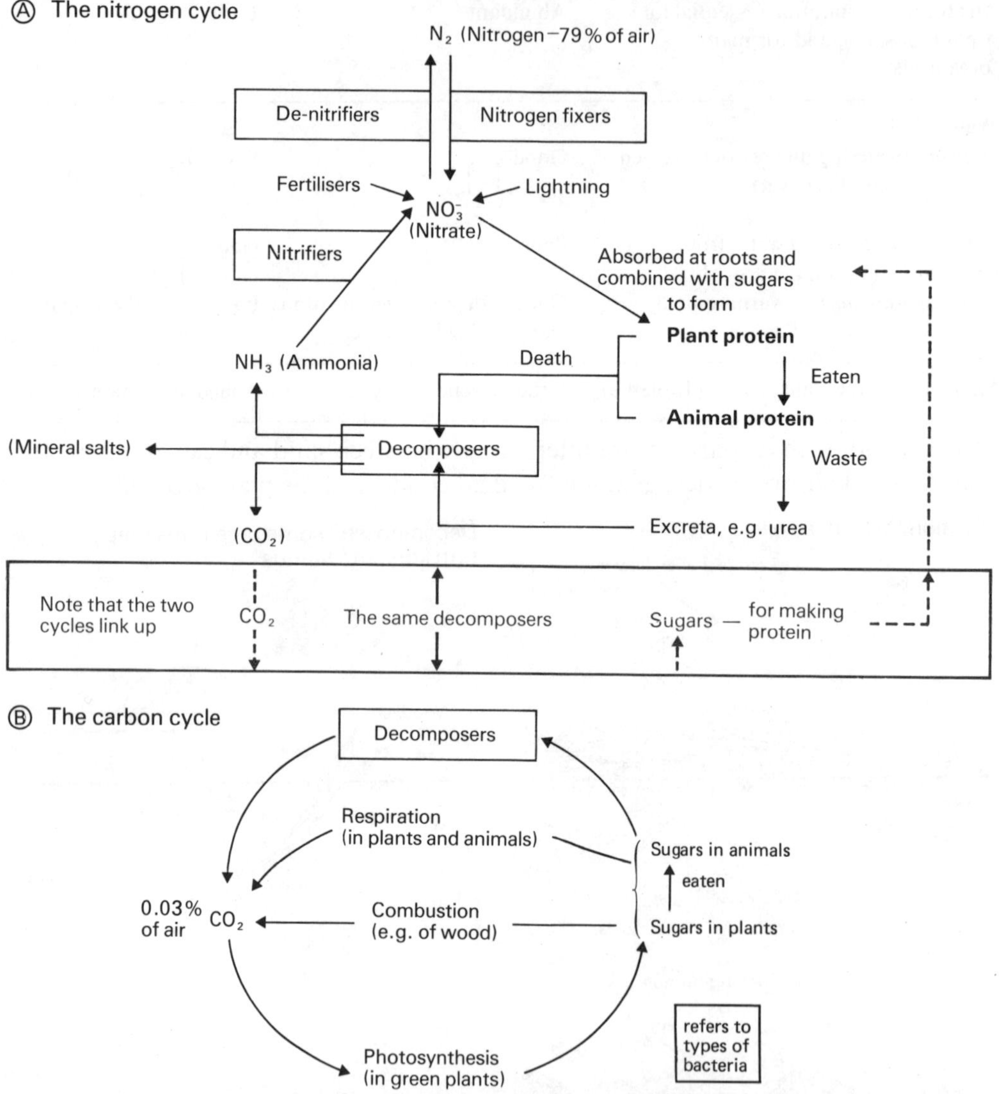

Fig. 15.8 (A) The nitrogen cycle (B) The carbon cycle

In green plants, nitrates and sugars form amino acids; these become proteins. Animals convert plant proteins into their own, but in doing so waste some, e.g. as urea, which is excreted.

Decomposers break down dead organisms and their wastes. Nitrogen compounds in them, e.g. proteins, end up as ammonia and then ammonium compounds.

15.7 CARBON CYCLE

Green plants *photosynthesise* CO_2 into sugars. Most other organic molecules are made using sugar, e.g. cellulose in wood or proteins and oils in seeds and leaves. When these are eaten by animals, the digested products are turned into animal carbohydrates, fats and proteins.

This variety of organic molecules is returned to air as CO_2 during respiration in plants, animals, and bacteria of *decay*; or by *combustion*.

Fuels include wood and the 'fossil fuels' coal, petroleum and natural gas. Fossil fuels were formed by the partial decay and compression by earth-forces of plants millions of years ago.

15.8   EARTHWORMS AND SOIL

Earthworms *(see also* unit 17.7):

(*a*) *aerate* and *drain* soil by tunnelling;
(*b*) *fertilise* soil by:

>   (*i*) pulling litter down into tunnels for bacteria to decompose;
>   (*ii*) excreting urine;
> (*iii*) decomposing when dead;

(*c*) bring *salts,* leached to lower layers, up again to roots (in worm casts);
(*d*) *neutralise* soil acidity by secreting lime into it (from gut glands);
(*e*) *grind* coarse soil finer in gut (in gizzard).

These activities are exactly what a farmer aims to do to make a *loam* (cultivated soil, with all six soil components in proportions suitable for good plant growth).

15.9   WATER CYCLE

In the *water cycle* most of the water circulated does not go through organisms:

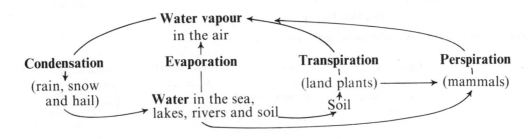

---

16 Man and his environment

Man has two environments: that outside his skin and the other inside it. He must manage both if he is to stay alive as an individual and as a species.

Man produces more food for himself than nature alone could provide, by farming the land. Farming depends on producing a fertile soil (see unit 15.5); on breeding good plant and animal food-species (see unit 14.6); and on reducing their pests and diseases (see unit 16.4).

Agricultural practices

1   Ploughing
2   Liming   4   Crop rotation
3   Manuring (= Fertilising)   5   Pest control

16.1   PLOUGHING

(*a*) aerates and drains soil by creating ridges and furrows;
(*b*) brings leached salts up to near the surface for roots;
(*c*) brings pests, sheltering deep down, up to the surface for frost to kill;
(*d*) allows frost to break up the ridges of soil;
(*e*) turns organic matter, e.g. wheat stubble, into the ground to decay.

16.2   LIMING AND FERTILISING

Liming – addition of powdered $CaCO_3$:

(a) neutralises acidity;

(b) allows efficient application of fertilisers
(see Fig. 16.1);

(c) flocculates ('clumps') clay particles
together into larger groups ('crumbs')
with air spaces between them.

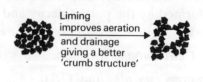

Liming improves aeration and drainage giving a better 'crumb structure'

Fertilising – restoring mineral salts (lost in crops) to the soil.

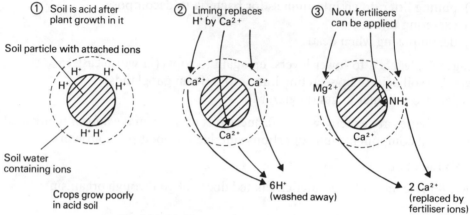

Fig. 16.1 Liming and fertilising – chemical effects

Table 16.1   Comparison of organic and inorganic fertilisers

	Organic: 'green manure' = legumes ploughed in to decay 'Brown manure' = animal dung + urine	**Inorganic:** factory products, e.g. $(NH_4)_2SO_4$ or wastes, e.g. basic slag
Cost	Cheap	Expensive
Application	Difficult (bulky, sticky)	Easy (powders, granules)
Action	Slow but long-lasting	Quick but short-lasting
Soil structure	Improved (see 'humus')	Not improved
Earthworms	Encouraged	·Often detrimental to them

16.3   CROP ROTATION

Crop rotation – growth of different crops on the same land in successive years without manuring each year. The two harvested crops have different mineral requirements and often obtain them from different soil depths. In the 'fallow year' legumes, e.g. clover, are sown to restore *nitrogen compounds* to the soil when the plants decay after being ploughed in. Other minerals (removed in crops) are restored by fertilising. (See Fig. 16.2 on page 131.)

16.4   PEST CONTROL

Pest organisms, e.g. locusts, termites, weeds, reduce man's agricultural efforts or other interests. *Man* created pests by providing organisms, normally held in check in their ecosystems, with unusual opportunities for increase in numbers in a monoculture (e.g. of corn, cotton or cows).

Chemical control – expensive. May eliminate pest but also kills harmless organisms too. Examples: DDT (insects); 2-4D (weeds) (see unit 16.6).

Biological control – cheap. Use of a natural enemy of pest to *control* numbers (some damage must be expected), e.g. guppy fish eat mosquito larvae in ponds (see also unit 17.19).

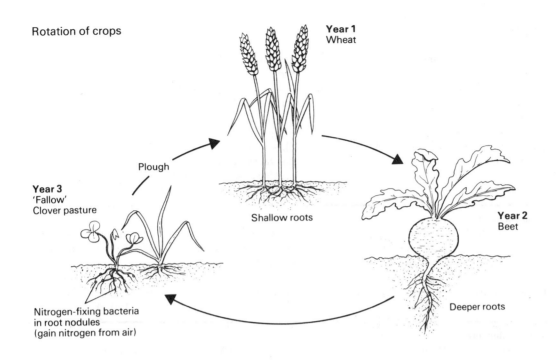

Rotation of crops

Year 1 Wheat

Plough

Year 3 'Fallow' Clover pasture

Shallow roots

Year 2 Beet

Nitrogen-fixing bacteria in root nodules (gain nitrogen from air)

Deeper roots

16.5 HUMAN POPULATION CRISIS (PROBLEMS)

Man's population growth has been *exponential*:

Year	Population	
1630 (estimated)	500 million	
1830	1000 million	200 years
1930	2000 million	100 years
1975	4000 million	estimated to rise to 6000 million by 2000.

This has been possible because of improvements in:

1 **Agriculture:** improved strains of crops and livestock; mechanisation and fertilisers– more food.

2 **Sanitation:** disposal of excreta, finally via sewage farms.

3 **Water supply:** filtration, finally chlorination.

4 **Medicine:** inoculation, drugs, antibiotics, aseptic surgery.

reduced death rate from disease

Consequences

Bacteria on an agar plate show exponential growth (log phase). This leads to exhaustion of food and self-pollution resulting in mass death (crash phase) (see Fig. 16.3, graph 1). Man is on the log phase still, but he is both polluting the biosphere and reducing its resources. Unlike bacteria, man has the ability to avoid the crash phase by using a variety of solutions.

16.6 POLLUTION

Pollution: waste substances or energy from human activities which upset the normal balances in the biosphere. Anything from noise (aircraft), and heat (atomic power stations) to various substances in excess (sewage, DDT).

Table 16.2 Air, land and water pollutants

Air pollutants	Origin	Effect	Solution
(a) Sulphur dioxide (SO_2)	Coal burning; sulphide ore smelting	Smog; bronchitis	Burn smokeless fuels; SO_2 extraction units in factories
(b) Soot	Factories, steam engines	Smog; coats leaves, reducing photosynthesis	Smokeless fuels; factory chimney filters

Table 16.2 – (*cont'd*)

(c) Carbon monoxide (CO)	Car exhausts	Prevents O_2 being carried by haemoglobin	After-burners in car exhausts turn $CO \rightarrow CO_2$
(d) Lead (Pb)	Anti-knock in petrol	Harms nervous system	Low-compression engines
(e) Chloro-fluoro-methanes	Aerosol propellants	Allow more u.v. light to penetrate stratosphere by breaking down ozone: may increase skin cancer incidence.	Not yet devised
Land pollutants			
(a) Insecticides	Crop protection; control of disease vectors, e.g. mosquito	May kill top consumers*; may lower photosynthesis rate of marine algae	Ban undesirable ones, e.g. DDT, as UK has done†
(b) Radioactive wastes	Nuclear reactor accidents and wastes; atom bombs	Mutations‡	Nuclear waste silos – but some have leaked
Water pollutants			
(a) Sewage	Human	Eutrophication§	Sewage treatment
(b) Artificial fertilisers	Excessive agricultural use	Eutrophication§	Use of green and brown manures (Units 16.2, 16.3)
(c) Petroleum	Tanker accidents	Oiled sea birds, beaches	Effective accident prevention
(d) Mercury (organic)	Chemical works; fungicides on seeds, wood	Minamata disease (paralysis, idiots born)	Effluent purification

* Tiny amounts in producers are concentrated along a food chain into top consumers. Thus in 1950's eagles had very high DDT levels and laid thin-shelled eggs that broke easily. Their population fell.

† Poor countries cannot afford to do this in the tropics – famine or disease would result. DDT is cheap, effective.

‡ Cobalt is part of vitamin B_{12}, strontium is part of bone. If ^{60}Co or ^{90}Sr enter body, radiations emitted can cause leukaemia.

§ *Eutrophication:* excess sewage creates population explosion in bacteria decaying it. This depletes O_2, killing aquatic animals – which provide even more matter for decay. Decay produces abundant mineral salts which encourage algae to multiply – water goes green.

16.7   DEPLETION OF RESOURCES

Resources are of two types: non-renewable (non-living) and renewable (living)

(a) *Non-renewable,* e.g. **minerals:** zinc – may last another 10 years; natural gas – 30 years, at present rates of use from *known* resources;

e.g. **soil:** removed by erosion following unwise land use such as over-grazing or clear-felling of forest (thus removing the binding action of roots). New soil takes centuries to form through weathering of rock and the action of organisms (see unit 15.5).

(b) *Renewable,* e.g. **foods:** herring and whales have been over-fished. Cutting down of forests exceeds planting. Harvesting should not exceed replacement rate.

Destruction of wild-life

Agricultural needs destroy natural habitats; pesticides, poison; and hunting for 'sport' or fashionable items, e.g. skins, ivory, may all lead to extinction of species, e.g. moa, Cape lion.

Food shortage

Two thirds of the world population lack either enough calories or protein or both in their diet. Poor nations are unable to pay for the surplus food of rich ones.

Reduced living space

Overcrowded populations lead to greater chance of epidemic diseases and social diseases, e.g. vandalism, baby-bashing, drug-taking, alcoholism.

16.8 HUMAN POPULATION CRISIS (SOLUTIONS)

Solutions

1 **Contraception** (see unit 12.19) and abortion (removing unwanted embryos) would by themselves reduce the rate of increase in population if used world-wide.

2 **Conservation of minerals:** use of substitutes for metals, e.g. carbon-fibre plastics; reversing the throw-away mentality by making durable products, e.g. cars that last; recycling metals in discarded items.

Note: Lowered industrial production (and fewer jobs) must be accepted as a result of these policies.

3 **Conservation of wild-life and natural scenery:** strict guardianship of nature reserves; acceptance that minerals in a mountain may be less valuable than the beauty it affords. Man's need for recreation and enjoyment of nature is as necessary for health as meeting his material needs.

4 **Conservation of renewable resources:** by never taking more than can be replaced (by reproduction).

5 **Finding new (acceptable) energy sources,** e.g. solar power, tide power. Fast-breeder reactors will produce very much more dangerous waste than conventional reactors – a possible mutation hazard. But using fossil fuels (coal, oil) to a greater extent may raise CO_2 levels in air causing a *'greenhouse effect'* that raises global temperature. This could melt polar ice caps, thus raising sea level and flooding many major coastal cities, e.g. London, New York. To re-cycle metals, produce substitutes for them, and make artificial fertilisers is very energy-consuming.

6 **New sources of food:** greater dependence on micro-organisms, e.g. 'SCP' (see unit 17.2) and soya bean meat-substitutes.

16.9 PREDICTIONS FOR THE FUTURE OF MANKIND

An international group of scientists called the 'Club of Rome', concerned at the misuse of the biosphere by man, gathered data from 1900–1970 on population, pollution, food and mineral resources in the world. Using a computer they made predictions about present and possible future trends in the world (see Fig. 16.3, graphs 2, 3 and 4).

These predictions do not have to come to pass. Hopefully, solutions will be implemented to avoid the fate of the bacteria shown in Fig. 16.3, graph 1 (see page 134).

MAN'S INTERNAL ENVIRONMENT

Hormones and nerves (see unit 9.9) help to stabilise the body's internal environment (achieve homeostasis). Any change from normal is called **disease.**

16.10 TYPES OF DISEASE IN MAN

1 **Genetic:** since these diseases are inherited, they are *incurable.*
Examples: **haemophilia** – a gene mutation (see unit 13.11); **mongolism:** baby has an extra chromosome, i.e. $46 + 1$ owing to faulty meiosis in mother. Person has retarded development and dies usually before 40.

2 **Diet deficiency:** curable by eating a balanced diet.
Examples: lack of iodine (**goitre,** see unit 4.3); or vitamin C (**scurvy,** see unit 4.5); or protein (**kwashiorkor** – matchstick limbs, pot belly, see unit 4.21).

3 **Hormonal:** curable by artificial supply of hormone.
Examples: lack of thyroxin (**cretinism**) or insulin (**diabetes**) (see unit 9.8).

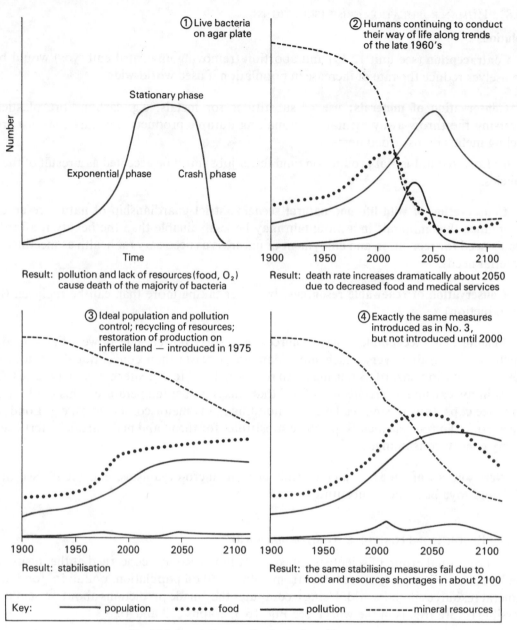

Fig. 16.3 Population graphs: bacteria and humans

Graphs based on those in THE LIMITS TO GROWTH: A report for THE CLUB OF ROME'S Project on the Predicament of Mankind, by Donella H Meadows, Dennis L Meadows, Jørgen Randers, William W Behrens III. A Potomac Associates book published by Universe Books, New York, 1972.

4   Pathogenic: entry of parasites (pathogens) into body which upset its metabolism.

Examples: viruses (see unit 17.1); bacteria (see unit 17.2); protozoa (see unit 17.4).

(*a*) For **prevention** (better than cure):

    (*i*) **kill vectors,** e.g. mosquitoes carrying malaria; or intermediate hosts, e.g. snails carrying bilharzia;

    (*ii*) **prevent access** of parasite by hygiene, water chlorination, cooking food or protective measures, e.g. mosquito nets;

    (*iii*) employ **preventive medicine** (prophylaxis) using immunisation (see below) or drugs, e.g. mepacrine for malaria;

    (*iv*) **quarantine** those who are ill (isolate sources of infection).

(*b*) A **cure** requires:

    (*i*) **hospitalisation:** rest and good food assist body's own defences;

    (*ii*) **medicines:** drugs, antibiotics kill pathogens.

16.11 NATURAL DEFENCES OF THE BODY AGAINST PATHOGENS

1 Skin: keratin; sweat (which is antiseptic) – (see unit 7.7).

2 Blood clotting: provides a temporary barrier before wound heals (see unit 5.8).

3 Phagocytes: ingest micro-organisms (see unit 5.8).

4 Lymphocytes: make antibodies (see unit 5.8) to kill pathogens or neutralise their poisons (with anti-toxins), thus making body immune (protected). There are two methods of immunisation:

Table 16.3 **Comparison of active and passive immunity**

	Active immunity (body participates)	**Passive immunity** (body passive)
Method	Weakened or dead strain of pathogen introduced, e.g. polio **vaccine**	Antibodies made by another animal, e.g. horse, are injected
Protection	(*a*) long-lasting ('boosters' prolong protection e.g. anti-tetanus every 3 years) (*b*) takes weeks to develop	(*a*) short-lived (body destroys the foreign antibodies) (*b*) immediate

16.12 NOTABLE CONTRIBUTORS TO HEALTH AND HYGIENE

Edward Jenner (1749–1823): practised *vaccination:* scratching cowpox (spots from vaccinia virus on cows) into skin protects person from smallpox. Cowpox – mild spots in dairy maids; smallpox – disfiguring or lethal disease.

Louis Pasteur (1822–1895): father of *bacteriology.* Discovered the bacterial nature of putrefaction and many diseases. Saved silk industry (pebrine disease of silkworms), brewers ('ropy' beer) poultry farmers (chicken cholera) and cattle farmers (anthrax) from severe losses by developing sterile techniques and vaccines. Finally, developed a rabies vaccine to protect humans.

Joseph Lister (1827–1912): developed *antiseptic surgery.* Used fine phenol spray to kill bacteria during operations, dramatically reducing hospital deaths. Today *aseptic* surgery is used – sterilisation of all equipment before use, in autoclaves (see unit 17.2).

Alexander Fleming (1881–1955): discovered lysozyme (natural antiseptic in tears and saliva) and the *antibiotic* penicillin (see unit 17.5).

DRUGS, ANTIBIOTICS, DISINFECTANTS AND ANTISEPTICS

'Drugs' are chemicals made by man or organisms. Some are harmful and possession of them is illegal, e.g. LSD – which has no medical purpose. Others (in the right doses) assist medically, e.g. sulphonamides for curing bacterial infections; aspirin for headaches; and belladonna for helping people with ailing hearts. The term 'drug' is thus too vague to be very useful.

Antibiotics are chemicals secreted by bacteria or fungi and extracted by man for his own use in killing micro-organisms in his body. *Examples:* penicillin, aureomycin.

Disinfectants are chemicals made by chemists to kill micro-organisms, e.g. neat 'Dettol' in latrines.

Antiseptics are chemicals used in such a dose that they kill micro-organisms but not human cells with which they make contact. May be diluted disinfectants, e.g. weak 'Dettol' for gargling or bathing cuts.

17 A variety of life

17.1 VIRUSES

Size: approximately 0.00001 mm, i.e. 10 nm (1/100 size of bacteria)–visible only with electron microscope.

Structure: protein coat around a DNA strand (a few genes) (see Fig. 17.1).

Living?: no; are not cells; having no metabolism of their own (see unit 2.1).

All are *parasites*, killing host cells as they reproduce within them, using the cell's energy and materials. This causes disease, e.g. rabies.

Disease transmission

(*a*) by water, e.g. polio;
(*b*) by droplet (sneezing), e.g. colds, 'flu;
(*c*) by vector, e.g. mosquito transmits yellow fever and greenfly transmits the TMV (see Fig. 17.1).

Useful: for biological control of rabbits – myxomatosis virus.

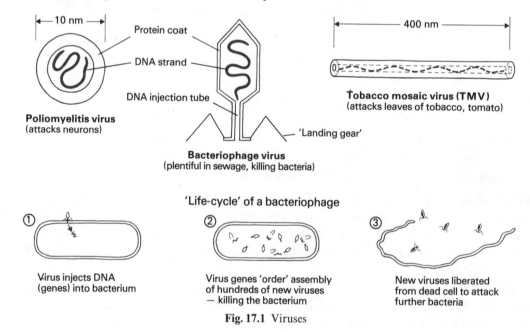

Fig. 17.1 Viruses

17.2 BACTERIA

Size: approximately 1μm, i.e. 1000 nm (1/100 size of mammal cheek cell) – the smallest cell.

Structure: Cell is unique in not having:

(*a*) nuclear membrane around its single loop chromosome;
(*b*) mitochondria (cell membrane has the same function);
(*c*) endoplasmic reticulum (see unit 2.2).

Cell is unlike a green plant cell in having no:

(*a*) chloroplasts (therefore bacteria are either saprophytes or parasites) (see unit 4.11);
(*b*) cellulose in cell walls (made of nitrogenous compounds instead) (see Fig. 17.2)

Reproduction

(*a*) by binary fission, every 20 minutes in suitable conditions.
(*b*) use a conjugation tube to transfer DNA from one bacterium to another. Bacteria do *not* reproduce by forming spores. Some bacilli, only, form spores (endospores) for survival when conditions become unfavourable.

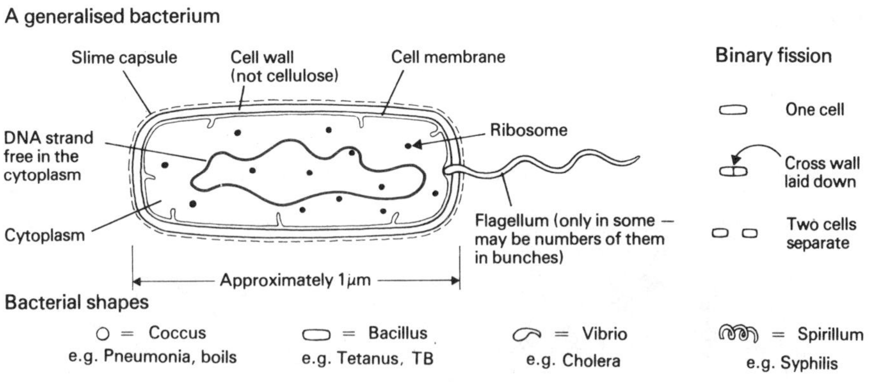

Fig. 17.2 *Bacteria*

Importance of bacteria

Helpful

(*a*) in decay, releasing nutrients for green plants (see unit 4.2);
(*b*) in fixing nitrogen for green plants (see unit 15.6);
(*c*) in industrial processes, e.g. making butter, cheese, vinegar;
(*d*) as food source – single cell protein ('SCP') fed to animals.

Harmful

(*a*) in decaying food (rotting, putrefying);
(*b*) in de-nitrifying the soil, reducing fertility (see unit 15.6);
(*c*) in causing disease to man and his animals;
(*d*) in causing food-poisoning (e.g. *Salmonella*).

Requirements

1 Moisture;
2 Organic food;
3 A suitable temperature (warmth);
4 No ultra-violet light (it kills by damaging DNA).

If these conditions are not met, bacteria die (see **1–4** below).

Man's control of harmful bacteria

1 **Dried foods:** peas, raisins, milk, meat – keep for ever.

Salting: e.g. ham, or *syruping*, e.g. peaches, plasmolyses (see unit 5.3) bacteria.

2 **Hygiene:** removal of bacterial foods by washing body, clothes, food-utensils; by disposing of refuse, excreta and hospital dressings; cleaning homes.

3 **Temperature treatment**

(*a*) *refrigeration:* deep-freeze ($-20°C$) suspends life; fridge ($+4°C$) slows rotting to acceptable level;
(*b*) *boiling:* kills most, but not spores;
(*c*) *pressure-cooking* ('sterilising' or 'autoclaving') for 10 minutes at 10 kN/m^2 (15lbs/in^2) kills all, including spores;
(*d*) *pasteurisation* (of milk): heat to 77°C for seconds and rapidly cool to 4°C.

4 **Irradiate with ultra-violet light** (thin sliced food, surgical instruments) and plan sunny homes (sunlight contains u.v. light).

5 **Chemicals** are also used to kill bacteria:

(*a*) *chlorine* in drinking water and swimming baths;
(*b*) *disinfectants* in loos;
(*c*) *medical use* of antiseptics, antibiotics, antibodies and drugs in or on man's body (see unit 16.12);
(*d*) *vinegar* for pickling food (pH too acid for bacteria).

17.3 SPIROGYRA

Spirogyra – a filamentous alga living in ponds (see Fig. 17.3).

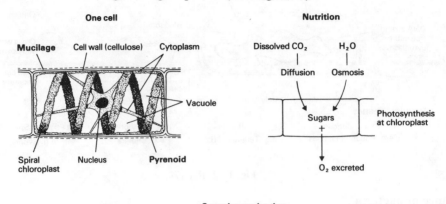

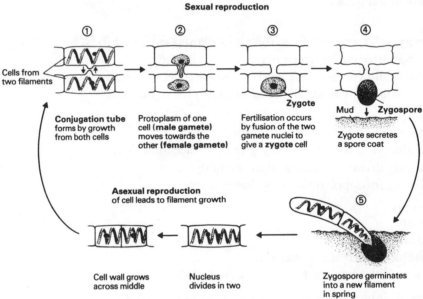

Fig. 17.3 *Spirogyra*

Structure: *Mucilage* stops *Spirogyra* drying out at surface of water, when trapped O_2 from photosynthesis causes tangled mass of filaments to float up during the day.

Pyrenoids turn sugars, made in chloroplasts, into starch.

Functions of other parts are as in any green plant cell (see unit 2.1).

Nutrition: holophytic (see unit 4.2).

Reproduction: since all cells in the filament are identical, and able to reproduce, each one may be regarded as an individual organism that happens not to have separated from its neighbour at cell division. This *asexual* reproduction occurs in summer: *sexual* occurs in autumn.

Zygospore ensures *dispersal* (carried to other ponds in mud on animals) and *survival* over the winter.

Importance of algae

1   **Diatoms** (unicellular algae) are the main plant component of plankton (phytoplankton):
(*a*) provide majority of world's O_2;
(*b*) are at base of marine food chains.

2   Some **sea-weeds** are eaten, e.g. 'Irish moss' by Irish and Japanese.

3   **Extracts:** 'agar' for bacterial culture methods; 'alginates' for ice-cream.

17.4 AMOEBA

Amoeba – a large fresh-water protozoan (up to 1 mm in diameter) (see Fig. 17.4).

Locomotion: cytoplasm in centre (plasmasol) flows forward forming a pseudopodium. At the front plasmasol fountains out, solidifying to a jelly-like tube (plasmagel) through which the centre flows. Plasmagel re-liquefies at rear end, flowing into centre.

Nutrition: holozoic (see unit 4.2). Pursues prey (algae, bacteria, other protozoa) by following the trail of chemicals they exude (chemotaxis, see unit 19.11). Ingests prey using pseudopodia; digests it in food vacuole; egests indigestible matter, e.g. cellulose.

Osmoregulation: water entering continually by osmosis, is channelled to the contractile vacuole. When full, this bursts, squirting water out. Process uses energy.

Respiration: gaseous exchange (O_2 in, CO_2 out) occurs over whole surface area (see p 58).

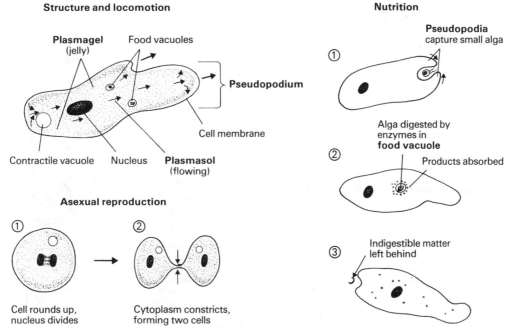

Fig. 17.4 *Amoeba*

Reproduction: asexually by binary fission; no sexual method.

Sensitivity: moves towards food; away from strong light, harmful chemicals and sharp objects.

Importance of protozoa

1 Malaria parasite (*Plasmodium*), transmitted by mosquito, kills millions of people by fever unless protected by drugs, like quinacrine.

2 Sleeping sickness parasite (*Trypanosoma*), transmitted by tse-tse fly, kills millions of people, cattle and pigs in Africa. No drug protection against some types.

3 Dysentery parasite (*Entamoeba*), transmitted by house-fly, causes dysentery (intestinal bleeding and upsets) and liver abscesses.

17.5 RHIZOPUS AND MUCOR

Rhizopus (mould on bread) and *Mucor* (mould on dung) – both 'pin-moulds' (see Fig. 17.5).

Structure: The cytoplasm, with many nuclei in it, lines the cell wall – a continuous tube (of chitin) with no partitions forming separate cells. Inside the cytoplasm is a continuous vacuole. Threads of fungus (hyphae) make up a mycelium.

Nutrition: saprophytic (see unit 4.2). Rootlet hyphae branch through the food secreting digestive enzymes and absorbing the soluble products.

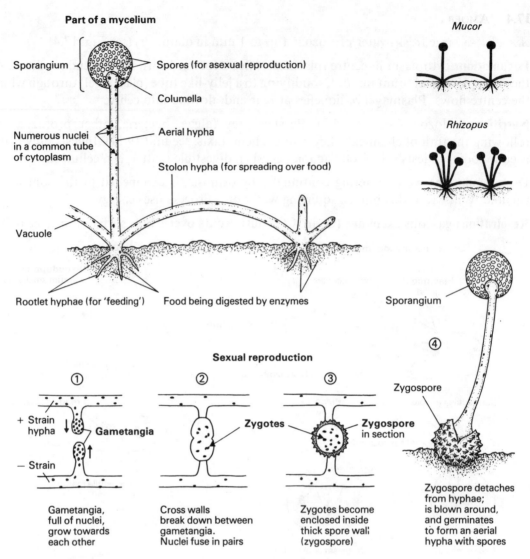

Fig. 17.5 *Mucor*

Reproduction:

(*a*) **asexually** by hundreds of spores from each sporangium. In *Mucor*, sporangium wall dissolves in moisture and spores are distributed in a slime-drop by rain or animals. In *Rhizopus*, wall cracks open when dry and wind distributes dry spores.

(*b*) **sexually** using gamete-nuclei in gametangia of two different strains. A zygospore results – allowing dispersal and survival in unfavourable conditions.

Importance of fungi

Helpful

1   **Decay fungi** liberate nutrients for green plants from dead organisms.

2   **Yeasts,** respiring anaerobically, provide:

(*a*) alcohol for brewers and wine-makers: this may be distilled to make spirits, e.g. gin;

(*b*) CO_2 for bakers (yeast acts on sugar in dough, making it rise).

$$C_6H_{12}O_6 \xrightarrow{\text{enzymes}} 2C_2H_5OH + 2CO_2$$

glucose   alcohol (ethanol)   carbon dioxide

The yeast cells themselves also yield vitamin B extracts (e.g. 'Marmite').

3   **Antibiotic-producers,** e.g. *Penicillium* produces penicillin.

4   **Food fungi,** e.g. mushrooms, chanterelles and single cell protein (from yeasts).

Harmful

1 Decay fungi spoil food, e.g. *Rhizopus, Pencillium* on bread, cakes and jam.

2 Plant diseases, e.g. potato blight caused millions to die in the Irish potato famine; 'rust' fungi damage cereal crops seriously.

3 Dry rot fungus destroys house timbers.

17.6 HYDRA

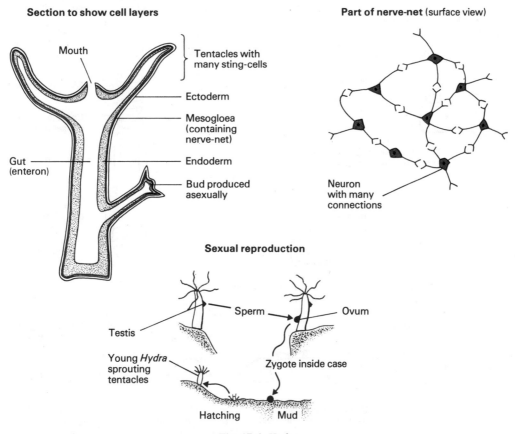

Fig. 17.6 *Hydra*

Hydra is a fresh-water coelenterate (see Fig. 17.6).

Structure: body has only two cell-layers (*ectoderm* and *endoderm*) forming a sack with tentacles at the open end. A *nerve-net* (no nerves or brain) lies between ectoderm and endoderm, in a thin layer of jelly (mesogloea).

Feeding

1 Prey, e.g. *Daphnia* (water flea), is paralysed by sting-cells on tentacles and moved through mouth into gut. Here, gland-cells secrete digestive enzymes to break up food; other cells ingest the bits (as Amoebae do) to finish off digestion. Indigestible food is egested through the mouth.

2 Some *Hydra* species have algae living in **symbiosis** within endoderm cells. *Hydra* gains photosynthesised food and O_2; algae gain CO_2 and nitrogenous wastes from *Hydra*.

Reproduction:

1 asexually by budding; buds detach.

2 sexually by forming testes and an ovary (containing one ovum) on the same *Hydra,* but ripening at different times. Sperm fertilises the ovum. Zygote secretes a chitin case and falls into the mud. Later the case splits and from it a hollow ball of cells grows into a *Hydra*. Parent usually dies.

17.7 EARTHWORM

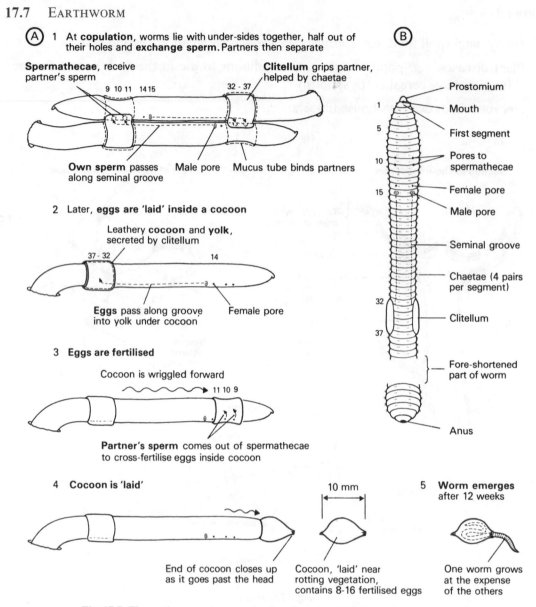

Fig. 17.7 The earthworm. A – reproduction, B – external features from underneath

Earthworm (*Lumbricus terrestris*) is a terrestrial annelid (see Fig. 17.7).

Reproduction

1   Worm is *hermaphrodite* (both male and female).

2   It *copulates* on warm moist nights to receive and store another worm's sperm in its spermathecae.

3   Later, it *cross-fertilises* its eggs within a cocoon which it lays.

Locomotion

1   Burrows through soil.

2   Alternately contracts longitudinal muscles (to become short and fat) and circular muscles (to become long and thin), using an internal liquid skeleton (see unit 10.5).

3   Chaetae (bristles) provide anchorage.

4   Mucus (slime) provides lubrication as it slides through tunnel.

Importance of earthworms

Improve soil fertility by their actions (see unit 15.8).

17.8   MOSS AND FERN

Moss and fern – green plants requiring water for sexual reproduction (see Figs. 17.8, 17.9). Life cycle shows **alternation of generations:**

1   Gametophyte generation: reproduces *sexually* using sperm that swim in water to the ovum. Zygote gives rise to sporophyte by growth.

2   Sporophyte generation: reproduces *asexually* by spores requiring dry air for dispersal. Spore germinates into gametophyte.

Moss plant is the *gametophyte;* sporophyte is short-lived.

Fern plant is the *sporophyte;* gametophyte is small and short-lived.

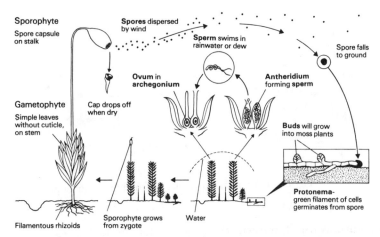

Fig. 17.8 Life cycle of a moss (showing alternation of generations)

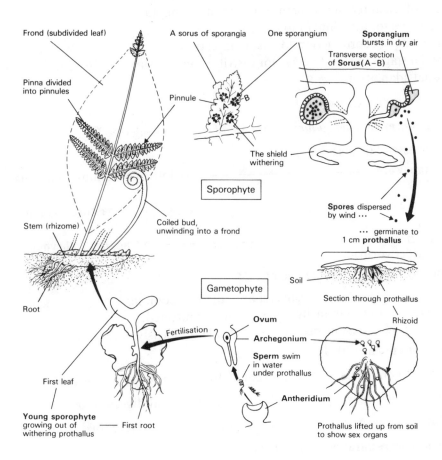

Fig. 17.9 Life cycle of a fern (showing alternation of generations)

17.9 ANGIOSPERMS (GENERAL STRUCTURE)

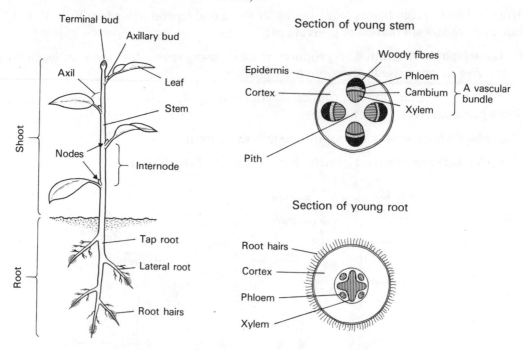

Fig. 17.10 Angiosperm – general structure of a dicot plant

17.10 PARASITIC ADAPTATIONS

Parasitic adaptations (of all parasites)

1   Specialised feeding structures.
2   Lack of usual feeding structures found in the phylum.
3   Structures for attachment to the host.
4   High rate of reproduction to ensure infection.
5   Special stages in the life cycle for distribution and survival. In addition, parasites show individual adaptations.

17.11 PORK TAPEWORM

Pork tapeworm (*Taenia solium*) – parasite of man and pig (see Fig. 17.11).

Life cycle essentials are:

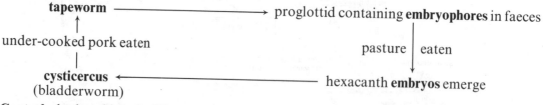

Control – by breaking the life-cycle:

(*a*) *Cook pork thoroughly* – cysticerci are killed by cooking.
(*b*) *Dispose of faeces* sanitarily – pigs cannot be infected.
(*c*) *Inspect pork* – meat inspectors prevent sale of 'measly pork'.

Adaptations to parasitic life

1   **Scolex:** hooks and suckers prevent dislodgement by food flowing in intestine.

2   **Thick cuticle** (perhaps also anti-enzymes): prevent digestion of worm by host.

3   **Flat shape:** large surface area for absorption of food (digested by man).

4   **Anaerobic respiration:** little O_2 in intestine.

5   **Hermaphrodite and self-fertilising:** essential because worm is large (2–8 metres), so only one can be accommodated at a time.

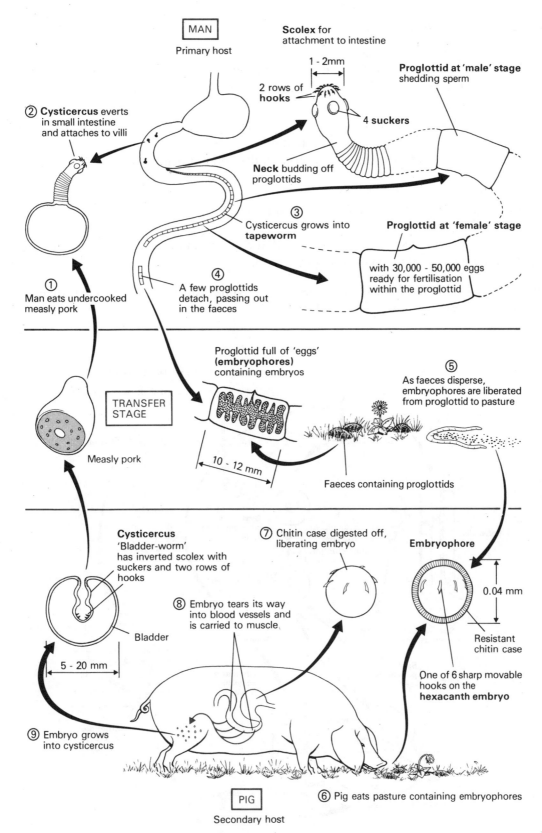

Fig. 17.11 Life cycle of the pork tapeworm, *Taenia solium*

6 High reproductive rate: makes up for the enormous chances *against* infection of hosts. In a worm's life span of over 25 years it produces over 2000 proglottids per year each containing 30–50 000 hexacanth embryos, each capable of forming a cysticercus to infect man.

7 Embryophore case: permits survival of embryo for many weeks.

8 Two hosts: gives a double chance of survival and distribution to new hosts.

17.12 PYTHIUM DEBARYANUM

Pythium debaryanum, the 'damping off' fungus – a plant parasite (see Fig. 17.12). Kills seedlings and weak plants grown in humid conditions; causes millions of pounds in losses and control measures in the horticultural industry. Difficult to control since:

(*a*) fungus is both parasitic on live plants and saprophytic on dead ones;
(*b*) humid, well-watered conditions in greenhouses favour rapid spread of fungus by zoospores (swim by flagella in minute films of water);
(*c*) zygospores survive for long periods even in dry soil not being used.

Control measures therefore include:

(*a*) growing seedlings in well ventilated conditions (zoospores not formed);
(*b*) burning all infected seedlings;
(*c*) using fungicides or steam-sterilising soil that contained infected plants before re-use in seedling boxes (to kill zygospores especially).

Feeding in parasitic fungi usually requires rootlet hyphae called **haustoria** penetrate into or between the host cells, absorbing food from them.

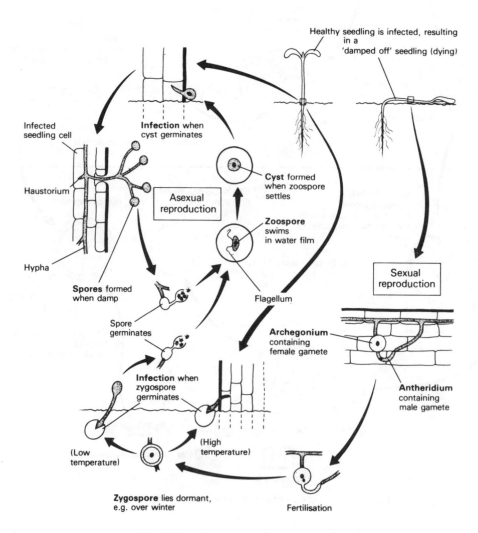

Fig. 17.12 Life cycle of *Pythium debaryanum*

17.13 DODDER

The dodder (*Cuscuta epithymum*) – parasite of gorse, broom, clover and heather.

Leaves: small scales without chlorophyll.

Stem: a pink thread twining around the host's stem and sending haustoria ('suckers') into it (see Fig. 17.13). Parasite's conducting tissue joins up with host's, gaining water and mineral salts from xylem and organic food from phloem.

Roots: none.

Flowers: pink-petalled, small and numerous; produced in second year.

Seeds: large numbers, germinate only in summer, giving time for spring growth of hosts.

Seedling: sends down root; shoot nutates (twists in a wide arc as it grows) so as to contact a suitable host stem to penetrate with a haustorium. If successful, root withers; otherwise seedling dies.

Cuscuta overwinters as nodules of tissue around each haustorium. Lives for two years or more. Not a parasite of economic importance.

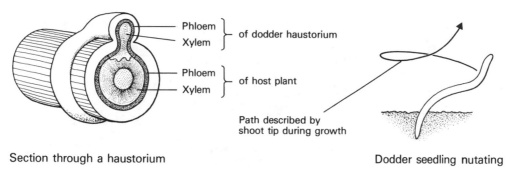

Section through a haustorium   Dodder seedling nutating

Fig. 17.13 Parasitic adaptations of the dodder, *Cuscuta epithymum*

17.14 INSECTS (LIFE CYCLES AND EXTERNAL FEATURES)

Insect characteristics

Adults have (in addition to Arthropod features, p. 23):
1 *A 3-part body:* head, thorax and abdomen.
2 *Six legs* on the thorax.
3 *Two pairs of wings* on the thorax (1 pair in flies).
4 One pair of *compound eyes* and one pair of antennae on the head.
5 One pair of *spiracles* on each abdominal segment.
6 *Life cycle* with egg, growing stages and metamorphosis (change) to adult.

Insects have two contrasting life cycles (see Fig. 17.14):

1 Incomplete metamorphosis, e.g. locust, cockroach, dragonfly. Growing stage (**nymph**) is similar to adult, lacking only wings and ability to reproduce. Last moult gives adult.

2 Complete metamorphosis, e.g. fly, butterfly, bee (most insects). Growing stage (**larva**) so unlike adult that reorganisation into an adult must be achieved as a **pupa**.

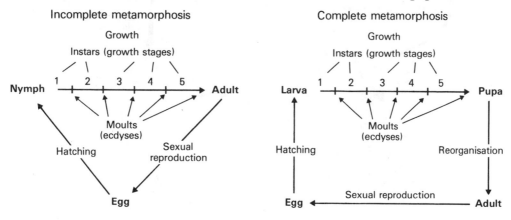

Fig. 17.14 Two kinds of life cycle in insects

17.15   Locust

The desert locust (*Schistocerca gregaria*) – found from North Africa to India. Devastates vegetation of all kinds, both as 'hopper' (nymph) and adult. Controlled by laying bran, soaked in insecticide, in path of hoppers (see Fig. 17.15).

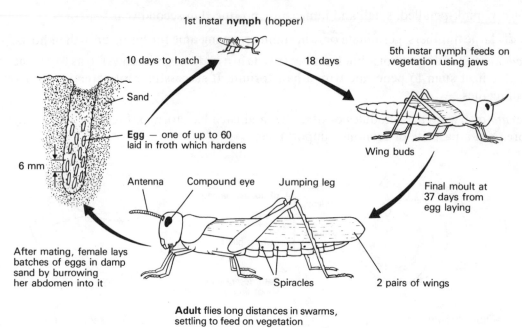

Fig. 17.15 The locust, *Schistocerca gregaria*

17.16   House fly

House fly (*Musca domestica*) (see Fig. 17.16).

Adults transmit diseases (e.g. dysentery, certain worms) by visiting faeces and then human food. Here they deposit the infecting organisms via their feet or saliva (see Fig. 4.10) or by their own droppings ('fly-spots'). Flies controlled by good garbage disposal and sanitation (removes breeding sites); insecticides. In tropics: use muslin or wire gauze fly-screens to cover food and drink.

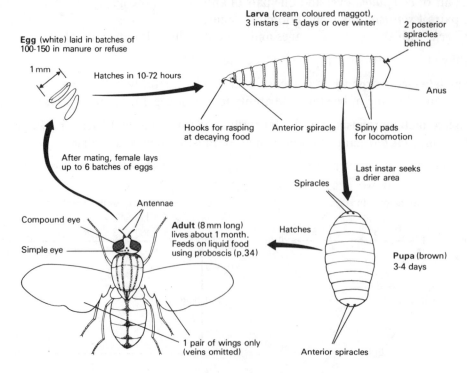

Fig. 17.16 House fly, *Musca domestica*

17.17 LARGE CABBAGE WHITE BUTTERFLY

Large cabbage white butterfly (*Pieris brassicae*) (see Fig. 17.17). Damages cabbage-family plants. Controlled by insecticides and a parasitic 3 mm black wasp (*Apanteles glomerata*). Its eggs, injected into caterpillar, hatch into larvae feeding on caterpillar's tissues, thus killing it. Pupates within bright yellow cocoons on caterpillar's skin.

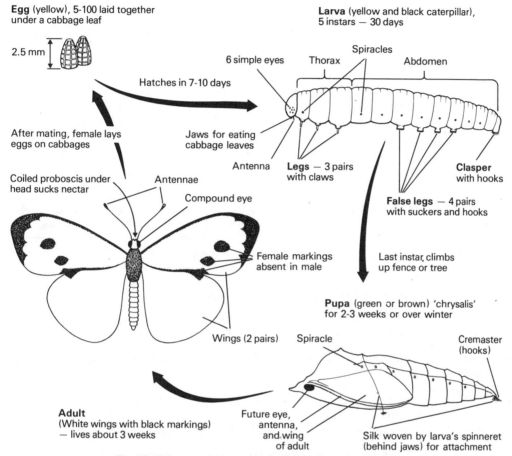

Egg (yellow), 5-100 laid together under a cabbage leaf

2.5 mm

Hatches in 7-10 days

After mating, female lays eggs on cabbages

Coiled proboscis under head sucks nectar

Antennae

Compound eye

Female markings absent in male

Wings (2 pairs)

Adult (White wings with black markings) — lives about 3 weeks

Larva (yellow and black caterpillar), 5 instars — 30 days

6 simple eyes   Thorax   Spiracles   Abdomen

Jaws for eating cabbage leaves

Antenna   **Legs** — 3 pairs with claws   **Clasper** with hooks

False legs — 4 pairs with suckers and hooks

Last instar, climbs up fence or tree

Pupa (green or brown) 'chrysalis' for 2-3 weeks or over winter

Spiracle   Cremaster (hooks)

Future eye, antenna, and wing of adult   Silk woven by larva's spinneret (behind jaws) for attachment

Fig. 17.17 Large cabbage white butterfly, *Pieris brassicae*

17.18 HONEY BEE

Honey bee (*Apis mellifera*) (see Fig. 17.18).

Organisation in the hive

No individual bee can live for long without assistance from the others. Thus, the hive, with its 5000–100 000 bees, is comparable to a socially-organised unit, e.g. a town, or to a multi-cellular organism (bee ≡ cell).

The queen is the only fertile female (*a*) laying eggs and (*b*) secreting 'queen substance', which is passed from bee to bee by mouth and keeps the colony working together.

Drones are fertile males; do no hive work; fed by workers; driven out to die in autumn.

Workers are infertile females with a sequence of duties as they get older:
(*a*) *nurse:* cleans out used cells; secretes protein-rich 'royal jelly' from head-glands to feed young larvae; feeds honey and pollen to older larvae.
(*b*) *food storer:* receives from foragers and stores in cells: pollen ('bee bread'); and nectar (mainly sucrose solution), which they change to honey by:
  (*i*) digesting sucrose to simple sugars.
  (*ii*) evaporating its water (at 84% sugar, no bacteria or fungi can ferment it).
(*c*) *comb builder:* secretes wax, oozing out as plates between abdominal segments; chews these into hexagonal cylinder shaped cells.

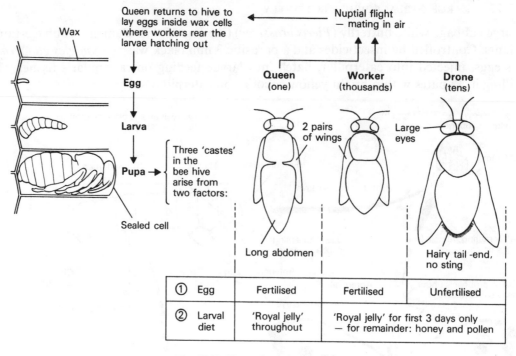

Fig. 17.18 Honey bee, *Apis mellifera*

(*d*) *ventilator:* stands, beating wings at hive entrance to:

   (*i*) create outward air current.

   (*ii*) carry scent from abdominal glands, to assist foragers in hive-recognition.

(*e*) *guard:* challenges incomers, stinging invading animals or bees unladen with food (usually robber bees).

(*f*) *forager:* gathers:

   (*i*) nectar in special crop.

   (*ii*) pollen stuck together with nectar in 'pollen baskets' of hind legs.

Communicates distance and angle from hive of good food sources by 'bee dances' (see Fig. 17.19). Returning forager bees 'tell' others of good food sources by agitated movements. Other bees understand the messages as follows:

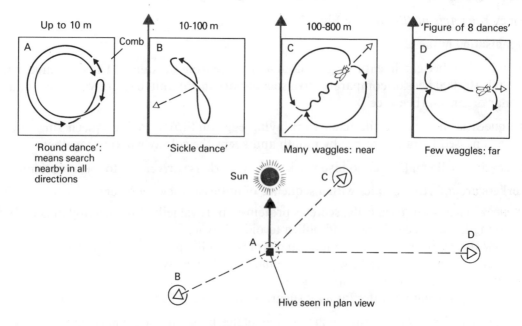

Fig. 17.19 Bee 'dances' on honey combs. Messages A–D are translated into bee flight paths

(*i*) vertically up the comb means the **direction of the sun;**

(*ii*) pattern of the dance in relation to the vertical means the **angle from the sun** at which bees must set off;

(*iii*) number of waggles of the abdomen means **distance of the food source;**

(*iv*) regurgitation of some nectar to bees nearby tells them **what flower to seek.**

Most bees die while working within six weeks.

(*g*) *old forager:* gathers:

(*i*) plant resins to make 'propolis' (to seal up cracks in the hive).

(*ii*) water to wet cells (evaporation cools them in hot weather, cf. sweating in mammals). Hive temperature usually maintained at 31–33°C.

17.19 IMPORTANCE OF INSECTS TO MAN

Helpful

1 Bees: pollinators (without which orchard fruit yields are greatly reduced) and **suppliers of honey** (sweetener) and **beeswax** (for high-grade polishes and lipstick).

2 Biological control of pests, by *lady-birds* (control aphids, mealy-bugs and scale insects in garden, coffee and citrus plantations); *Cactus moth* caterpillars (eat prickly-pear cactus invading agricultural land).

Harmful

1 Food destroyers, e.g. *locust* (crops), *grain weevil* (stored grain).

2 Materials destroyers, e.g. *termites* (wooden buildings), *cotton boll weevil* (cotton flower), *clothes moth* (woollen clothes).

3 Disease vectors, e.g. *mosquitoes* (yellow fever virus, malaria protozoan and elephantiasis nematode worm), *tse-tse flies* (human sleeping sickness and similar sicknesses in domesticated animals), *housefly* (dysentery protozoa and bacteria), *fleas* (plague bacteria), *wood-boring beetle* (dutch-elm disease fungus), *aphids* (plant virus disease).

4 Nuisances, e.g. *cockroaches* and *ants* (spoiling food).

The mosquito can only lay its eggs on stagnant water. The aquatic larvae breathe air through spiracles at the surface of the water; so do the pupae. The adults may emerge within a week after egg-laying in tropical countries. The females need a meal of blood to ensure proper egg development before fertilisation. They tend to 'bite' humans at night, sheltering by day in dark places in houses. These habits give opportunities for controlling mosquitoes:

1 drain marshes or otherwise remove stagnant water (prevents egg-laying);

2 spray light oils containing insecticide on water that cannot be removed (oils block spiracles, suffocating the aquatic stages; the insecticide kills females landing to lay eggs);

3 introduce 'mosquito fish', e.g. *Gambusia* or guppy, into the water (to eat larvae and pupae);

4 spray walls of houses with long-lasting insecticides, e.g. DDT (kills adults sheltering there).

Mosquitoes only transmit **diseases** (see above) if they are given the opportunity to suck up the parasites of an infected person. When mosquitoes 'bite' they inject saliva to prevent the blood clotting. It is with this saliva that the parasites enter healthy people. It is therefore wise in the tropics to:

1 sleep under a mosquito net (prevents getting 'bitten');

2 take, regularly, drugs that kill the parasites that do get injected (prophylaxis, see p. 134);

3 quarantine (isolate) those who become diseased, away from other people and under mosquito nets (to prevent infecting mosquitoes).

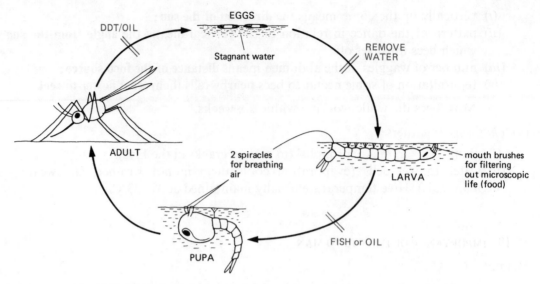

Fig. 17.20 Life cycle of the Anopheline mosquito and methods of controlling it

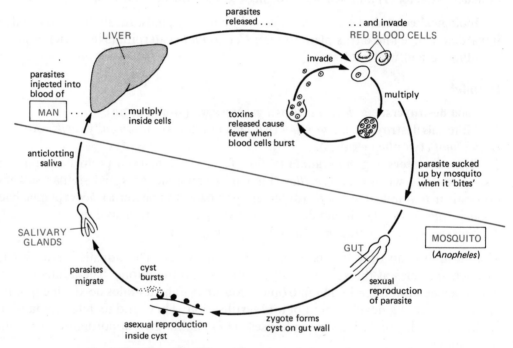

Fig. 17.21 Life cycle of *Plasmodium*, the malaria parasite

17.20   BONY FISH

Adaptations to an aquatic environment

1   Locomotion (see Fig. 17.22)

(a) *Shape:* streamlined. Skin, secreting mucus, covers overlapping bony scales.

(b) *Propulsion:* sideways movement of muscular body exerts a backward and sideways force on the water via the large surface area of the *tail*. Vertebrae have balls of cartilage between them allowing great flexibility; muscles on either side contract alternately to give sideways movement. In fast swimming, side fins kept flat against body. When static, thrusts from pectoral (and pelvic) fins adjust position.

(c) *Stability: fins* prevent roll, pitch and yaw (see Fig. 17.23).

(d) *Control:* pectoral and pelvic fins act as *hydroplanes* according to angle; when both are held at right angles to body, act as *brakes*.

(e) *Buoyancy: air-bladder* (contents adjustable) keeps fish at required depth. Saves energy (cartilaginous fish, e.g. sharks, have no air-bladders and must keep swimming to prevent sinking).

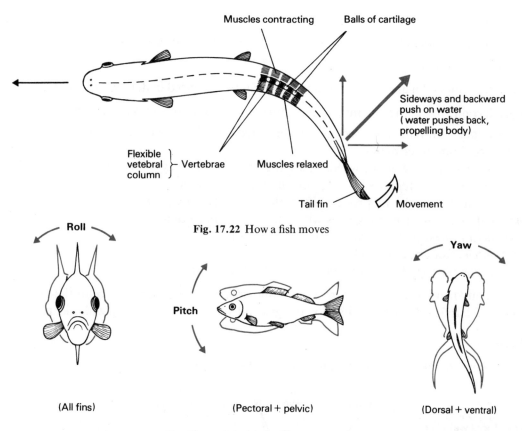

Fig. 17.22 How a fish moves

Fig. 17.23 How fish fins prevent instability

2 Respiration

Water enters mouth, is sieved by gill-rakers, allowing gaseous exchange over gills, and leaves under bony operculum. Rakers may provide feeding method too (see Fig. 4.8b).

3 Sensitivity

(*a*) *'Smelling': two nostrils* are double, leading water through a U-shaped cavity lined with cells sensing chemicals.

(*b*) *Seeing:* two unblinking *eyes*.

(*c*) *'Hearing': lateral line* canal contains hair-cells, in bunches, sensitive to pressure waves in water – from obstacles and from moving organisms.

The *cloaca* (a chamber) receives faeces, urine and gametes from separate tubes; discharges to the water via a single opening.

17.21 THREE-SPINED STICKLEBACK

The three-spined stickleback (*Gasterosteus aculeatus*) (see Fig. 17.24).

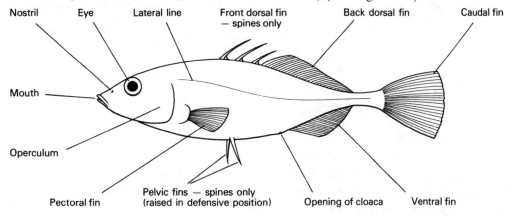

Fig. 17.24 Three-spined stickleback, *Gasterosteus aculeatus*

Habitat: margins of rivers, lakes – amongst weeds.

Food: worms, crustacea and insect larvae (carnivorous). Is eaten by perch, pike and heron.

Specialised in two ways:

1 **Fins:** front dorsal fin and pelvic fins have no webs (spines used in defence when erected).

2 **Reproduction:** has elaborate instinctive courtship behaviour and parental care:

(a) In February – March, *males* become red-breasted and blue-eyed and take up a *territory* (defended from other males).
(b) Build a *nest*-tunnel of water-weeds stuck together by a kidney secretion.
(c) Lead fat, egg-laden females by a *zig-zag dance* to the tunnel.
(d) Female enters tunnel and, prodded by male, lays a few *eggs;* she then leaves.
(e) Male enters tunnel, squirting eggs with sperm to *fertilise* them.
(f) Male *aerates* nest by fin movements and *defends* it.
(g) Eggs *hatch* after about a week.
(h) Male keeps *fry* together in a defended shoal for another week.

(Most bony fish lay large numbers of eggs and sperm into the same place in the water, trusting to luck that sufficient fertilisation of eggs and survival of the young will take place.)

17.22 FROG

The frog (*Rana temporaria*) – an amphibian (see Fig. 17.25).

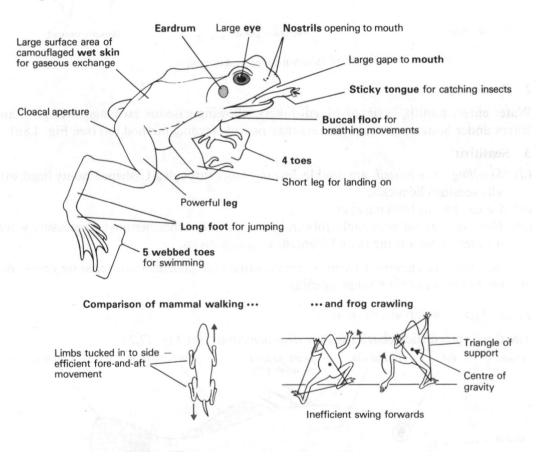

Fig. 17.25 Frog, *Rana temporaria* – external features

Adaptations for jumping

1 Long hind limbs with powerful muscles.
2 Strong pelvic girdle strengthened by a central rod, the urostyle.
3 Stout pectoral girdle with large sternum cartilage to protect heart on landing.
4 Forelimbs designed to take impact of landing.
5 Very short vertebral column to avoid dislocation on take-off and landing.

Life cycle

(*a*) In March, male frogs croak, inviting females into shallow water.

(*b*) Male grips female under arm-pits with swollen black 'nuptial pads' on thumbs.

(*c*) Female lays a few hundred *eggs;* male squirts *sperm* over them as they emerge in a continuous stream.

(*d*) Sperm must penetrate eggs to effect *fertilisation* before albumen swells.

(*e*) Albumen gives egg *protection* from injury and predators; *camouflage* (by being transparent); and a *large surface area* for gaseous exchange.

(*f*) *Larvae* hatch (according to temperature) in about 10 days. In a *continuous* process of change (little happens overnight) larvae go through *three stages* (see Table 17.1 and Fig. 17.26).

(*g*) After about 90 days *young frogs* with stumpy tails hop onto land and start to catch insects with a sticky tongue. Hibernate in mud at bottom of ponds or in sheltered crevices, to avoid freezing each winter.

(*h*) Frogs are *adult* by their fourth season.

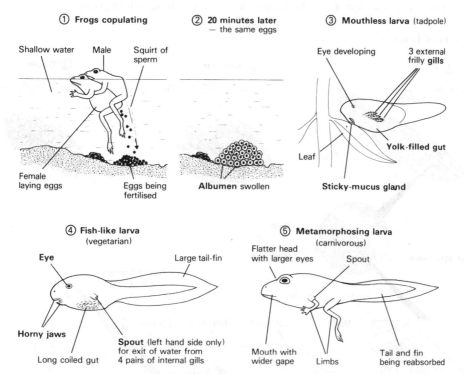

Fig. 17.26 Frog – life history

Table 17.1   The three larval stages of a frog

	Mouthless	*Fish-like*	*Metamorphosing*
Size	6 mm long	20 mm long	40 mm long
Duration	2-3 days	40 days	40 days
Feeding	On yolk in gut only	Herbivorous: uses horny jaws to scrape off algae	Carnivorous: scavenger and even cannibal
Breathing (*gas exchange*)	3 pairs of external gills; skin	4 pairs of internal gills next to gill slits; skin	Lungs; buccal cavity: skin
Locomotion	Nil (stuck by mucus to water weed)	Uses tail with broad fin to swim	Tail swimming; hind limbs at times
Sense organs	Nil (still developing)	Lateral line (Fig. 17.24); eyes	Eyes very large

Metamorphosis is the change of an immature or larval stage into an adult form. In the frog, metamorphosis is started by secretion of increasing amounts of *thyroxin* (hormone, see unit 9.8) from the thyroid gland.

17.23 BIRDS

Adaptations for flight (see Fig. 17.27)

(*a*) *Light bones* – some air-filled and linked to air sacs; no teeth (heavy).

(*b*) *Streamlined* – general body shape, contour feathers smoothing outline.

(*c*) *Feathered wings* – large surface area to exert force on air.

(*d*) *Large flight muscles* – big ones for down-flap; smaller ones for up-flap, together 20% of body weight.

(*e*) *Large keeled sternum* – for attachment of flight muscles.

(*f*) *Breathing system* (see unit 6.5) and *large heart* – highly efficient at supplying food and O_2 to flight muscles at a rate high enough to provide sufficient energy for flight.

(*g*) *High body temperature* – ensures rapid respiration.

Flightless birds, e.g. ostrich, kiwi, lack one or more of these adaptations.

Three kinds of feather:

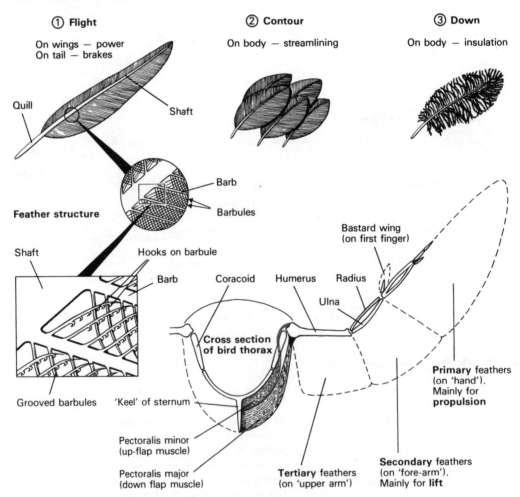

Fig. 17.27 Structures required for flight in birds

Flight

Birds cannot develop buoyancy (compare air-bladder of fishes, see unit 17.20).

Lift is generated by creating low pressure above wing and higher pressure below it. This requires (*a*) an aerofoil wing and (*b*) movement of air over aerofoil. Movement of air over the wing can be produced in three ways:

1 **Gliding:** wing rigid, *air still;* bird moves through air because it is falling.
2 **Soaring:** wing rigid, *air moving,* e.g. cliff-side winds or hot up-currents from the ground.
3 **Flapping flight:** *wing moves,* exerting forces on air.

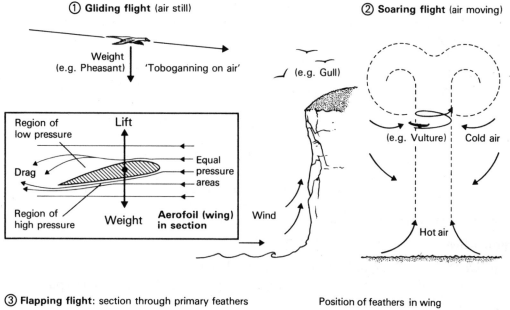

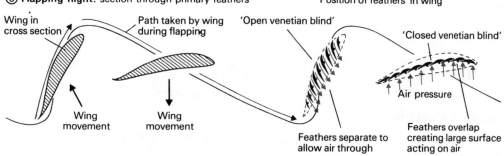

Fig. 17.28 Three methods of flight

Flapping flight can result in fast, slow and even hovering flight – all modifications of the following essentials:

(*a*) *down-flap:* primary feathers overlap giving maximum air-resistance as arm is brought down; primaries move forward (giving lift) and downward with ends curled upwards (giving forward propulsion).

(*b*) *up-flap:* arm is raised with the wrist *rotated* forward allowing air in between the primaries (like an open Venetian blind); this reduces air resistance.

Reproduction

(*a*) Male birds of some species, e.g. robin, take up and defend *territories.*

(*b*) Courtship and display leads to *pairing* for the breeding season.

(*c*) One or both of the pair achieve *nest building* in trees, holes or on the ground.

(*d*) Further display leads to *mating* and internal fertilisation.

(*e*) *Eggs* are laid in nest singly, over a period of days, till clutch is complete.

(*f*) Eggs gain O_2 through shell from environment, and warmth from female's featherless brood-patches. She also turns the eggs daily, before *incubation* ('sitting').

(*g*) Embryo develops, cushioned within the *amnion* (water bag), getting food from *yolk-sac. Allantois* stores excreted uric acid; absorbs O_2 (see Fig. 17.29).

(*h*) Chick *hatches* with help of egg-tooth (discarded after use).

(*i*) *Parental care* of young extends to removal of droppings, defence and feeding (instinctive behaviour induced by yellow gape of chick's mouth and chirruping, see unit 12.17).

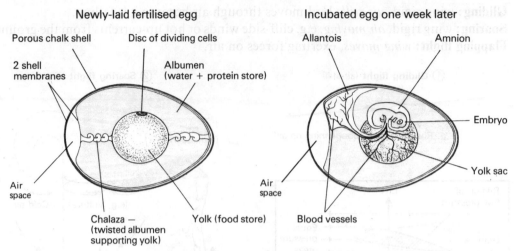

Newly-laid fertilised egg

Porous chalk shell   Disc of dividing cells

2 shell membranes   Albumen (water + protein store)

Air space

Chalaza — (twisted albumen supporting yolk)   Yolk (food store)

Incubated egg one week later

Allantois   Amnion

Embryo

Yolk sac

Air space

Blood vessels

Fig. 17.29 Bird's egg – internal features

17.24 MAMMAL CHARACTERISTICS

Reproduction

1 *Suckle* their young on milk from mammary glands.
2 *Viviparous* – give birth to young, not eggs (exceptions: Echidna and Platypus).

In the head

3 *Large cerebrum* – the most intelligent vertebrates.
4 *Ear pinna* – external ear.
5 *Three ear ossicles* – in the middle ear.
6 *Four kinds of teeth* – incisors, canines, premolars and molars.
7 *Hard palate* – allows chewing and breathing simultaneously.

Temperature regulation

8 *Endothermic* (homeothermic) – constant body temperature (birds also).
9 *Hair* – for insulation.
10 *Sweat glands* – for cooling.

Respiration

11 *Diaphragm* – muscular sheet separating heart and lungs from other organs.
12 *Erythrocytes* (red blood cells) – lack nuclei.

Most mammals are **placentals** – embryos are grown inside uterus (womb), nourished via the placenta. Others are **marsupials** – embryos are born early and grow mainly within a pouch, e.g. kangaroo. Two types only (Echidna and Platypus) lay eggs much like those of reptiles, but then give milk to the hatched young. These egg-layers are the **monotremes.**

17.25 RABBIT

The rabbit (*Oryctolagus cuniculus*)

Life history:

(a) Males pursue females in *'courtship' chases*.
(b) *Mating* occurs mainly in January–June (but can be in any month).
(c) Female often digs a short (30–90 cm) 'stop' burrow away from warren at blind end of which she makes a *nest* of hay, straw and her own chest fur.
(d) *Gestation* of young takes 28–31 days; 3–7 blind young born.
(e) Female is often *mated* again within 12 hours of dropping litter.
(f) Young are *suckled* for about 21 days; fiercely protected from enemies.
(g) Young are *sexually mature* at 3–4 months; fully grown by 9 months.
(h) *Life expectancy* in wild about 1 year.

Section III Self-test units

Do not attempt these tests until you have worked through the relevant unit in Section II.
Answers appear on page 189.

Test on unit 2 Life

1 Nutrition means:
   A building up sugars **B** intake of food to build up living matter **C** eating food
   D absorbing vitamins ___

2 The main purpose of respiration is to:
   A use oxygen in cells **B** burn sugars **C** provide energy for cells
   D give off carbon dioxide ___

3 Maintaining a suitable quantity of water in cells is called:
   A excretion **B** drinking **C** osmoregulation **D** hydration ___

4 Metabolism does *not* take place in:
   A death **B** digestion **C** growth **D** respiration ___

5 A cell wall is *not*:
   A freely permeable **B** non-living **C** selectively permeable **D** found in plants ___

6 Chloroplasts are found in:
   A animal cells **B** all plant cells **C** the vacuole **D** green plant cells ___

7 Protoplasm does not include:
   A cytoplasm **B** nucleus **C** cell wall **D** protein and water ___

8 The organelle which 'controls' the cell is the:
   A cell membrane **B** nucleus **C** cytoplasm **D** ribosome ___

9 Name plant and animal cells which fit the descriptions below:

	Plant	Animal
(*a*) long and thin	_____	_____
(*b*) have no nucleus	_____	_____
(*c*) are not green (plant) are red (animal)	_____	_____

10 The following are various sub-units into which a species of plant or animal can be divided:

   A cell **B** organ **C** organelle **D** organism **E** organ system **F** tissue

   (*a*) Arrange them in order starting with the simplest and ending with the most complex:

   ___ ___ ___ ___ ___ ___

   (*b*) Which of the above can be applied to the following?
       (*i*) cat_____ (*ii*) *Amoeba*_____ (*iii*) leaf_____ (*iv*) chloroplast_____
       (*v*) muscle_____ (*vi*) alimentary canal (gut)_____

Test on unit 3 Classification

1 Which of the following is an animal?
   A sea-anemone **B** sea-weed **C** bee-orchid **D** horse-tail ___

2 Which of the following possesses no chlorophyll?
   A copper-beech tree **B** dandelion **C** lichens **D** *Penicillium* mould ___

3 Which of the following is a mammal?
   A sea-horse **B** dolphin **C** sea-butterfly **D** tarantula ___

4 Which plant reproduces by forming seeds?
   A fern **B** mushroom **C** oak **D** moss ___

5 Here is a range of animals:
A spider B starfish C Protozoa D tapeworm E locust
F *Lumbricus terrestris* G crab H snail

   (*i*) To which of the above do the following descriptions apply?
       (*a*) is the name of a phylum   ___
       (*b*) is the name of a species   ___
       (*c*) has eight legs   ___
       (*d*) belongs to the phylum Mollusca   ___
       (*e*) belongs to the phylum Arthropoda   ___ ___ ___
       (*f*) is a flat-bodied worm   ___
       (*g*) has a body built on a five-rayed plan   ___
   (*ii*) What kind of animals are **A–H**?   _____

6 Here is a range of organisms:
A bat B bacterium C blue whale D frog E sea-anemone
F sparrow G alligator H salmon J *Amoeba*

To which of the above do the following descriptions apply?

   (*a*) unicellular   ___ ___
   (*b*) feathered   ___
   (*c*) mammal   ___ ___
   (*d*) body temperature is constant and warm   ___ ___ ___
   (*e*) larva uses gills for gaseous exchange   ___ ___
   (*f*) lays eggs out of water   ___ ___
   (*g*) belongs to class Amphibia   ___
   (*h*) animals not in the phylum Chordata   ___ ___ ___
   (*j*) has cell walls   ___

Test on unit 4 Foods and feeding

1 The following terms describe various methods of nutrition:
A autotrophic B heterotrophic C parasitic D saprophytic E holozoic F carnivorous
   (*i*) With which of the above are the following statements about organisms associated?
       (*a*) All their energy comes from respiration.   ___(includes ___ ___ ___ ___)
       (*b*) They require only inorganic food.   ___
       (*c*) They digest their food externally but have no gut.   ___
       (*d*) A dog's method of nutrition.   ___ ___ ___
       (*e*) Food is taken from a living organism, which survives.   ___ ___
   (*ii*) Apart from **B** and **E**, what term not mentioned above best
       describes man's nutrition?   _____

2 The following kinds of substances may be found in organisms:
A fats B carbohydrates C water D salts E protein

   (*a*) Which are organic?   ___ ___ ___
   (*b*) Which of the organic substances contain C, H and O alone?   ___ ___
   (*c*) Which of the organic substances contains N?   ___
   (*d*) Which substance forms the major part of living cells?   ___
   (*e*) Which possess H and O in the ratio of 2 to 1?   ___ ___
   (*f*) Name an organic food class not mentioned in **A–E** above   _____

3 The following are items of diet for man:
A oranges B butter C lean steak D table salt E boiled potatoes

   (*a*) Which is mainly protein?   ___
   (*b*) Which is mainly carbohydrate?   ___
   (*c*) Which is mainly fat?   ___
   (*d*) Which contain cellulose?   ___ ___

(*e*) Which are 'energy' foods?   — —
(*f*) Which contains iodine?   —
(*g*) Which contains vitamin C?   —
(*h*) Which is a body-building food?   —

4 The following substances may be found in the mammal gut:
   A amino acids **B** vitamins B and C **C** fatty acids **D** starch **E** vitamins A and D
   F glucose

   (*a*) Which can be absorbed into villi?   — — — — —
   (*b*) Which are absorbed into lacteals in the villi?   — —
   (*c*) Which are simple units of proteins?   —
   (*d*) Which are digested by ptyalin (salivary amylase)?   —
   (*e*) Which are simple units of carbohydrates?   —
   (*f*) Which are required in diets in minute amounts?   — —

5 The following are included in man's diet in small quantities:
   A calcium **B** fluorine **C** iron **D** vitamin C **E** vitamin D **F** vitamin A **G** iodine

   (*i*) Which of these are needed for:
      (*a*) making red blood cells?   —
      (*b*) making strong bones   — —
      (*c*) good vision at night?   —
      (*d*) making hard teeth?   —
      (*e*) preventing scurvy?   —
      (*f*) addition to margarine (by law)?   — —
      (*g*) making the hormone thyroxin?   —
   (*ii*) Which of the above can man synthesise by sunbathing?   —

6 The following terms are associated with the way in which mammals deal with their
   food:
   A physical digestion **B** chemical digestion **C** canines **D** cellulases **E** hydrolysis
   F condensation **G** egestion **H** rumen or caecum

   (*a*) enzymes in the gut of all mammals   — —
   (*b*) digestion of plant cell walls   — — — — —
   (*c*) bile   —
   (*d*) killing prey   —
   (*e*) storing glucose as glycogen   —
   (*f*) molars   —
   (*g*) elimination of roughage and excess gut bacteria   —

7 The following are parts of the mammal gut:
   A stomach **B** colon **C** duodenum **D** rectum **E** lower part of small intestine
   F buccal cavity **G** oesophagus

   (*a*) Place them in sequence, starting at the mouth end   _____
   (*b*) Where would you find teeth?   —
   (*c*) Where would you find villi?   — —
   (*d*) Between which parts is the epiglottis?   — —
   (*e*) Between which parts is the pyloric sphincter?   — —
   (*f*) Between which parts is the caecum?   — —
   (*g*) Which parts of the intestine are long and narrow?   — —
   (*h*) Which parts of the intestine are short and wide?   — —
   (*j*) Which part receives bile?   —
   (*k*) Which part receives gastric juice?   —

8 Parts concerned with digestion in the buccal cavity include:
   A salivary glands **B** enamel **C** pulp cavity **D** dentine **E** molars **F** incisors
   G premolars **H** canines.

(*a*) Arrange the types of teeth in sequence from front to back.   ___ ___ ___ ___

(*b*) Arrange the parts of a tooth in order of hardness starting with the hardest part.   ___ ___ ___

(*c*) Which type of tooth is not present in the milk set?   ___

(*d*) Which type of tooth is not present in herbivores?   ___

(*e*) Which part contains ptyalin?   ___

(*f*) Which part of a tooth contains blood vessels?   ___

(*g*) Which class of food is digested by the secretion from **A**?   ___

9   Green plant nutrition is affected by the following factors:
A water **B** chlorophyll **C** nitrates **D** carbon dioxide **E** sunlight **F** darkness
G magnesium ions

(*a*) Which are essential for making sugars?   ___ ___ ___ ___

(*b*) Which additional factor is needed to make amino acids, once sugars have been made?   ___

(*c*) Which supplies the energy for photosynthesis?   ___

(*d*) Which are 'food' for the plant?   ___ ___ ___

(*e*) Which of the 'foods' will not be absorbed efficiently unless there is oxygen around the roots?   ___ ___

(*f*) For which factor, needed for photosynthesis, is **G** particularly important?   ___

(*g*) Which factor stops photosynthesis every 24 hours?   ___

(*h*) Which foods enter by diffusion alone?   ___

10   Experiments on photosynthesis may involve the following:
A variegated leaves **B** soda lime or caustic soda **C** ethanol **D** iodine **E** oxygen
F starch

(*i*) Which would you use to:

(*a*) prevent leaves getting carbon dioxide?   ___

(*b*) remove chlorophyll from leaves?   ___

(*c*) test whether chlorophyll is essential for photosynthesis?   ___

(*d*) test a decolourised leaf for starch?   ___

(*ii*) Which are products of photosynthesis?   ___ ___

(*iii*) If water containing ^{18}O were fed to a photosynthesising plant, in which product would the ^{18}O appear?   ___

(*iv*) Before doing any photosynthesis experiment with a pot plant, what must first be removed from its leaves?   ___

11   The following are parts of leaves:
A stomata **B** palisade cells **C** xylem cells **D** spongy cells **E** epidermis cells
F phloem cells **G** cuticle **H** guard cells

(*i*) Which cells allow transport of:

(*a*) water into the leaf?   ___

(*b*) gases out of the leaf?   ___

(*c*) sucrose out of the leaf?   ___

(*ii*) After excluding your answers to (*i*) (*a*)–(*c*), arrange the remaining parts in the correct sequence to label a vertical section of a leaf, starting with the upper surface: ___ ___ ___ ___ ___

(*iii*) Which cells can photosynthesise?   ___ ___

(*iv*) Which cells provide most of the strength in veins?   ___

(*v*) Which are small pores?   ___

Choose the best answer to the alternatives given in questions 12–19.

12   Assimilation is the process in which food is:
A taken in **B** used or stored within the body **C** excreted **D** broken up   ___

13 The elements carbon, hydrogen, oxygen and nitrogen can all be found in:
A fats **B** glycogen **C** proteins **D** carbohydrates   ___

14 Glycogen is stored in the:
A liver **B** stomach **C** pancreas **D** brain   ___

15 The liver does not:
A break down red blood cells **B** make urea **C** make bile **D** make insulin   ___

16 A food tested by boiling with Benedict's (or Fehling's) solution gave an orange precipitate. This showed it contained some:
A protein **B** fat **C** reducing sugar **D** sucrose   ___

17 A protein when boiled with Millon's reagent gives the following colour:
A brick red **B** blue-black **C** orange **D** brown   ___

18 Fats and oils do not:
A leave translucent stains on paper **B** taste sweet **C** float in water
D dissolve in ethanol and reappear as a white emulsion when water is added   ___

19 Chlorophyll is removed from leaves before they are tested for starch because:
A otherwise the iodine would not react.
B the green colour would make it difficult to see any blue-black colour.
C this helps the alcohol to penetrate the leaf.
D boiling in water kills the leaf.   ___

Test on unit 5 Water and transport systems

1 Match the biological functions of water given as **A**–**E** below with processes (*a*)–(*g*) by putting the correct letters in the spaces provided (you may use **A**–**E** more than once):
A reactant **B** glucose transporter **C** lubricant **D** coolant **E** supporter

(*a*) blood flowing   ___
(*b*) sweating   ___
(*c*) digestion   ___
(*d*) plant cells becoming turgid   ___
(*e*) movement at a synovial joint   ___
(*f*) photosynthesis   ___
(*g*) transpiration   ___

2 (*i*) State the name of the process by which plant cells gain most of their:

(*a*) mineral salts;   _____
(*b*) water;   _____
(*c*) carbon dioxide.   _____

(*ii*) Which of the above processes:

(*a*) requires a semi-permeable membrane?   _____
(*b*) is slow?   _____
(*c*) requires cell respiration?   _____

3 A strip of epidermis was taken from a leaf and cut into three parts. Each piece was placed for 5 minutes in one of three beakers containing either distilled water, or 0.5 molar sugar solution, or 1.0 molar sugar solution. After 5 minutes a representative cell from each piece of epidermis was drawn – as shown in the diagram:

Which cell(s):
(a) had been in the distilled water? ___
(b) had been in the 1.0 M sugar solution? ___
(c) has a high wall pressure? ___
(d) are plasmolysed? ___ ___
(e) has the most concentrated cell sap? ___
(f) is turgid? ___ ___
(g) could have come from a wilted leaf (rather than from this experiment)? ___ ___

4 (i) Match the plant parts **A—F** below with their descriptions (a)—(f):
   A xylem **B** stomata **C** cork **D** phloem **E** cuticle **F** lenticels

   (a) external holes in an old stem ___
   (b) woody cells (vessels) ___
   (c) wax secreted by cells ___
   (d) cells of outer bark ___
   (e) leaf pores ___
   (f) sieve tube cells ___
   (ii) Which pairs of plant parts **A–F** above are associated with (a)–(e) below?
   (a) are transporting tissues ___ ___
   (b) allow gaseous exchange ___ ___
   (c) waterproof the plant ___ ___
   (d) permit supply of raw material for photosynthesis ___ ___
   (e) are dead cells ___ ___

5 Which of the following is *not* a process linked with transpiration?
   A transporting sugars **B** absorption of water by roots **C** cooling the leaf
   D evaporation of water at leaves ___

6 Which of the following factors increases the rate of loss of water vapour at the surface of leaves?
   A still air **B** sunlight **C** high humidity **D** cool temperature ___

7 Select from **A–M** those items which apply to (a)–(d):
   A epidermis cell **B** guard cell **C** CO_2 **D** O_2 **E** spongy mesophyll cell
   F xylem vessel **G** dry soil **H** palisade cell **J** phloem sieve tube **K** cuticle
   L water vapour **M** closed stoma

   (a) three types of cell that photosynthesise ___ ___ ___
   (b) three types of cell that cannot photosynthesise ___ ___ ___
   (c) three factors that reduce transpiration ___ ___ ___
   (d) stomata during the day allow the entry of ___ into the leaf
       and the exit of ___ and ___

8 Which of the following is the correct definition of osmosis?
   A absorption of water by roots
   B diffusion of water from where it is in high concentration to where it is in low concentration across a semi-permeable membrane
   C diffusion of a weak solution into a strong one across a semi-permeable membrane
   D absorption of salts into a weak solution across a cell membrane ___

9 Write **T** (for true) or **F** (for false) against the following statements about a sea-water algae the cells of which are becoming turgid:

   (a) The cells will shortly burst. ___
   (b) The sea water is a stronger solution than that inside the cell vacuoles. ___
   (c) The cell membrane is fully permeable to the water but not to the salts. ___
   (d) The cell wall is fully permeable to sea water. ___

10 Which of the following is the principal reason why multicellular animals have a blood system?
   A They need to cool themselves when they are active.
   B Diffusion alone is too slow a process to supply food and remove wastes from their cells.
   C Hormones cannot be transported any other way.
   D The heart would have nothing to do otherwise. ____

11 Mammal blood can be separated into various components.
   (*i*) What is the main chemical component of:
      (*a*) whole blood? _____
      (*b*) dried plasma? _____
      (*c*) dried erythrocytes? _____

   (*ii*) What is the main type of cell in
      (*a*) the cellular part of blood? _____
      (*b*) the leucocyte portion? _____

12 In mammal blood, name:
   (*a*) a gas transported mainly as bicarbonate ions; _____
   (*b*) a gas transported mainly in red cells; _____
   (*c*) a waste made principally in the liver; _____
   (*d*) the main food respired in cells. _____

13 Which of the statements below apply to lymph nodes?
   A they produce white blood cells **B** they filter out bacteria from lymph
   C they store carbohydrates **D** they pump lymph **E** they assist in making antibodies

   ___ ___ ___

14 Where appropriate, match statements **A–G** with blood vessels (*a*)–(*c*):
   A non-return valves **B** blood under low pressure **C** thick walls with muscle
   D walls one-cell thick **E** blood loses volume **F** blood flows in pulses
   G provide a very large surface area

   (*a*) arteries ___ ___   (*b*) veins ___ ___   (*c*) capillaries ___ ___ ___

15 Which of the following is the medium which carries dissolved food to the cell membranes of tissues?
   A serum **B** lymph **C** blood **D** water **E** extracellular fluid (tissue fluid) **F** plasma ___

16 Which of items **A–H** below in the blood are:
   (*a*) lost at the lungs? ___ ___ ___
   (*b*) used by growing muscles? ___ ___
   (*c*) removed permanently from blood in the kidneys? ___ ___ ___ ___
   (*d*) gained at a sunbather's skin? ___ ___

   A O_2 **B** CO_2 **C** urea **D** amino acids **E** water **F** vitamin D **G** glucose **H** heat

17 A blood cell is on the point of entering the mammal heart. Trace the route it will take to reach the aorta by arranging those of the following letters that apply, in the correct sequence:
   A lung **B** left ventricle **C** right ventricle **D** pulmonary vein **E** right auricle
   F left auricle **G** hepatic portal vein **H** pulmonary artery **J** renal artery

   ___ ___ ___ ___ ___ ___ ___

18 Trace the journey of a blood cell from the aorta to just outside the heart assuming that it contributes to the processes involved in the absorption of digested food and its storage in the liver on the way. Arrange those of the following letters that apply in the correct sequence:
   A renal artery **B** hepatic portal vein **C** mesenteric artery (to intestine)
   D hepatic vein **E** vena cava **F** hepatic artery **G** villi **H** liver **J** lungs

   ___ ___ ___ ___ ___ ___

19   Which of the following blood vessels **A–H** are associated with (*a*)–(*e*) below?
A renal artery **B** leg vein of a sprinting man **C** pulmonary artery **D** renal vein
E hepatic portal vein **F** aorta **G** hepatic vein **H** pulmonary vein

(*a*) lowest urea content   ___   (*d*) warmest blood   ___
(*b*) highest food content after a meal   ___   (*e*) highest blood pressure   ___
(*c*) lowest oxygen content   ___

20   Select the figures from the right-hand column which most closely approximate to the
statements in the left-hand column and insert them in the spaces provided, as they
apply to man:

(*a*) _____ : number of red blood cells per mm³ of blood   70
(*b*) _____ : number of white blood cells per mm³ of blood   98.4
(*c*) _____ : resting adult heart-beat rate per minute   0
(*d*) _____ : number of heart chambers   1
(*e*) _____ : number of nuclei in a red blood cell   4
(*f*) _____ : man's 'normal' under-tongue temperature in °C   10 000
                                                                       5 000 000
                                                                       37

Test on unit 6 Respiration

1   Pair terms **A–E** with the descriptions (*a*)–(*e*):
A internal respiration **B** breathing **C** external respiration **D** respiration
E gaseous exchange

(*a*) movements in animals bringing oxygen to where it can be absorbed
     into the body   ___
(*b*) a physical process which includes **B** and **E**   ___
(*c*) exchange of O_2 for CO_2 ___
(*d*) chemical reactions in cells that release energy from organic molecules   ___
(*e*) a process which includes **A**, **B** and **E**   ___

2   Below is a list of structures in organisms. Against them write the appropriate letter
from **A** and **E** in question 1 above to signify their main purpose in respiration:

(*a*) gills   ___   (*e*) tracheoles   ___
(*b*) mitochondria   ___   (*f*) ribs   ___
(*c*) capillaries   ___   (*g*) *Amoeba's* cell membrane   ___
(*d*) diaphragm   ___   (*h*) leaves   ___

3   Small animals like *Amoeba* and *Paramoecium* do not need gills because:
A they would get in the way
B there is no oxygen in the water in which they live
C only fish evolved with gills
D their surface area for obtaining oxygen is large in relation to
     their volume.
E they do not move very far and so need little oxygen.   ___

4   Air inhaled by man on a dry day differs from air exhaled in the following respects.
It contains:
A more CO_2 **B** less CO_2 **D** less water vapour **E** more water vapour
F more O_2 **G** more nitrogen **H** same amount of nitrogen **J** more dust

___ ___ ___ ___

5   Air breathed in by man passes the structures of the respiratory system listed below
in what order?
A bronchioles **B** bronchi **C** nostrils **D** pharynx **E** alveoli **F** epiglottis **G** trachea

___ ___ ___ ___ ___ ___ ___

6   Write **T** (true) or **F** (false) against the following statements. As a man breathes in:

   (*a*) the volume of his chest cavity increases.   ___
   (*b*) the pressure within his chest cavity decreases.   ___
   (*c*) the lungs expand, pushing out the ribs.   ___
   (*d*) the diaphragm becomes flatter.   ___
   (*e*) the ribs move downwards and inwards.   ___
   (*f*) the deflated alveoli fill with air.   ___

7   (*i*) Which of the following statements do you feel is the *most* accurate?   ___
      A Man breathes out carbon dioxide.   ___
      B Man breathes in oxygen.   ___
      C Man breathes out nitrogen.   ___
      D Man breathes out air.   ___

   (*ii*) In the spaces provided above indicate the approximate percentage of gases applicable to statements **A** to **C**.
   (*iii*) If statements **A** and **B** above were *literally* true what would happen to:
      (in **A**) a man being revived by the 'kiss of life'?

      _____

      (in **B**) a man smoking a cigarette?

      _____

8   Write **T** (true) or **F** (false) against the following statements. Anaerobic respiration in yeast:

   (*a*) produces CO_2.   ___   (*d*) needs O_2.   ___
   (*b*) produces bread.   ___   (*e*) liberates more energy
   (*c*) uses glucose.   ___   than aerobic respiration.   ___

9   If an animal is respiring aerobically, which of the following is it *not* doing?
   A using glucose **B** performing gaseous exchange **C** using O_2 **D** giving out CO_2
   E making ethanol **F** releasing heat   ___

10 Pair organisms **A–H** with their structures for gaseous exchange (*a*)–(*e*):
   A earthworm **B** *Amoeba* **C** insect **D** mammal **E** fish **F** frog **G** flowering plant
   H yeast

   (*a*) tracheoles   ___   (*d*) cell membranes only   ___
   (*b*) alveoli   ___   (*e*) skin capillaries   ___ ___
   (*c*) gill lamellae   ___

11 From the list of organisms in question 10 above select those that:

   (*a*) assist their gaseous exchange by breathing.   ___ ___ ___ ___
   (*b*) do *not* use blood to assist gaseous exchange.   ___ ___ ___ ___
   (*c*) respire aerobically.   ___

12 The cells (*a*)–(*c*) of an angiosperm perform some of the processes **A–F**. Insert the appropriate letters from **A–F** in the spaces provided:
   A respire at all times **B** produce O_2 at all times **C** produce CO_2 at night
   D absorb CO_2 in sunlight **E** produce O_2 by day **F** do none of these

   (*a*) green cells in a leaf   ___ ___ ___ ___
   (*b*) non-green cells of pith   ___ ___
   (*c*) xylem vessels of wood   ___

Test on unit 7 Excretion, temperature regulation and homeostasis

1   Select from **A–F** below those that are *not* major excretory products in:

   (*a*)   an insect.   — — — —
   (*b*)   an oak tree by day.   — — — —
   (*c*)   a mammal.   — — — —
   A O_2 **B** CO_2 **C** water **D** autumn leaves **E** uric acid **F** urea

2   Select from **A–E** below those that are *not* excretory organs in man:
   A liver **B** anus **C** kidneys **D** salivary glands **E** lungs   — —

3   Urea is excreted by mammals. Name the organ where it is:

   (*a*)   made.   _____
   (*b*)   stored temporarily.   _____
   (*c*)   excreted.   _____

4   Trace the pathway of a urea molecule from a person's aorta to its elimination from the
   body by arranging structures **A–L** in the correct sequence:
   A   collecting duct   **E**   renal vein   **J**   bladder
   B   Bowman's capsule   **F**   loop of Henlé   **K**   urethra
   C   glomerulus   **G**   first coiled tubule   **L**   ureter
   D   renal arterioles   **H**   second coiled tubule

   (*a*)   inside the kidney.   — — — — — — —
   (*b*)   beyond the kidney.   — — —

5   Match the items **A–F** below with (*a*)–(*f*) – biological materials present in man's
   kidney:
   A 2–4% solution of urea **B** pressure-filtrate of blood
   C hormone ADH influences its uptake **D** blood in renal vein
   E totally reabsorbed in first coiled tubule **F** blood leaving glomerulus

   (*a*)   water   —
   (*b*)   urine   —
   (*c*)   tissue fluid   —
   (*d*)   small food molecules   —
   (*e*)   blood unusually rich in blood cells   —
   (*f*)   blood containing almost no urea   —

6   Which of the following are *not* normally present in urine?
   A glucose **B** amino acids **C** fatty acids **D** water **E** sodium chloride **F** protein
   G blood cells **H** bile pigments

                                                         — — — —

7   More glucose enters the kidney than leaves it because:
   A the kidney cells use glucose in respiration.
   B the kidney converts glucose to amino acids.
   C glucose is retained by the kidney to maintain a high osmotic pressure.
   D the kidney stores glucose as glycogen.   —

8   No glucose is normally present in urine. This is because:
   A glucose is not filtered out into Bowman's capsules.
   B the glucose is excreted as sucrose.
   C the bladder reabsorbs the glucose.
   D kidney tubules reabsorb glucose.   —

9 The volume of urine produced by a healthy person fluctuates. Assuming no extra drinking takes place, indicate the effect of factors (*a*)–(*e*) on urine volume by inserting **I** (increase), **D** (decrease) or **O** (no change) in the spaces provided:

(*a*) strenuous exercise   —
(*b*) drinking a litre of water   —
(*c*) eating a lot of salted peanuts   —
(*d*) a hot day   —
(*e*) eating 1 kg of steak   —

10 (*i*) Water loss accompanies most forms of excretion. Name the processes **A**–**E** described below and an excretory product which is lost at the same time:

	Process	*Product*
A water vapour loss by a daisy in sunlight	_____	_____
B water vapour loss at skin in man	_____	_____
C water vapour loss from lungs in man	_____	_____
D water loss by a bear in winter	_____	_____
E water loss by *Amoeba*	_____	_____

(*ii*) Select from **A**–**E** above pairs of processes which have as a main function:
(*a*) keeping the strength of body fluids stable.   — —
(*b*) causing loss of heat.   — —

(*iii*) Select from **A**–**E** above pairs of processes in which:
(*a*) loss of excretory substances is of minor importance.   — —
(*b*) the excretory substances are gases.   — —

11 Heat can be gained or lost from an organism's environment in a number of ways. By which of the following methods can heat only be *lost*?
A evaporation of water **B** radiation **C** conduction **D** convection   —

12 Which of the descriptions of organisms **A**–**D** below *best* describes:

(*a*) an insect?   —   (*b*) a mammal?   —

A body temperature remains constant **B** ectotherm (poikilotherm) **C** cold-blooded **D** warm-blooded

(*c*) If an insect experiences a warm sunny day followed by a chilly night, which of the following terms best describes it during those 24 hours?

A warm-blooded **B** cold-blooded **C** warm- and cold-blooded   —

13 The methods of temperature regulation used by a mammal are listed below as (*a*) to (*d*). Indicate which of items **A**–**F** below assist in methods (*a*)–(*d*):
A shivering **B** vaso-constriction **C** subcutaneous fat **D** radiation **E** sweating **F** liver metabolism **G** contact with warm rocks

(*a*) heat loss   — —
(*b*) heat generation   — —
(*c*) heat conservation   — —
(*d*) heat gain from outside   — —

14 The basic reason for the inactivity of ectotherms (poikilotherms) during cold weather is:
A they are hibernating **B** there is no food available **C** their enzymes work slowly **D** their body water is frozen   —

15 The following activity in an organism does *not* contribute to homeostasis:
A removal of CO_2 **B** provision of adequate food **C** provision of adequate O_2 **D** removal of excess water **E** continuance of growth   —

Test on unit 8 Sensitivity

1   The structures of the eye listed as (a)–(g) have various properties and functions listed as A–N. Match the two by putting the letters A–N in the spaces provided:
A is very sensitive to touch B regulates amount of light reaching back of eye
C does most of the light focusing D is tough and opaque E is black
F is tough and translucent G nourishes the retina H is muscular
J is attached at the blind spot K is light-sensitive L is white
M is the front surface layer N is the innermost surface

(a) sclera ___ ___   (d) choroid ___ ___   (f) iris ___ ___
(b) cornea ___ ___   (e) retina ___ ___   (g) optic nerve ___
(c) conjunctiva ___ ___

2   Which of the following is true?
When an eye of a mammal focuses on a near object:
A the lens becomes thinner B the lens becomes a fatter shape once the tension is taken off it C the cornea is bent further by the ciliary muscles D the ciliary muscles contract, squashing the lens into a more convex shape   ___

3   Which of the following statements about the fovea is untrue?
A contains rods and cones B contains cones only C is on the optical axis of the eye
D is where objects being viewed are normally in focus   ___

4   Pair up structures (a)–(d) with properties A–D:
A region of acutest vision B allow colour vision only
C allow black and white vision only D where retina is absent

(a) cones   ___
(b) rods   ___
(c) optic nerve   ___
(d) fovea   ___

5   Fill in the blanks in the following table:

Focusing abnormalities of the human eye

	Abnormality	Eyeball length	Eye lens	Corrective lens
(a)			Cannot get fat enough to focus on a nearby object	
(b)		Normal		Bifocal lenses
(c)			Cannot get thin enough to focus on a high-flying jet	

6   Arrange letters A–G in the spaces provided to convey the roles that each structure plays in hearing processes (a)–(e):
A ear ossicles B hair cells in cochlea C perilymph D tympanum E endolymph
F pinna G auditory centre of brain

(a) sound gathering   ___   (d) sound detection   ___
(b) sound conduction ___ ___ ___ ___   (e) sound appreciation   ___
(c) sound amplification   ___ ___

7   By arranging letters A–J in sequence, indicate the order in which a noise would affect the parts of the ear:
A endolymph B perilymph C round window D oval window E hair cells F stapes
G ear drum H malleus J incus

___ ___ ___ ___ ___ ___ ___ ___ ___

8 The parts of the ear that assist in telling a person he is changing position are:
A endolymph B perilymph C cochlea D semicircular canals E ampullae F cupula
G cones H hair cells J cerebellum

— — — — —

Test on unit 9 Co-ordination and response

1 Organisms gather information about their environment using sensory cells which send
'messages' to other parts of their bodies which, in turn, respond. Compare this chain of
events in respect of gravity acting on a pot plant that has been knocked over, and a cat
which has overbalanced, by filling in the table below.

	(a) Location of sensory cells	(b) Type of 'message' sent	(c) Speed of 'message'	(d) Main response
Plant				
Cat				

2 The following terms **A–G** are associated with the reception and response to stimuli in
plants and animals. Select those which do *not* apply to:
(a) flowering plants.   — — — —
(b) insects.   —
A sensory cells B sense organs C nerves D hormones E reflexes F tropisms G taxis

3 Select from **A–E** below the kinds of cell in a mammal that:

(a) are sensitive to their environment.   —
(b) receive 'messages' from sensory cells.   —
(c) transmit 'messages' to effectors.   —
(d) take 'messages' to the brain from the spinal cord.   —
(e) store information.   —
A sensory cells B relay neurons C brain cells D sensory neurons E motor neurons

4 (i) Arrange the appropriate four kinds of cell from A–E in question 3 above in the
       correct sequence to make up the main part of a reflex arc: — — — —
   (ii) Name a fifth kind of cell needed to complete the arc: _____

5 Which parts of the mammal brain, **A–F** below, are concerned principally with:
(a) sense of balance?   —   (d) controlling breathing rhythm?   —
(b) intelligent decisions?   —   (e) secreting hormones?   —
(c) controlling body temperature? —   (f) interpreting what is seen?   —
A hypothalamus B pituitary C cerebrum D optic lobes E medulla oblongata
F cerebellum

6 Which description from **A–E** best fits the parts of a neuron listed (a)–(e)?
A secrete a chemical into a gap B long, in sensory neurons C long, in motor neurons
D major part of white matter in spinal cord E major part of grey matter in spinal cord

(a) cell bodies   —   (c) synaptic knobs   —   (e) fatty sheaths   —
(b) dendrons   —   (d) axons   —

7 Arrange parts (a)–(d) in question 6 in the order in which they would pass an impulse:

— — — —

8 State which of **A–D** below does *not* describe a conditioned reflex action:
A rapid B unlearned C inappropriate response D response to a stimulus   —

9   State which of **A**–**D** below does *not* apply to a reflex action:
    A is an inherited response **B** involves a maximum of three kinds of neuron
    C always involves the brain **D** for example blinking **E** is of high survival value ___

10 During the control of blood sugar in a mammal two antagonistic hormones are
    employed. Fill in the table about them:

	Raises blood sugar	Lowers blood sugar
(a) Hormone's name		
(b) Hormone's source (gland)		
(c) Means of stimulating gland to secrete		
(d) Main organ stimulated by hormone		

11 The maintenance of a constant internal environment in an organism is called:
    A osmoregulation **B** homeostasis **C** temperature control **D** enteritis   ___

12 A number of metabolic diseases in mammals arise as a result of abnormal endocrine
    function. Complete the table below concerned with this:

Name of abnormality	Caused by lack of (hormone)	From (gland)
(a) Dwarfism		
(b)	Insulin	
(c) Water diabetes (diabetes insipidus)		
(d)		Thyroid of baby
(e) Goitre		

13 Choose from the items **A**–**H** below those that apply to secretion of:
    (a) hormones   __ __ __ __ __
    (b) digestive enzymes.   __ __ __
    A organic **B** inorganic **C** secreted in minute quantities
    D secreted in relatively large quantities **E** secreted into ducts
    F secreted into blood **G** secreted from endocrine glands
    H amount secreted often subject to 'feedback'

Test on unit 10 Support and locomotion

1 (*i*) Select the component *not* concerned with support of aerial parts of a currant-bush:
   A turgor pressure **B** xylem **C** cellulose **D** cork   ___

   (*ii*) which of the above provide the *main* support for:

   (*a*) leaves?   ___ ___   (*b*) stem?   ___

2 Select the component *not* concerned with support in a mammal:
   A protein fibres **B** chitin **C** bone **D** cartilage   ___

3 **A–E** below are functions of skeletons. Select those that are *exclusively* functions of:
   (*a*) mammal skeletons.   ___
   (*b*) insect skeletons.   ___ ___

   A levers for locomotion **B** protection **C** making red blood cells
   D providing camouflage **E** determining body shape exactly

4 Name the materials in an insect's skeleton that perform the following functions:
   (*a*) waterproofing   _____
   (*b*) hardness   _____
   (*c*) flexibility   _____

5 Name the part of a mammal's locomotory system that:
   (*a*) links bone to bone.   _____
   (*b*) links bone to muscle.   _____
   (*c*) provides lubricating fluid at joints.   _____
   (*d*) provides cushioning at movable joints   _____

6 When a human forearm is raised, certain events take place. From the following, select those that are true:
   A Triceps muscle pushes the elbow down.
   B Nerve impulses go to biceps muscle causing contraction.
   C Nerve impulses pass to both biceps and triceps.
   D Biceps shortens.
   E Triceps shortens.
   F Triceps is prevented from shortening by reflex action.   ___ ___ ___ ___

7 Select from the following descriptions those that are *not* true concerning locomotion of an earthworm in its burrow:
   A Has no skeleton.
   B Pulls itself up to its anchored prostomium.
   C When circular body-muscles contract, body becomes short and fat.
   D Segments can be anchored with eight chaetae each.
   E When circular muscles contract, longitudinal muscles relax.
   F Segments that are extending pull in their chaetae.   ___ ___ ___

8 (*i*) Vertebrae consist of a number of parts each of which performs an important function. Fill in the name of the part and its function against the descriptions given below:

Description	Name	Function
A main cylinder of bone		
B largest hole		
C main dorsal projection of bone		
D small projections of bone in pairs, front and back		

(*ii*) Which of **A**–**D** above is nearest to the:

(*a*) dorsal aorta   ——   (*b*) intervertebral disc   ——

9   Name the type of vertebrae or individual vertebra in mammals which:

  (*a*) allows most of the mobility in the back.   _____

  (*b*) is fused to the pelvic girdle.   _____

  (*c*) allows swivelling of the head right and left.   _____

  (*d*) is behind the anus.   _____

  (*e*) bears ribs.   _____

10   State as precisely as you can where in a human you would find:

  A the radius.   _____

  B synovial fluid.   _____

  C the humerus.   _____

  D the tibia.   _____

  E phalanges.   _____

  F the femur.   _____

  G carpals.   _____

  H the scapula.   _____

11   Between which bones in question 10 would you find the following kinds of joint?

  (*a*) hinge   _____   (*c*) slipping   _____

  (*b*) ball and socket   _____   (*d*) fixed (suture)   _____

Test on unit 11 Growth

1   Growth includes certain of the following processes, depending on the organism concerned:

  A mitosis **B** meiosis **C** formation of protein **D** formation of new cell walls
  E vacuolation **F** differentiation

  Fill in the appropriate letters as the processes apply to:

  (*a*) most animals   —— —— ——   (*b*) most plants   —— —— —— —— ——

2   Complete the following passage by inserting suitable words in the blanks:

  Angiosperms grow into a _____ shape with a _____ surface area
  to assist in absorption of _____ and _____ through their
  leaves and of _____ and _____ from the soil in which
  they are anchored. By contrast animals have _____ bodies
  with limbs to assist them in _____ to get their food.

3   Study **A**–**G** below as they apply to primary and secondary growth in angiosperms:
  A growth in length **B** cambium divides **C** apical meristem divides **D** growth in
  diameter **E** cork formed **F** some cortex splits off **G** forms xylem and phloem

  Enter letters **A**–**G** as they apply mainly to:

  (*a*) primary growth —— —— ——   (*b*) secondary growth —— —— —— —— ——

4   **A**–**H** below apply to seeds. Enter the correct letters in the spaces provided where they
  are associated with structures (*a*)–(*d*):

  (*a*) cotyledon   —— ——   (*c*) plumule   —— ——

  (*b*) radicle   —— ——   (*d*) testa   —— ——

  A root **B** hilum **C** shoot **D** micropyle **E** grows out first on germination
  F are the first true leaves **G** leaf that absorbs endosperm **H** there are two in bean seed

5   Which of the items (*a*)–(*d*) in question 4:

  (*i*) make up the embryo in a seed?   _____

  (*ii*) grow from the ovule?   _____

6 Complete the following passage:

When an endospermic seed is germinating it gets its food from the _____ by digesting it with_____ and absorbing it via the_____.
For these processes to occur the seed needs three essential conditions:
_____,_____, and_____.

7 When a seed germinates epigeally, certain events occur. Which of the following do these include?:
A the testa splits **B** the hypocotyl grows fast **C** the cambium divides
D the epicotyl grows fast **E** the cotyledons appear above ground
F the apical meristems divide **G** the cotyledons remain below ground
H new cells vacuolate

___ ___ ___ ___ ___

8 State which of items **A–H** in question 7 apply to:

(*a*) *all* types of germination ___ ___ ___   (*b*) hypogeal germination only ___ ___

9 Which of the following do *not* apply to the way an insect grows?
A Skeleton and other tissues grow at the same rate.
B Skeleton does not grow but is replaced.
C Animal's mass increases gradually to adulthood.
D Mass increases suddenly at each moult.
E Length of the body increases suddenly at each moult.

___ ___

Test on unit 12 Reproduction

1 Gametes can never be:
A the protoplasm of *Spirogyra* cells **B** pollen grains **C** spermatozoa
D nuclei inside the gametangia of *Mucor* **E** haploid **F** the whole egg of a hen

___ ___

2 Zygotes are:
A certain kinds of gamete **B** cells produced when gametes fuse **C** dividing cells
D certain kinds of spore **E** the first cells of asexually produced organisms   ___

3 Fertilisation has occurred when:
A a sperm has just reached an ovum.
B pollen grains of the right species have reached a stigma.
C a zygote has just been formed.
D the pollen tube nucleus has reached the ovule.
E nuclei of the male and female gametes have become one.   ___ ___

4 State which of the terms **A–F** you would associate with:
(*a*) asexual (non-sexual) reproduction   ___ ___ ___
(*b*) sexual reproduction   ___ ___ ___
A meiosis **B** identical offspring **C** spores **D** flowers **E** a variety of offspring **F** tubers

5 State which of the following would *not* be produced by mitosis:
A fungal spores **B** sperm **C** bulbs **D** runners **E** pollen **F** zygospores.   ___ ___

6 Pair organisms (*a*)–(*e*) with descriptions **A–G**:
A reproduces both sexually and asexually **B** does not reproduce asexually
C does not reproduce sexually **D** male gamete does not swim
E 'conjugation' precedes fertilisation **F** reproduces by 'budding'
G reproduces by binary fission

(*a*) *Amoeba*   ___ ___   (*d*) *Spirogyra*   ___ ___ ___
(*b*) daffodil   ___ ___   (*e*) rat   ___
(*c*) *Hydra*   ___ ___

7   In a winter twig, name the parts that:

   (*a*) protect delicate parts of a bud.   _____

   (*b*) permit gaseous exchange.   _____

   (*c*) have waterproof scars.   _____

   (*d*) show where the flower stalks fell off. _____

   (*e*) show where leaves fell off at bud-burst. _____

8   Apply the appropriate descriptions **A–D** to the terms (*a*)–(*c*) (which concern plants):
   A survives winter as seed in its second year **B** flowers twice a year
   C survives winter as seed each year **D** survives for many years

   (*a*) perennial   ___   (*b*) biennial   ___   (*c*) annual   ___

9   Name the part(s) of an insect-pollinated flower that usually:

   (*a*) 'advertises' by colour and scent.   _____

   (*b*) rewards insects with sugar solution.   _____

   (*c*) enables the stigma to brush against the visiting insect. _____

   (*d*) protects the flower in bud.   _____

   (*e*) contains ova (female gametes).   _____

   (*f*) contains ovules.   _____

10   Cross-pollination is best described as:
   A   the arrival of pollen on a stigma from a second flower.
   B   the liberation of gametes at the ovule.
   C   pollen transfer from one species to the next.
   D   pollen reaching the stigma of a flower from a second plant of the same kind.
   E   none of these.   ___

11   Indicate the origin of (*a*)–(*d*) by pairing them up with **A–D**
   A receptacle **B** integuments **C** ovary **D** ovule

   (*a*) seed   ___   (*c*) false fruit   ___
   (*b*) true fruit   ___   (*d*) testa   ___

12   Opposite the following parts of a wind pollinated flower write *two* descriptive terms
   which might indicate what the parts would look like:

   (*a*) stigma   _____ _____

   (*b*) pollen   _____ _____

   (*c*) petals   _____ _____

13   (*a*)–(*c*) below describe stages in mammal reproduction. Select from **A–D** the location
   of those stages within the reproductive tract of the female:
   A ovary **B** uterus **C** oviduct **D** vagina

   (*a*) Fertilisation takes place.   ___

   (*b*) A blastula develops into an embryo.   ___

   (*c*) New ova are shed.   ___

14   Name the parts of an angiosperm and of a mammal which:

	Angiosperm	*Mammal*
(*a*) make pollen/sperm.	_____	_____
(*b*) receive pollen/sperm.	_____	_____
(*c*) allow development of the embryo within.	_____	_____
(*d*) are the immediate source of food for the embryo.	_____	_____
(*e*) are responsible for expulsion of the embryo when it is fully developed.	_____	_____

15 At the stage when a mammal is a developing embryo, name the part(s) which:

(*a*) cushion the embryo from blows.   _____

(*b*) passes wastes from embryo to mother.   _____

(*c*) will be severed after birth.   _____

(*d*) receives oxygen from the mother.   _____

(*e*) is normally the first to appear outside the mother at birth._____

(*f*) will be the very last to leave the uterus at birth.   _____

Test on unit 13   Genes, chromosomes and heredity

1 Put the following in increasing order of size (volume):

A nucleus **B** DNA thread **C** protoplasm **D** chromosome **E** gene   _____

2 Choose from **A–E** in question **1** the item which:

(*a*) determines synthesis of an enzyme.   ___

(*b*) is visible under a light microscope only at cell division.   ___

(*c*) becomes divided into two after the nucleus has divided.   ___

(*d*) is diploid after fertilisation.   ___

3 Link (*a*)–(*g*) with the appropriate items from **A–J** by filling in the blanks:
A phenotype **B** dominant **C** homozygous **D** environment **E** co-dominant
F genotype **G** heterozygous **H** recessive **J** alleles

(*a*) determines characteristics   ___ ___

(*b*) the appearance of an organism   ___

(*c*) gene that expresses itself as a characteristic   ___

(*d*) gene that only expresses itself if there are two of them   ___

(*e*) two identical genes at a locus   ___

(*f*) name given to two alternative genes at a locus   ___

(*g*) two alternative genes at a locus which both express themselves   ___ ___

4 The number of chromosomes in a gorilla's cheek cell is 48. The number in a gorilla's ovum is:
A 24 **B** 48 **C** 96 **D** 23   ___

5 Choose the type of cell division that reduces the chromosome number by half:
A mitosis **B** meiosis **C** growth cell divisions **D** binary fission   ___

6 Choose from the following those that do *not* apply to meiosis:
A products are haploid **B** there are four products from each original cell
C there are two products from each original cell **D** products are not identical
E ensures that a species does not double its diploid number **F** occurs at growing points

___ ___

7 A certain mollusc can be either striped or unstriped. If an organism of genotype **Bb** is crossed with a homozygous dominant having a striped shell:

(*i*) the expected ratio of genotypes in the offspring is
A all **BB** **B** ½**Bb**:½**BB** **C** all **bb** **D** all **Bb**   ___

(*ii*) the expected ratio of phenotypes is
A all striped   **B** all unstriped   **C** ½ striped and ½ unstriped   **D** all faintly striped ___

8 Pure lines of red flowers crossed with white ones give only pink offspring.

(*i*) What will be the ratio of red, white and pink flowers if the following crosses are made:

(*a*) white × pink?   _____

(*b*) red × pink?   _____

(*c*) pink × pink?   _____

(*ii*) Show your reasoning for answer (*i*) (*a*)–(*c*) by drawing Punnett squares for each
cross: (*a*)   (*b*)   (*c*)

9   Eye colour is determined by a dominant/recessive relationship in a certain mammal.
The following results were obtained from crosses made. Fill in the *genotypes* of the
organisms indicated by letters (*a*)–(*c*) in the family tree below, using B = brown,
b = blue:

Blue-eyed × Blue-eyed

(*a*) Brown × Blue   Blue   (*b*) Blue   Blue   Blue × (*c*) Brown
(*a*) . . . .   (*b*) . . . .   (*c*) . . . . .

Brown Brown Brown Brown   Brown Blue Brown Blue Blue

10   Two male animals, **A** and **B**, both with brown fur, were crossed (at different times) with
a grey-furred female, **C**. Whereas mating **A** with **C** gave offspring that were all brown,
the offspring of **B** with **C** were 31 brown and 29 grey. State the genotype of each of the
animals:
A: __   **B:**   __   **C:**   __

11   Statements **A**–**G** below refer to activity within the nucleus of a cell. Insert, in the table,
those activities going on at the three stages of mitosis and meiosis indicated:

	mitosis	*meiosis* (first division)
(*a*) interphase		
(*b*) metaphase		
(*c*) anaphase		

A gene number is being duplicated **B** gene number is being halved
C gene number is remaining the same **D** genes are making enzymes
E centromeres divide **F** centromeres do not divide
G pairs of homologous chromosomes line up on the equator of the cell
H individual chromosomes line up on the equator of the cell

12   Plant A with 2n = 16 is grafted onto another plant, B, with 12 chromosomes as the
diploid number. State the number of chromosomes in the nuclei of:

(*a*) the pollen of plant A.   __   (*c*) the zygotes formed in plant A. __
(*b*) the vegetative growth of plant B. __   (*d*) the petals of plant A.   __

Test on unit 14 Evolution

1   The theory of evolution by natural selection was originated by:
A Malthus **B** Lamarck **C** Mendel **D** Darwin   __

2   Arrange the following statements concerning evolution in a logical order:
A   In any population of organisms there is a variety of individuals.
B   Populations remain reasonably constant in numbers.
C   All organisms could, theoretically, show an exponential rise in numbers.
D   Those varieties best adapted to the environment survive.
E   There must be a 'struggle for existence' which keeps populations down.

__ __ __ __ __

3   The forces of natural selection acting on an insect population might include:
    A pollination **B** frosts **C** spiders **D** insecticide-resistance **E** scarcity of food
    F other insects with similar food requirements   — — — —

4   Which of the following could not be an adaptation?
    A inherited features **B** a wing for flying **C** mutations **D** ability to reason out a solution
    E haemoglobin for carrying oxygen **F** sun-tanning of the European skin   —

5   The following are possible causes of variation in organisms. Select those that are un-
    likely to affect their evolution:
    A cutting human hair different ways **B** sexual reproduction in mice
    C using different levels of fertiliser on crops **D** mutant cells being used in repro-
    duction **F** exercising horses to make them sleek.   — — —

6   Complete the following sentences:

    Irradiation of cells by _____ may cause _____ in them.

    These are changes in the_____ of the nuclei of cells and often kill them.

    However, sometimes such _____ cells survive.

    Only if these cells are _____ or_____ can the changes in them be passed to
    future generations.

    Only helpful changes of this type have any chance of becoming widespread in a popula-
    tion, thus affecting _____ of the species.

7   The diagram below shows a 'family tree' of organisms evolving. Each *letter*, e.g. **C** or **D**
    represents a species:

    By reference to the diagram select those
    species which:

    (*a*) have become extinct.   — —
    (*b*) are common ancestors to more
          than one species.   —
    (*c*) show great variety.   —

8   The types of organism C^1, C^2, C^3, C^4 shown in question 7 could become new species if
    breeding between them was prevented. Assuming that these organisms are water
    beetles introduced by man to the various lakes in North and South America, list, with
    a sentence of explanation, three reasons which might prevent the beetles from inter-
    breeding from lake to lake:

    (*a*) _____

    (*b*) _____

    (*c*) _____

9   Select an appropriate example from **A**–**E** below for each of (*a*)–(*e*):

    A leg of insect and of cow **B** Shetland pony **C** black (melanic) variety of peppered
    moth **D** eye of monkey and of whale **E** *Archaeopteryx*

    (*a*) analogous   —   (*d*) mutant   —
    (*b*) homologous   —   (*e*) product of man's selective breeding   —
    (*c*) link-animal   —

10   Select from the following the item that could *not* be regarded as evidence for Darwin's theory of evolution:
A fossils B selective breeding C acquired characteristics in a lifetime
D similarity of embryos of different species   ___

11   Which of the following statements about fossils are incorrect?
A are found in igneous rocks B are found in sedimentary rocks
C are found in amber D none found in rocks older than 600 million years
E usually have mineralised hard parts F have preserved soft parts   ___ ___ ___

12   Which of the statements below do *not* describe the pentadactyl limb accurately?
A is present in all terrestrial animals B is present in almost all vertebrates
C is present in all mammals
D consists of a five-fingered hand, wrist bones and three long bones
E consists of a five-fingered hand, wrist bones and two long bones
F present only in pterodactyls   ___ ___ ___

13   Arrange the following groups in order of increasing age (i.e. starting with the most recently evolved):
A fish B dinosaurs C algae D man E birds   ___ ___ ___ ___ ___

Test on unit 15 Ecology

1   From the environmental factors A–H select those that are:

(*a*) abiotic   ___ ___ ___ ___   (*b*) biotic   ___ ___ ___ ___

A sunlight B parasites C symbionts D wind E snow F competitors G mineral salts
H predators

2   From the biotic factors in question 1 select:

(*i*) those biotic factors that:
(*a*) do harm to other organisms.   ___ ___ ___
(*b*) do good to other organisms.   ___

(*ii*) those abiotic factors that:
(*a*) influence plant nutrition.   ___ ___ ___
(*b*) might harm a tree if it were not deciduous.   ___ ___

3   Link definitions (*a*)–(*e*) below with terms A–E:
(*a*) place where an organism lives   ___
(*b*) influence of one organism on another   ___
(*c*) a number of species interacting in a locality   ___
(*d*) nutritional interrelationships of organisms   ___
(*e*) interaction of forest organisms both with each other and with their abiotic environment   ___

A community B ecosystem C food web D biotic factor E habitat

4   Explain the difference between the following pairs of terms by stating what the first term lacks to make the second:

(*a*) food chain and food cycle   _____
(*b*) food chain and food web   _____
(*c*) community and ecosystem   _____

5   Look at Fig. 15.4 (p.125) again.

(*i*) Write down two food chains of four members, each of which includes a different parasite. (Do *not* repeat the food chain in Fig. 15.3):

(*a*) _____
(*b*) _____

    (*ii*) Write down:
        (*a*) two competitors *of* the rabbits.   _____   _____
        (*b*) two competitors *for* the voles.   _____   _____
   (*iii*) Assuming that the food web is complete, as drawn, what definite *immediate* changes would there be to the number of each kind of organism if:
        (*a*) sow-thistles and dandelions died? _____

          _____

        (*a*) all rabbits died of myxomatosis?

            more _____
            fewer _____
            no _____

6 Study Fig. 15.1 (p. 123) again. From it write down:

    (*a*) one food chain with three members in it. _____
    (*b*) one food chain with five members in it. _____

    (*c*) two decomposer organisms.   _____   _____
    (*d*) a filter-feeder.   _____
    (*e*) the organism most likely to be harmed, through
         the food chain, by DDT in the aquarium.   _____
    (*f*) two ways in which bacteria might benefit from
         the fish over a period of time.   _____   _____
    (*g*) two ways in which *Elodea* might benefit from the
         bacteria.   _____   _____
    (*h*) two ways in which the abiotic part of this ecosystem might
         benefit *named* organisms (other than through nutrition).

          _____
          _____

7 The biosphere does *not* include:
A whole mountains **B** deepest ocean depths **C** air at 8000 metres **D** soil   __ __

8 Write down an influence from outer space that:

    (*a*) might change future generations of organisms genetically. _____
    (*b*) affects the nutrition of the world. _____
    (*c*) affects distribution of organisms on shores. _____
    (*d*) causes synthesis of vitamin D in skin. _____
    (*e*) adds to the earth's mass. _____

9 Sandy soil does not:
A contain a lot of air **B** hold water well **C** have many earthworms **D** warm quickly

                                          __ __

10 The following constituents of soil are organic:
A water **B** humus **C** rock particles **D** earthworms **E** decay bacteria **F** air

                                      __ __ __

11 Humus improves soil and crop growth by:
A discouraging earthworms **B** helping to drain sandy soil **C** helping to aerate clay soil
D providing mineral salts on decaying **E** neutralising acidity
F liberating CO_2 as it decays   __ __ __

12 **A–D** are types of bacterium that cause changes in the nitrogen chemistry of soil. Match each with the changes (*a*)–(*d*) that cause

    (*a*) nitrates to nitrogen   __   (*c*) ammonia to nitrite and nitrate __
    (*b*) nitrogen to nitrates   __   (*d*) protein to ammonia   __

    A nitrifying **B** nitrogen fixing **C** putrefying (decay) **D** denitrifying

13   Select from the types of bacterium in question **12** those which:

    (*a*) are harmful to a farmer's interests.   ———

    (*b*) may be present in legume roots.   ———

    (*c*) make meat go bad.   ———

    (*d*) are present particularly in *fresh* manure heaps.   ———

    (*e*) are active in un-drained soil.   ———

14   Name the raw materials that the following organisms need to make their proteins:

    (*a*) animals   _____

    (*b*) green plants   _____

    (*c*) nitrogen fixing bacteria   _____

15   Certain activities in the world cause an increase of CO_2 in the air, others a decrease.

    (*i*) Name the activities that are principally:

        (*a*) human, increasing CO_2.   _____

        (*b*) bacterial and fungal, increasing CO_2.   _____

        (*c*) holophytic, reducing CO_2.   _____

    (*ii*) Name two organelles in cells whose activities affect the levels of CO_2 in the air, and state their effects:

        (*a*) _____ _____

        (*b*) _____ _____

    (*iii*) Select the average level of CO_2 in the air:
        A 0.3% **B** 3.0% **C** 0.03% **D** 0.003%   ———

16   Select those of the following activities of earthworms which are helpful to crop growth:
    A tunnelling **B** eating humus **C** dying and decaying **D** secreting lime
    E being eaten by birds **F** pulling leaves into tunnels   —— —— —— ——

17   Complete the following sentence:
    A cultivated soil or '_____' has a range of sizes of rock particles ranging from
    0.2mm (called_____) to _____ mm (called clay).
    This allows it to contain a good supply of_____,_____, and_____ all
    of which encourage plant growth. In addition it includes_____ which makes
    it darker in colour and encourages a variety of_____to feed on it, helping it to
    decay.

_____

Test on unit 16   Man and his environment

1   Liming the soil is *not* designed to:
    A kill pests **B** help to drain clay **C** neutralise soil acidity
    D give heavy soils a good 'crumb structure'   ———

2   Rotation of crops is practised principally to:
    A eliminate pests **B** replace lost nitrogen compounds **C** give cattle different pastures
    D enrich soil with fertilisers   ———

3   Artificial fertilisers do *not* have the disadvantage of:
    A leaching away into streams easily when it is rainy **B** benefiting plants slowly
    C expensiveness **D** not improving soil structure   ———

4   The present human population is about 4000 million. By the year 2000 it is expected,
    on present trends, to reach:
    A 7000 million **B** 8000 million **C** 4000 million **D** 6000 million   ———

5 Give *one* example of a pollutant, and its effects, arising from each of the following:

                    pollutant   *effect*

    (*a*) petrol motor car   _____   _____

    (*b*) jet aircraft   _____   _____

    (*c*) farmer   _____   _____

    (*d*) atomic power plant   _____   _____

6 There were no agricultural pests before man became agricultural. This was because the organisms that are now pests:
A kept hidden **B** had less plentiful food supplies
C were controlled by natural insecticides
D were controlled by numerous parasitic wasps   ___

7 One species of animal that humans have not yet managed to make extinct is:
A the dodo **B** Tasmanian wolf **C** the tiger **D** the moa   ___

8 Group the following resources in the world into the categories:
(*a*) renewable   __ __ __   (*b*) non-renewable   __ __ __

A soil **B** copper ores **C** ebony trees **D** coal **E** blue whales **F** ivory

9 Most of the world's population is already undernourished. This is because:
A there is not enough food produced **B** people will not eat single-cell protein
C there is enough food, but it is not distributed well enough **D** fertilisers are expensive   ___

10 From **A**–**F** select two diseases that cannot be treated successfully:
A malaria **B** goitre **C** diabetes **D** mongolism **E** mumps or influenza
F tuberculosis (TB)   __ __

11 Select from the diseases named in question **10** those that are caused by:

    (*a*) hormone deficiency.   __   (*d*) a virus.   __
    (*b*) dietary deficiency.   __   (*e*) a bacterium.   __
    (*c*) faulty chromosome number.   __   (*f*) a protozoan.   __

12 House flies in the Middle East too easily transfer dysentery (disease) bacteria and protozoa from faeces to food by visiting both. Assuming that an abundance of flies and exposed faeces is usual in such places, how could you prevent yourself from getting dysentery if you went to live there? State three methods you would use, each different in principle:

    (*a*) _____
    (*b*) _____
    (*c*) _____

13 Immunity to a disease *cannot* be achieved by:
A catching the disease and recovering **B** inoculation with a mild strain of the pathogen
C injection with antibodies to the disease obtained from a rabbit
D taking a preventive drug   ___

14 Passive immunity is:
A long lasting and offers immediate protection
B short lasting but offers immediate protection
C long lasting but offers protection only after some time **D** vaccination   ___

15 Link the man to the invention he is associated with:
A aseptic surgery **B** vaccination **C** polio vaccine **D** rabies vaccine **E** brewing
F antiseptic surgery **G** anti-malarial drugs **H** penicillin

    (*a*) Pasteur   __   (*c*) Jenner   __
    (*b*) Lister   __   (*d*) Fleming   __

Test on unit 17 A variety of life

In addition to questions requiring straight **recall** of facts about organisms, this unit has questions which will give you practice in **comparison** and **contrast** of organisms. This type of question is common in examinations.

1   Select from the following statements **A–F** those that apply to:
    (*a*) viruses ___ ___ ___   (*b*) bacteria ___ ___ ___

    A the smallest cellular organisms **B** invisible under the best light microscopes
    C made of nucleic acid and protein only **D** all are parasitic
    E many are saprophytic **F** reproduce by binary fission

2   (*a*)–(*d*) below are features of both bacteria and algae such as *Spirogyra*. State in the space provided how these features differ in the two groups:

	Bacteria	*Algae*
(*a*) cell wall composition		
(*b*) position of the chromosome material in the cell		
(*c*) type of nutrition		
(*d*) response to direct sunlight		

3   Pair up **A–E** concerning *Spirogyra* with items (*a*)–(*e*):
    A made in pyrenoids **B** spiral and green **C** by-product from nutrition
    D stores mineral salts and water **E** covered by mucilage

    (*a*) oxygen   ___   (*d*) chloroplasts   ___
    (*b*) starch   ___   (*e*) vacuole   ___
    (*c*) cell walls   ___

4   *Spirogyra* differs from *Amoeba* in a number of respects, indicated (*a*)–(*f*) below. Say what the *differences* are:

	Spirogyra	*Amoeba*
(*a*) phylum		
(*b*) three major structural features of the cell		
(*c*) means of osmo-regulation		
(*d*) main gas absorbed from solution by day		
(*e*) reproduction methods		
(*f*) structures for locomotion		

5   Compare and contrast the following organisms as far as features **A–G** are concerned by placing the appropriate letters against the organism's name:
    A reproduce by binary fission **B** reproduce by spores **C** reproduce by conjugation
    D germinate from zygospores **E** use enzymes to digest food **F** digest food externally
    G have no cell wall

    (*a*) Bacteria   ___ ___ ___ ___
    (*b*) *Spirogyra*   ___ ___
    (*c*) *Mucor*   ___ ___ ___ ___ ___
    (*d*) *Amoeba*   ___ ___ ___

6 Name and give the phylum of the organisms which have the following effects on health:

                                           Name   *Phylum*
   (*a*) cause malaria   _____   _____
   (*b*) transmit malaria   _____   _____
   (*c*) cause influenza   _____
   (*d*) cause athlete's foot   _____   _____
   (*e*) provide man with a rich
       source of B vitamins _____   _____
   (*f*) provide penicillin   _____   _____
   (*g*) cause tetanus   _____
   (*h*) transmit venereal disease _____   _____

7 Complete the following passage which refers to *Hydra*:

Hydra is a simple_____ which lives in_____. It catches prey such as

_____ with special_____ cells on its_____, which paralyse the prey.

The food is digested by_____ secreted into the_____ and waste material

is egested (eliminated) via the_____. Green species of *Hydra* also gain food and

_____ from algae living in symbiosis within its_____ cells. Well-fed *Hydra*

usually reproduce asexually by_____. The young are copies of the parent with

_____ layers of cells and a nervous system called a_____ without nerves

or a_____.

8 Both mosses and ferns show 'alternation of generations' in their life cycles. Link structures (*a*)–(*f*) concerning this with the appropriate descriptions **A**–**H**:

A reproduces sexually **B** reproduces asexually **C** needs water to reach the ovum **D** needs wind for dispersal **E** grows from the zygote **F** grows into the gametophyte **G** produces sperm **H** contains the ovum

  (*a*) sporophyte   __ __   (*d*) spore   __ __
  (*b*) gametophyte   __ __ __   (*e*) sperm   __
  (*c*) antheridium   __   (*f*) archegonium   __

9 Name the structures in a bony fish that fulfil the following functions:

  (*a*) move the tail from side to side _____
  (*b*) can act as hydroplanes _____
  (*c*) provides buoyancy _____
  (*d*) prevent roll _____
  (*e*) sense obstacles _____
  (*f*) sieve out matter that might damage gills _____
  (*g*) protects gills externally _____

10 Name the structures in a bird that assist flight by:

  (*a*) streamlining the body. _____
  (*b*) providing a large surface area for 'lift'. _____
  (*c*) providing the power for wing-flapping. _____
  (*d*) providing the muscles with enough oxygen (two organs). _____

11 (*a*) Fill in the blanks in the diagram below which shows an *aerofoil* in section.

(*b*) What is missing from the diagram if flight of the aerofoil is to be achieved?

_____

12 Contrast the methods of gaseous exchange, locomotion, feeding and 'hearing' in a fish (such as the minnow or stickleback) with those of an adult frog by naming the structures involved in each case below:

	fish	*frog*
(*a*) gaseous exchange		
(*b*) locomotion		
(*c*) feeding		
(*d*) hearing		

13 In a developing bird's egg name the structures within the shell that:

(*a*) enable gaseous exchange.   _____
(*b*) supply water to the embryo.   _____
(*c*) provide a food store for the embryo.   _____
(*d*) allow the embryo to float in 'water'.   _____

14 Name the stage, after the egg, in the life cycle of insects such as flies, butterflies and bees at which:

(*a*) ecdysis occurs.   _____
(*b*) sexual maturity is attained.   _____
(*c*) feeding for growth occurs.   _____
(*d*) wings appear.   _____
(*e*) a period of immobility (other than hibernation) occurs.   _____

15 Name the stage, after the egg, in the life cycle of insects such as the locust or cockroach at which:

(*a*) ecdysis occurs.   _____
(*b*) sexual maturity is attained.   _____
(*c*) feeding for growth occurs.   _____
(*d*) wings appear.   _____
(*e*) a period of immobility (other than hibernation) occurs.   _____

16 Apply descriptions **A–G** to the three types of honey-bee (*a*)–(*c*):
A female **B** male **C** fertile **D** infertile **E** longest lived **F** lacking sting **G** smallest

(*a*) drone   __ __ __   (*b*) worker __ __ __   (*c*) queen __ __ __

17 Contrast the characteristics of insects with those of mammals by filling in the blanks below:

	insect	*mammal*
(*a*) position of skeleton in body		
(*b*) main material of skeleton		
(*c*) temperature control		
(*d*) number of walking limbs		
(*e*) where gaseous exchange occurs		
(*f*) source of developing embryo's food		

18 Compare any two parasites that you have studied by filling in the blanks below:

name		
(a) primary host (A)		
(b) secondary host (B)		
(c) means of transmission:		
(i) from A to B		
(ii) from B to A		
(d) means of reproduction:		
(i) in/on primary host		
(ii) in/on secondary host		
(e) food and means of feeding from primary host		
(f) example of a non-parasitic member of the same group (phylum)		
(g) food and means of feeding of (f)		

19 **A**–**F** below are stages in the reproduction and early development of the frog. Arrange them in the sequence in which they occur in the frog's life cycle:
A fertilisation occurs **B** albumen swells **C** eggs are laid
D male grips female under armpits **E** sperm is shed into water
F zygote develops into a ball of cells   — — — — — —

20 (i) **A**–**D** below are descriptions of the method of feeding at four stages in the life cycle of the frog after it has hatched from the egg. Name the structures that would be used at each stage to obtain oxygen:
A scavenging on dead animals   _____
B *not* feeding   _____
C catching live animals on tongue _____
D feeding on water plants   _____

(ii) Arrange letters **A**–**D** in the sequence in which the stages of the frog's life cycle described above occur: — — — —

21 (i) **A**–**F** below concern stages in the reproduction of an earthworm. Fill in the blanks alongside each to indicate the structures involved:
A Eggs appear from inside the body at _____.
B Eggs develop into worms in _____.
C Two worms copulate head to tail, _____ surfaces together.
D The other worm's sperm fertilises the eggs inside _____.
E Sperm is transferred to the other worm along _____.
F The cocoon is secreted by _____.

(ii) Arrange stages **A**–**F** above in the sequence in which they occur:

          — — — — — —

Answers to Self-test units

Below you will find answers to all the self-test questions. Each answer is keyed back into the relevant topic(s) in the text. After each answer there is a reference in brackets to the unit(s) in the book, (e.g. § 2.2 means see unit 2.2 Organelles).

Unit 2

1 **B** (§ 2.1)
2 **C** (§ 2.1)
3 **C** (§ 2.1)
4 **A** (§ 2.1)
5 **C** (§ 2.2)
6 **D** (§ 2.2)
7 **C** (§ 2.2)
8 **B** (§ 2.3)
9 (*a*) e.g. xylem vessel/e.g. neuron or muscle, (*b*) xylem vessel/red blood cell, (*c*) any cell without chloroplasts/red blood cell (§ 2.5, 5.5, 5.8, 9.2, 10.7)
10 (*a*) **CAFBED**, (*b*) (*i*) **D**, (*ii*) **AD**, (*iii*) **B**, (*iv*) **C**, (*v*) **F**, (*vi*) **E** (§ 2.5)

Unit 3

1 **A** (§ 3.1)
2 **D** (Fig. 3.2, § 17.5)
3 **B** (§ 3.1)
4 **C** (Fig. 3.2)
5 (*i*) (*a*) **C**, (*b*) **F**, (*c*) **A**, (*d*) **H**, (*e*) **AEG**, (*f*) **D**, (*g*) **B**; (*ii*) invertebrate (§ 3.1)
6 (*a*) **BJ**, (*b*) **F**, (*c*) **AC**, (*d*) **ACF**, (*e*) **DH**, (*f*) **FG**, (*g*) **D**, (*h*) **BEJ**, (*j*) **B** (Figs. 3.2, 3.3)

Unit 4

1 (*i*) (*a*) **B (CDEF)**, (*b*) **A**, (*c*) **D**, (*d*) **BEF**, (*e*) **BC**; (*ii*) omnivorous (§ 4.2)
2 (*a*) **ABE**, (*b*) **AB**, (*c*) **E**, (*d*) **C**, (*e*) **BC**, (*f*) vitamins (§ 4.4, 4.5)
3 (*a*) **C**, (*b*) **E**, (*c*) **B**, (*d*) **AE**, (*e*) **EB**, (*f*) **D**, (*g*) **A**, (*h*) **C** (§ 4.4, 4.5)
4 (*a*) **ABCEF**, (*b*) **CE**, (*c*) **A**, (*d*) **D**, (*e*) **F**, (*f*) **BE** (§ 4.4, 4.5, 4.13)
5 (*i*) (*a*) **C**, (*b*) **AE**, (*c*) **F**, (*d*) **B**, (*e*) **D**, (*f*) **EF**, (*g*) **G**; (*ii*) **E** (§ 4.2, 4.5)
6 (*a*) **BE**, (*b*) **ABDEH**, (*c*) **A**, (*d*) **C**, (*e*) **F**, (*f*) **A**, (*g*) **G** (§ 4.11, 4.12, 4.14)
7 (*a*) **FGACEBD**, (*b*) **F**, (*c*) **EC**, (*d*) **FG**, (*e*) **AC**, (*f*) **EB**, (*g*) **EC**, (*h*) **BD**, (*j*) **C**, (*k*) **A** (Fig. 4.14)
8 (*a*) **FHGE**, (*b*) **BDC**, (*c*) **E**, (*d*) **H**, (*e*) **A**, (*f*) **C**, (*g*) carbohydrate (starch) (§ 4.14, Fig. 4.13)
9 (*a*) **ABDE**, (*b*) **C**, (*c*) **E**, (*d*) **ACDG**, (*e*) **CG**, (*f*) **B**, (*g*) **F**, (*h*) **D** (§ 4.6, 4.7, 4.10)
10 (*i*) (*a*) **B**, (*b*) **C**, (*c*) **A**, (*d*) **D**; (*ii*) **EF**; (*iii*) **E**; (*iv*) **F** (§ 4.6)
11 (*i*) (*a*) **C**, (*b*) **H**, (*c*) **F**; (*ii*) **GEBDEG**; (*iii*) **BDH**; (*iv*) **C**; (*v*) **A** (§ 4.8, Fig. 4.5)
12 **B** (§ 4.12)
13 **C** (§ 4.4)
14 **A** (§ 4.20)
15 **D** (§ 4.20)
16 **C** (§ 4.4)
17 **A** (§ 4.4)
18 **B** (§ 4.4)
19 **B** (Fig. 4.1)

Unit 5

1 (*a*) **B**, (*b*) **D**, (*c*) **A**, (*d*) **E**, (*e*) **C**, (*f*) **A**, (*g*) **D** (§ 5.1)
2 (*i*) (*a*) active transport, (*b*) osmosis, (*c*) diffusion; (*ii*) (*a*) osmosis, (*b*) diffusion, (*c*) active transport (§ 5.2)
3 (*a*) **C**, (*b*) **B**, (*c*) **C**, (*d*) **A** and **B**, (*e*) **B**, (*f*) **C**, (*g*) **A** or **B** (§ 5.2)
4 (*i*) (*a*) **F**, (*b*) **A**, (*c*) **E**, (*d*) **C**, (*e*) **B**, (*f*) **D**; (*ii*) (*a*) **AD**, (*b*) **BF**, (*c*) **CE**, (*d*) **AB**, (*e*) **AC** (§ 5.3)
5 **A** (§ 5.4)
6 **B** (§ 5.4)

7 (*a*) **BEH,** (*b*) **AFJ,** (*c*) **GKM,** (*d*) **CDL** (Fig. 4.5)

8 **B** (§ 5.2)

9 (*a*) **F,** (*b*) **F,** (*c*) **T,** (*d*) **T** (§ 5.2)

10 **B** (§ 5.7)

11 (*i*) (*a*) water, (*b*) protein, (*c*) haemoglobin; (*ii*) (*a*) erythrocytes (red), (*b*) phagocytes (§ 5.8, Table 5.4)

12 (*a*) CO_2, (*b*) O_2, (*c*) urea, (*d*) glucose (§ 5.8)

13 **ABE** (§ 5.11)

14 (*a*) **CF,** (*b*) **AB,** (*c*) **DEG** (§ 5.9, Table 5.5)

15 **E** (§ 5.8)

16 (*a*) **BEH(G),** (*b*) **AD,** (*c*) **AGEC,** (*d*) **FH** (§ 7.1, 7.2, 7.4)

17 **ECHADFB** (Fig. 5.12)

18 **CGBHDE** (Fig. 5.12)

19 (*a*) **D,** (*b*) **E,** (*c*) **C,** (*d*) **B,** (*e*) **F** (Fig. 5.12, § 5.10)

20 (*a*) 5 000 000, (*b*) 10 000, (*c*) 70, (*d*) 4, (*e*) 0, (*f*) 37 (Table 5.4, § 5.9)

Unit 6

1 (*a*) **B,** (*b*) **C,** (*c*) **E,** (*d*) **A,** (*e*) **D** (§ 6.1)

2 (*a*) **E,** (*b*) **A,** (*c*) **E,** (*d*) **B(C),** (*e*) **E,** (*f*) **B(C),** (*g*) **E,** (*h*) **E** (§ 6.1, 6.2, 6.4, 6.6)

3 **D** (§ 6.3)

4 **BDFHJ** (§ 6.6)

5 **CDFGBAE** (§ 6.6)

6 (*a*) **T,** (*b*) **T,** (*c*) **F,** (*d*) **T,** (*e*) **F,** (*f*) **T** (§ 6.6)

7 (*i*) **D;** (*ii*) **A** 4%, **B** 21%, **C** 79%; (*iii*) **A** he would be suffocated, **B** he would be burnt by the cigarette bursting into flames (§6.6)

8 (*a*) **T,** (*b*) **F,** (*c*) **T,** (*d*) **F,** (*e*) **F** (§ 6.2)

9 **E** (§ 6.2)

10 (*a*) **C,** (*b*) **D,** (*c*) **E,** (*d*) **BH,** (*e*) **AF** (§ 6.4)

11 (*a*) **CDEF,** (*b*) **BCGH,** (*c*) **A – H** (§ 6.4)

12 (*a*) **ACDE,** (*b*) **AC,** (*c*) **F** (§ 6.7)

Unit 7

1 (*a*) **ACDF,** (*b*) **BCEF,** (*c*) **ACDE** (§ 7.1, 5.6)

2 **BD** (§ 7.1)

3 (*a*) liver, (*b*) bladder, (*c*) kidneys (§ 7.2)

4 (*a*) **DCBGFHA,** (*b*) **LJK** (§ 7.2)

5 (*a*) **C,** (*b*) **A,** (*c*) **B,** (*d*) **E,** (*e*) **F,** (*f*) **D** or **F** (§ 7.2)

6 **ABCFG** (§ 7.2)

7 **A** (§ 7.2)

8 **D** (§ 7.2)

9 (*a*) **D,** (*b*) **I,** (*c*) **I,** (*d*) **D,** (*e*) **I** (§ 7.2)

10 (*i*) **A** transpiration/O_2, **B** perspiration/heat or urea, **C** breathing/CO_2, **D** urination/urea, **E** osmoregulation/urea or CO_2 (not their main route); (*ii*) (*a*) **DE,** (*b*) **AB;** (*iii*) (*a*) **BE,** (*b*) **AC** (§ 7.1)

11 **A** (§ 7.4)

12 (*a*) **B,** (*b*) **A,** (*c*) **C** (§ 7.4)

13 (*a*) **DE,** (*b*) **AF,** (*c*) **BC,** (*d*) **DG** (§ 7.5)

14 **C** (§ 7.4)

15 **E** (§ 7.6)

Unit 8

1 (*a*) **DL,** (*b*) **FC,** (*c*) **AM,** (*d*) **EG,** (*e*) **KN,** (*f*) **BH,** (*g*) **J** (§ 8.3)

2 **B** (§ 8.3)

3 **A** (§ 8.3)

4 (*a*) **B,** (*b*) **C,** (*c*) **D,** (*d*) **AB** (§ 8.3)

5 (*a*) long sight/short/convex (converging) lenses, (*b*) old sight/lens has lost its elasticity (collapsibility), (*c*) short sight/long/concave (diverging) lenses (§ 8.3, Fig. 8.3)

6 (*a*) **F**, (*b*) **ACDE**, (*c*) **AD**, (*d*) **B**, (*e*) **G** (§ 8.5)

7 GHJ, FDB, AEBC (§ 8.5)

8 ADEFH (§ 8.5)

Unit 9

1 (*a*) root and shoot tips/inner ear (semi-circular canals), (*b*) hormonal/nervous, (*c*) slow/rapid, (*d*) geotropism (growth)/righting reflex action (muscular action) (§ 9.1, 9.7, 9.12)

2 (*a*) **BCEG,** (*b*) **F** (§ 9.1, 9.11)

3 (*a*) **A,** (*b*) **D,** (*c*) **E,** (*d*) **B,** (*e*) **C** (§ 9.2)

4 (*i*) **ABDE;** (*ii*) muscle *or* gland cells (Fig. 9.5)

5 (*a*) **F,** (*b*) **C,** (*c*) **A,** (*d*) **E,** (*e*) **B,** (*f*) **C** (§ 9.7)

6 (*a*) **E,** (*b*) **B,** (*c*) **A,** (*d*) **C,** (*e*) **D** (§ 9.2, 9.5)

7 *badc* (§ 9.2)

8 B (§ 9.5)

9 C (§ 9.5)

10 (*a*) adrenalin/insulin, (*b*) adrenal/islet tissue of pancreas, (*c*) nerves/hormone (from pituitary), (*d*) liver/liver (§ 9.8)

11 B (§ 7.6)

12 (*a*) growth hormone/pituitary,(*b*) sugar diabetes/islet tissue of pancreas, (*c*) ADH (antidiuretic hormone)/pituitary, (*d*) cretinism/thyroxin, (*e*) iodine/diet (§ 9.8, 9.10)

13 (*a*) **ACFGH,** (*b*) **ADE** (§ 9.8, Fig. 4.15)

Unit 10

1 (*i*) **D;** (*ii*) (*a*) **AC,** (*b*) **B** (§ 10.1)

2 B (§ 10.7)

3 (*a*) **C,** (*b*) **DE** (§ 10.10)

4 (*a*) wax cuticle, (*b*) protein + chitin, (*c*) chitin (§ 10.6)

5 (*a*) ligament, (*b*) tendon, (*c*) synovial membrane, (*d*) cartilage (§ 10,7, 10.8)

6 BCDF (§ 10.4, 10.8)

7 ABC (§ 10.5)

8 (*i*) **A** centrum/weight-bearing, **B** neural canal/protects nerve cord, **C** neural spine (dorsal process)/tendon and ligament attachment, **D** zygapophyses/prevent dislocation; (*ii*) (*a*) **A,** (*b*) **A** (§ 10.9)

9 (*a*) lumbar, (*b*) sacral, (*c*) axis, (*d*) caudal (coccyx in man), (*e*) thoracic (§ 10.9)

10 A forearm (front), **B** any movable joint, **C** upper arm, **D** lower leg, **E** fingers or toes, **F** upper leg, **G** wrist, **H** shoulder (Figs. 10.6, 10.10, 10.11)

11 (*a*) **A** and **C, D** and **F;** (*b*) **C** and **H;** (*c*) **G;** (*d*) none (§ 10.8)

Unit 11

1 (*a*) **ACF,** (*b*) **ACDEF** (§ 11.1)

2 branched, large, CO_2, sunlight, water, mineral salts, compact, moving (§ 11.1)

3 (*a*) **ACG,** (*b*) **BDEFG** (§ 11.2, 11.3)

4 (**a**) **GH,** (*b*) **AE,** (*c*) **CF,** (*d*) **BD** (§ 11.6)

5 (*i*) (*a*) – (*c*); (*ii*) (*a*) – (*d*) (§ 11.6, Fig. 12.9)

6 endosperm, enzymes, cotyledon(s), water, warmth, oxygen (§ 11.6)

7 ABEFH (§ 11.6)

8 (*a*) **AFH,** (*b*) **DG** (§ 11.6)

9 AD (§ 11.5, 10.3)

Unit 12

1 BF (§ 12.6, 12.11, 17.23)

2 B (§ 12.1)

3 CE (§ 12.1, 12.7)

4 (*a*) **BCF,** (*b*) **ADE** (§ 12.1, 12.2)

5 BE (§ 12.1)

6 (*a*) **CG,** (*b*) **AD,** (*c*) **AF,** (*d*) **ADE,** (*e*) **B** (§ 12.2, 12.7, 17.3)

7 (*a*) scale leaves, (*b*) lenticels, (*c*) bark (cork), (*d*) saddle (inflorescence) scar, (*e*) girdle scar (§ 12.3)

8 (*a*) **D**, (*b*) **A**, (*c*) **C** (§ 12.4)

9 (*a*) petals, (*b*) nectary, (*c*) style, (*d*) sepals, (*e*) ovules, (*f*) ovary (carpels) (§ 12.7, 12.8)

10 **D** (§ 12.9)

11 (*a*) **D**, (*b*) **C**, (*c*) **A**, (*d*) **B** (§ 12.11, 12.12)

12 (*a*) large surface area e.g. 'feathery'/exposed, (*b*) small/smooth/very plentiful, (*c*) small/unattractive, e.g. green, unscented, or missing (§ 12.8)

13 (*a*) **C**, (*b*) **B**, (*c*) **A** (§ 12.14)

14 (*a*) anther/testis, (*b*) stigma/vagina, (*c*) ovary (carpel)/uterus, (*d*) endosperm/placenta, (*e*) fruit/uterus (§ 12.7, 12.11, 12.14)

15 (*a*) amniotic fluid and mother's tissues, (*b*) placenta (villi), (*c*) umbilical cord, (*d*) placenta (villi, haemoglobin in embryo's erythrocytes), (*e*) head (of baby), (*f*) placenta (§ 12.14, 12.15)

Unit 13

1 **EBDAC** (§ 13.1)

2 (*a*) **E**, (*b*) **D**, (*c*) **C**, (*d*) **A** (§ 13.1)

3 (*a*) **DF**, (*b*) **A**, (*c*) **B**, (*d*) **H**, (*e*) **C**, (*f*) **J**, (*g*) **EG** (§ 13.2, 13.3)

4 **A** (§ 13.12)

5 **B** (§ 13.14)

6 **CF** (§ 13.14)

7 (*i*) **B**; (*ii*) **A** (§ 13.5)

8 (*a*) ½ pink : ½ white, (*b*) ½ red : ½ pink, (*c*) 1 red : 2 pink : 1 white (§13.4, 13.6)

9 (*a*) **BB**, (*b*) **bb**, (*c*) **Bb** (§ 13.4)

10 **A** : BB, **B** : Bb, **C** : bb (§ 13.4)

11 (*a*) **AD/AD**, (*b*) **EH/FG**, (*c*) **C/B** (§ 13.12, 13.13)

12 (*a*) 8, (*b*) 12, (*c*) 16, (*d*) 16 (§ 13.14)

Unit 14

1 **D** (§ 14.1, 14.2)

2 **CBEAD** (§ 14.3)

3 **BCEF** (§ 14.3)

4 **C** (§ 14.3)

5 **ACE** (§ 14.3)

6 ultra violet, gamma or X-rays; mutations; DNA (genes); mutant; sperm; ova (or equivalents, i.e. male or female gametes); evolution (§ 13.11)

7 (*a*) **AE**, (*b*) **E**, (*c*) **C** (§ 14.3 no. 8, 14.4 no. 1)

8 Any three of *space* (separating the lakes); *time* (different times at which the populations breed – especially on either side of the equator); *genetics* (they accumulate mutations that prevent successful fertilisation; or they may become physically very different so that their genitalia do not fit thus preventing copulation between large and small individuals) (§ 14.3)

9 (*a*) **A**, (*b*) **D**, (*c*) **E**, (*d*) **C**, (*e*) **B** (§ 14.4)

10 **C** (§ 14.4)

11 **ADF** (§ 14.4)

12 **AEF** (§ 14.4)

13 **DEBAC** (§ 14.4)

Unit 15

1 (*a*) **ADEG**, (*b*) **BCFH** (§ 15.1)

2 (*i*) (*a*) **BFH**, (*b*) **C**; (*ii*) (*a*) **AEG**, (*b*) **DE** (§ 15.3)

3 (*a*) **E**, (*b*) **D**, (*c*) **A**, (*d*) **C**, (*e*) **B** (§ 15.1)

4 (*a*) decomposers, (*b*) other related food chains, (*c*) abiotic factors in the environment (§ 15.2)

5 (*i*) (*a*) e.g. wheat → vole → fox → *tick*; (*b*) dandelion → rabbit → fox → *flea* (hound is *not* a parasite); (*ii*) (*a*) vole, leaf-miner insect, (*b*) owl, fox; (*iii*) (*a*) leaf-miners die, rabbits eat grass only; (*b*) more leaf-miners, grass, dandelions, sow-thistles; fewer voles; no stoats (Fig. 15.4)

6 (*a*) e.g. diatoms → *Daphnia* → fish, (*b*) diatoms → protozoa → *Daphnia* → *Hydra* → fish, (*c*) bacteria, *Asellus*, (*d*) *Daphnia*, (*e*) fish, (*f*) excreta, dead body, (*g*) CO_2, mineral salts, (*h*) e.g. gravel anchors *Elodea* roots; water gives organisms support, keeps them cool (Fig. 15.1)

7 A (Fig. 15.1)

8 (*a*) ultra violet light (mutation), (*b*) sunlight (photosynthesis), (*c*) sun and moon's gravity (tides), (*d*) ultra violet light, (*e*) meteorites (§ 15.1)

9 BC (§ 15.5)

10 BDE (§ 15.5)

11 CDF (§ 15.5)

12 (*a*) **D,** (*b*) **B,** (*c*) **A,** (*d*) **C** (§ 15.6)

13 (*a*) **D,** (*b*) **B,** (*c*) **C,** (*d*) **C,** (*e*) **D** (§ 15.6)

14 (*a*) amino acids, (*b*) nitrates and sugars, (*c*) nitrogen and organic matter, e.g. sugars (§ 15.6)

15 (*i*) (*a*) combustion, (*b*) decay (bacterial respiration), (*c*) photosynthesis; (*ii*) (*a*) chloroplast/photosynthesis tuns CO_2 into carbohydrates, (*b*) mitochondrion/respiration turns carbohydrates into CO_2; (*iii*) **C** (§ 15.7, 4.6, 2.2)

16 ACDF (§ 15.8)

17 'loam', sand, 0.0002, air (oxygen), water, mineral salts, humus, decomposers *or* earthworms *or* bacteria (i.e. organisms) (§ 15.5)

Unit 16

1 A (§ 16.2)

2 B (§ 16.3)

3 B (§ 16.2)

4 D (§ 16.5)

5 (*a*) CO/carboxyhaemoglobin, or Pb/effect on nervous system, (*b*) noise/irritation or possible deafness if no protection, (*c*) artificial fertilisers/eutrophication, or insecticides/predators, (*d*) radioactive elements/mutations, or heated water effluent/upset aquatic ecosystem (§ 16.6)

6 B (§ 16.4)

7 C (§ 16.7)

8 (*a*) **CEF,** (*b*) **ABD** (§ 16.7)

9 C (§ 16.7)

10 DE (§ 16.10)

11 (*a*) **C,** (*b*) **B,** (*c*) **D,** (*d*) **E,** (*e*) **F,** (*f*) **A** (§ 16.10)

12 (*a*) food covers, e.g. muslin, (*b*) insecticides in home, (*c*) preventive drug (prophylaxis) (§ 16.10)

13 D (§ 16.12, Table 16.3)

14 B (§ 16.11, Table 16.3)

15 (*a*) **D,** (*b*) **F,** (*c*) **B,** (*d*) **H** (§ 16.12)

Unit 17

1 (*a*) **BCD,** (*b*) **AEF** (§ 17.1, 17.2)

2 (*a*) nitrogenous/cellulose, (*b*) in cytoplasm, free/inside a nuclear membrane, (*c*) saprophytic or parasitic/holophytic, (*d*) killed by ultra violet light/photosynthesis (§ 17.2, 17.3)

3 (*a*) **C,** (*b*) **A,** (*c*) **E,** (*d*) **B,** (*e*) **D** (§ 17.3)

4 (*a*) Algae/protozoa, (*b*) cell wall, large vacuole, green chloroplast/no cell wall, contractile vacuole, no chloroplast, (*c*) cell wall resists water entry once cell is turgid/contractile vacuole ejects water, (*d*) CO_2/O_2, (*e*) (asexual growth) and sexual/asexual (binary fission) only, (*f*) none (does not move)/pseudopodia (§ 17.3, 17.4, 2.1)

5 (*a*) **ACEF,** (*b*) **CD,** (*c*) **BCDEF,** (*d*) **AEG** (§ 17.2, 17.3, 17.4, 17.5)

6 (*a*) *Plasmodium*/Protozoa, (*b*) e.g. *Aedes* (mosquito)/ Arthropoda, (*c*) virus, (*d*) *Tinea*/Fungi, (*e*) *Saccharomyces* (yeast)/Fungi, (*f*) *Penicillium* (green mould)/Fungi, (*g*) bacteria, (*h*) *Homo* (man)/Vertebrata (Chordata) (§ 17.1, 17.4, 17.5, 3.2, 3.3)

7 animal, fresh water, e.g. *Daphnia* (water-flea), sting, tentacles, enzymes, enteron (gut), mouth, oxygen, endoderm, budding, two, nerve net, brain (§ 17.6, 9.4)

8 (*a*) **BE,** (*b*) **AGH,** (*c*) **G,** (*d*) **DF,** (*e*) **C,** (*f*) **H** (§ 17.8)

9 (*a*) muscle blocks, (*b*) pectoral fins, (*c*) swim-bladder, (*d*) (dorsal) fins, (*e*) eyes/lateral line, (*f*) gill-raker, (*g*) operculum (§ 17.20)

10 (*a*) contour feathers, (*b*) flight feathers, (*c*) large pectoral muscles, (*d*) through-system lungs, large heart (§ 17.23)

11 (*a*) (*i*) lift; (*ii*) drag; (*iii*) mass, (*b*) air movement over aerofoil, left to right (§ 17.23, Fig. 17.28)

12 (*a*) gills/lungs, skin, buccal cavity, (*b*) tail, pectoral fins/4 legs, (*c*) jaws/sticky tongue, (*d*) lateral line organ/ear (§ 17.20, 17.22)

13 (*a*) allantois, (*b*) albumen, (*c*) yolk, (*d*) amnion (§ 17.23)

14 (*a*) larva, (*b*) adult, (*c*) larva, (*d*) adult, (*e*) pupa (§ 17.14)

15 (*a*) nymph, (*b*) adult, (*c*) nymph, (*d*) nymph, (*e*) none (no pupa stage) (§ 17.15)

16 (*a*) **BCF**, (*b*) **ADG**, (*c*) **ACE** (§ 17.18)

17 (*a*) outside (exoskeleton)/inside (endoskeleton), (*b*) chitin/bone, (*c*) none (ectothermic)/ constant (endothermic), (*d*) 6/4, (*e*) tracheoles/alveoli, (*f*) yolk (in egg)/placenta (within mother) (§ 6.4, 6.6, 7.4, 10.3, Fig 3.3)

18 Examples: pork tapeworm/dodder. Answers would then be: (*a*) man/clover, gorse etc, (*b*) pig/ none, (*c*) (*i*) 'eggs' (embryophores) eaten in pasture by pig/none; (*ii*) 'bladder-worms' (cysticerci) eaten in raw measly pork by man/none, (*d*) (*i*) asexually: budding off proglottids, sexually: within proglottid/sexually: by many flowers; (*ii*) none/none, (*e*) host's digested food absorbed through skin/food absorbed from host's vascular bundles via haustoria, (*f*) *Planaria* (pond flatworm)/any flowering plant, (*g*) uses mouth and gut to scavenge solid food/photo-synthesis (leaves) (§ 17.11, 17.13)

19 **DCEABF** (**C** and **E** actually occur at the *same* time) (§ 17.22)

20 (*i*) **A** skin, internal gills, lungs, **B** skin, external gills, **C** skin, lungs, buccal cavity, **D** skin, internal gills; (*ii*) **BDAC** (§ 17.22)

21 (*i*) **A** female pore (segment 14), **B**, cocoon, **C** ventral (underside), **D** cocoon, **E** seminal grooves, **F** clitellum; (*ii*) **CEFADB** (§ 17.7)

Section IV
Hints for candidates taking biology examinations

Students should not be entered for an examination that is beyond their ability. Success in examinations for which you have been entered (which assumes that you *do* have the ability) lies in good 'examination technique'. Your teacher will usually advise you on the type of examination you will sit by showing you past question papers. But certain principles of technique apply to all methods of examination:

1 Come fully equipped with pen, pencil, rubber, ruler and coloured pens or pencils.

2 Read the exam instructions carefully – do not leave out compulsory questions.

3 Plan your time for answering according to the marks allocated.

4 Do the maximum number of questions. If you are asked to do five questions at 20 marks each and you only do four, you can only score a maximum of 80. The first 50% of marks in each question are usually the easiest to gain; thereafter they become harder. Thus it is more likely that you will gain your best result by doing five questions reasonably well rather than by doing four questions – as you might think – very well. Five answers averaging a mark of 12 out of 20 = 60%. To gain the same 60% on four questions you must average 15 out of 20.

5 Choose the right questions to do. Often you can spot which ones will give you best marks from the mark allocation shown in brackets on the question paper. Add up what you think you would get from the sections you would attempt.

6 Understand what the question asks. Never twist the examiner's words into a meaning he did not intend. Perhaps half of those who fail exams do so because they answer a completely different question from that written on the examination paper. If someone asks you how to mend a bicycle puncture and you reply with an excellent description of how to raise the saddle, you have not answered their question, nor have you given them any help! In an examination, mis-information of this kind earns you no marks. And you fail. Perhaps you knew the correct answer all along. But you failed to show the examiner that you knew. What a reward for all your hours of work. What a waste!

7 Plan essay answers before writing. Organise key words into logical order or pattern (see below).

8 Only use large labelled diagrams in your answers if they *save* words and make your answer clearer.

9 Set out your work neatly. An examiner is human. If your written answers are neatly set out he is much more likely to give you the benefit of the doubt where your answers are not entirely clear.

10 Keep a cool head. You can only do this by getting plenty of sleep and some exercise over the examination period. You will reason better if you do *not* stay up all night revising.

Multiple choice questions
These are sometimes called fixed response or objective questions. At first sight these questions seem to be comparatively easy because answering them is simply a matter of choosing one correct answer from the possible answers given. However, the questions are designed to test how well you know specific topics and students do not always obtain as high a mark as they expected. But providing you know or can work out each answer (see below), the multiple choice questions in an examination should not be troublesome. (You will have had plenty of practice in answering these types of question if you have worked your way through most of the self-test questions in Section III of this book.)

If four choices of answer are offered, usually two are very obviously wrong. You now have a 50% chance of being right even if you don't know the answer. Don't leave the odds at 25% by a blind guess.

Suppose the question asks you to *recall* a name – for example the topmost bone in your vertebral column (backbone). The answer choices are: (*a*) radius, (*b*) humerus, (*c*) atlas, (*d*) axis. If you don't know the answer, but do at least remember that (*a*) and (*b*) are bones in the arm, you are left with a guess between (*c*) and (*d*). You *are* likely to know the answer, however, if you use one of the memory aids suggested in unit 1.4.

Suppose, however, the question requires you to *reason* from facts you should know. If the question is 'Which gas(es) are produced by a green plant's leaves in the dark?' and the answer choices are: (*a*) CO_2, (*b*) N_2, (*c*) CO_2 and O_2, (*d*) O_2, from these (*b*) can be eliminated because nitrogen gas is neither used nor produced by green plants on their own. Leaves readily suggest photosynthesis, a by-product of which is oxygen. But *light* is needed for photosynthesis and the question states that the leaves are in the *dark*. So (*c*) and (*d*) must be wrong because both include oxygen. That leaves (*a*) as the answer. There are also other types of 'choice' questions which are more testing.

Essay questions

Most essay questions today are 'structured' into sections which require paragraph answers. The principles for writing essays or paragraphs are the same. The examiner is looking for a number of facts that you should be remembering as key words – just how many is often suggested by the mark allocation. On rough paper write down the key words and join these by lines into a pattern-diagram where necessary. Number the key words according to the order in which you are going to use the facts in your answer. In this way your facts will be presented logically; and nothing will be left out. If examples make your answer clearer, use them.

Take the following example of a structured question:

'(*a*) Why are enzymes frequently referred to as "biological catalysts"?   (4)
(*b*) What are the effects of changing (*i*) pH upon the rate, (*ii*) temperature   (7)
    of action of any **named** enzyme?'
    (there followed a third section to complete the question.)   (*Oxford*)

The way to go about planning your answers is illustrated below:

Notice that this student used the key words from the question to build up this pattern-diagram

From this pattern-diagram, done in a minute or two, might come a written answer like:

(a) Catalysts are substances which in small amounts can greatly increase the rate of certain chemical reactions. Catalysts remain unchanged at the end of the reaction. Enzymes, unlike catalysts used in chemical works, are proteins. They control the rate of reactions in living things e.g. in respiration and digestion.

(i) Pepsin digests proteins in the stomach where conditions are acid. It will not do so if conditions are alkaline.

(ii) Pepsin works best at body temperature. If it is boiled it is destroyed and stops working. If it is cooled by ice it will also stop working but it is not destroyed.

'State' and 'explain' essays: 'state' or 'list' means put down as simple facts' – nothing else. 'Name' is a similar instruction: no explanations are required.

'Explain' requires not only the facts or principles but also the reasons behind them. When you are thinking out the answer to an 'explain' question, ask yourself 'which?', 'what?', 'where?', 'why?' and 'when?' about the subject. These questions will help you to avoid leaving out information that you know. You *must*, however, only give the information that is asked for – for example 'which?' and 'when?' may be irrelevant (unnecessary) in a particular question. Try these:

'State three features commonly shown by animals at their respiratory surfaces.'

The answer could be: 'Large surface area; wet surface; often associated with a blood system'– to give the bare essentials. No *reasons* are required; and only three lines were allocated for the answer.

'(*a*) *Name two* enzymes which are produced in the mammalian pancreas and which are used in the digestion of food in the alimentary canal.

(i)...

(ii)..

(*b*) Select *one* of these enzymes, *name* the substrate which it digests and the product or products formed.

Name of enzyme...

(i) Substrate...

(ii) Product or products ....,'

(AEB)

When reading through questions you have decided to answer, **underline vital words**.

Note that the examiners have been particularly helpful here by putting in italics vital words that *you* would have underlined. However, as you read through it would be worth underlining 'pancreas', to emphasise where the enzymes come from. The remaining words that you would have underlined are already emphasised for you after the numerals (i) and (ii). The answers may be found in unit 4.15.

'Compare' and 'contrast' essays: 'contrast' means pick out the *differences* between. If you are asked to do this you must use such words as 'Whereas...' and 'however...'. It is not sufficient to give two *separate* accounts of the two organisms or processes to be contrasted.

  'Compare' means pick out *differences* (contrasts) *and similarities*. Thus your answer will include not only 'whereas...' and 'however...' statements but also 'both...'.

In planning such answers it is vital to write down on rough paper, in three columns, the features to be compared or contrasted and, alongside, the comparison you have made mentally.

Feature, or characteristic	Organism, or process A	Organism, or process B
1 ... 2 ... etc	Differences (i.e. *contrasts*)	
1 ... 2 ... etc.	Similarities	

} *Comparison*

You will have seen ample examples of constructions of this sort if you have tried the self-test questions for unit 17. Try these:

'Contrast the actions of nerves and hormones in co-ordination in a mammal.   [10]'
(*O and C*)

The answers may be found in unit 9.9.
Distinguish carefully between the two terms in *each* of the following pairs:
(*a*) respiration: breathing,
(*b*) excretion: secretion,
(*c*) canine tooth: molar tooth,
(*d*) clay soil: sandy soil,
(*e*) stigma: anther.

Answers may be found in unit 6.1; units 7.1 and 9.8, unit 4.14, unit 15.5, and unit 12.7 respectively.
'Compare and contrast the external features of a bird, a fish and an amphibian, showing how each is adapted to its own particular way of life.'

(*SUJB*)

The words to underline here are, apart from 'compare and contrast', 'external' and 'adapted'. The question does *not* concern itself with the fact that all three animals have vertebrae (which are *internal*). for example. It *is* concerned with *why* birds have beaks; and *why* frogs (amphibians) have wide gapes to their mouths. Adaptations (see unit 14.3) are answers to biological problems; and beaks and wide gapes are indeed solutions to these animals' feeding needs. Points of similarity include two eyes and two nostrils. Finally, in any such *general* comparison, recall the mnemonic BERLIN GOD SEES (see units 1.4 and 2.1). The first nine of these letters do remind you, after all, of *functions;* and adaptations are very much concerned with function. With this lead, try constructing your 'compare and contrast' table using the features that B,E,R,L,I,N in BERLIN GOD remind you of.

Graphs, diagrams and experiments

Graphs: If you are asked to put information on a graph, it is vital that on both axes you state the relevant *units*, e.g. 'g' or 'cm³/h' or 'numbers of live insects'. Usually the title of the graph is implied by the question – but sometimes it is important that *you* should provide it. All plots must be precise and ringed. You will avoid wrong plots by using a ruler to lead your eye to the precise spot.

Diagrams:

1 *Draw in pencil* – in case you need to use an eraser.
2 *Draw large* – for clarity and easy labelling, then put down your pencil.
3 *Label* in ink or biro neatly and add a *title*.
4 *Rule your labelling lines* in biro, avoiding crosses. Biro does not smudge against the ruler.

Nor can the straight labelling lines be confused with being part of the detail of the drawing (which is in pencil).

If you follow this drill *in sequence* you will save time. And time is often marks!

Experiments

Experiments must be written up in a logical order under subheadings. The account usually includes a diagram which *saves* words. Do not duplicate the information in a diagram by also giving a *written* account of what it shows. Only write what the diagram does *not* say.

The following is an outline of the structure of such an account:

Aim: 'To discover...' or 'To investigate...'. If you start off with 'Experiment to prove...', it makes a mockery of what scientific investigation is all about. This start indicates to examiners that the 'experiments' you did were actually *demonstrations* of something you knew already – and some examiners may not give you much credit in consequence.

Materials and Method: 'The materials were set up as shown in the diagram' could be the opening sentence. There follows a fully labelled diagram. Only supplementary information is now needed, e.g. 'The plant used in the experiment had first been de-starched by keeping it in the dark for 48 hours' or, 'The length of the root was measured again after 24 hours'.

Note the use of the impersonal 'was measured' which is preferable to the personal 'I measured'. A list of the materials used is unnecessary. Do not forget to emphasise which was the *test* and which the *control* part of the experiment.

Results: a plain statement of what happened in both test *and* control – no discussion. The discussion can be left to a separate subheading, if it is necessary.

Conclusion: the *answer* to the 'aim'. This is a plain statement, not an essay. Thus the aim might have been 'to find out if light is necessary for photosynthesis', and the experiment's conclusion is likely to have been 'Light is necessary for photosynthesis'.

Too often candidates run out of their allocated time by giving rambling accounts which both score poorly and leave insufficient time for the remaining questions (so costing marks *both* ways). Try this:

'Describe, in detail, how it could be shown conclusively that light is necessary for the synthesis of carbohydrates in green plants'
(There followed a more theoretical part to the question)

(SUJB)

Here the 'aim' is supplied. As the question uses the words 'could be shown', the remaining subheadings 'Materials and method' and 'Results' must both be used; the conclusion is implied by the wording. Many other questions of this type simply ask for the method. For the answer, see Section 4.6.

Relevance

Sadly, a large number of reasonably knowledgeable candidates do not do themselves justice by writing irrelevant answers. Sheer length of an answer will not gain any marks. It is the key facts and principles that the examiner is looking for, *whatever* the length of the answer. So do not 'pad out' your answers.

The length of answer required is often suggested either by the marks awarded to it in the mark scheme (often stated alongside the question), or by the space allocated to it on an answer sheet. If your answer is about to be either much shorter or much longer than these two indicators suggest, think again. Re-read the question – and your underlining of the important words in it.

A composite question to end with:
'What is excretion? and why is it necessary in living organisms? Give the origins of the excretory compounds in (*a*) a flowering plant and (*b*) a mammal. Describe how the kidney functions as an excretory organ in a mammal.   **(2,2,6,4,11)**'

Analysis of the question:
Definition: 2 marks (see unit 2.1)

Reason for excretion: 2 marks. Chemical processes in the body (metabolism) are inefficient or produce by-products, e.g. not all the amino acids absorbed by a mammal can be used, so some are excreted as urea (see unit 4.20).

Excretory compounds (and origin) (see unit 7.1)
Mammal: 6 marks – H_2O, CO_2 (respiration); urea (excess protein); bile pigments (worn out red blood cells) would suffice.
Note: waste heat (from respiration) is *not* an excretory *compound*.

Flowering plant: 4 marks – O_2 (photosynthesis); CO_2 and H_2O (respiration) would suffice. Wastes (tannins) in fallen bark or leaves could gain credit.

Kidney function: 11 marks. Blood, containing wastes, enters the kidney in the renal artery and leaves 'purified' in the renal vein.

Draw a labelled diagram of a nephron (see unit 7.2) with explanation of the functions of its parts.

Urine, carrying wastes, drips into the pelvis of the kidney.

Note: a diagram of the whole urinary system is *not* required; nor does the question ask for details of the kidney's osmoregulatory function; nor does it ask about malfunction of the kidney.

Note: the skeleton answers provided above are only for the guidance of candidates. They do not necessarily represent what the Examination Boards themselves would require as adequate answers. The author himself is, however, an experienced examiner.

Section V Practice in answering examination questions

The questions that follow have been selected from GCE, SCE and CSE Biology papers of a range of Examination Boards. The answers which are given to these questions are not the official answers from Examination Board marking schemes, but have been written by the author. They are skeleton answers only. The length of answer required is sometimes suggested by the number of marks allocated in brackets after the question. This is not always the case, however, since not all the Boards supply marking schemes.

GCE AND SCE QUESTIONS (ANSWERS ON PAGE 206)

1 (a) By means of labelled diagrams **only** illustrate the structure of:

    (i) a cell from the mesophyll of a leaf;   (6 marks)
    (ii) a hypha of a named mould;   (5 marks)
    (iii) a **named** protozoon;   (6 marks)
    (iv) a **named** bacterium.   (2 marks)

(b) Give the function of six different structures which you have labelled in any of the cells.   (6 marks)

(Oxford Local Examinations)

2 (a) Give an explanation of the process of photosynthesis.

(b) Describe how the following organisms are dependent on this process:

(i) a mould (ii) a caterpillar (iii) a bird of prey.

(University of Cambridge Local Examinations)

3 (a) Distinguish between *saprophytic* and *parasitic* modes of nutrition.

(b) Give the name of one disease caused by a protozoan. Name the protozoan and indicate how this disease is transmitted.

(c) What methods can be used to control the spread of the disease named in (b)?

(University of Cambridge Local Examinations)

4 (a) List **two** chemical elements other than carbon, hydrogen, oxygen and nitrogen which are required by both green plants and mammals.   (2 marks)

(b) For each of the elements you have chosen give one reason why it is required (i) in green plants, and (ii) in mammals.   (2 marks)

(c) Choose one of the elements from your list and describe how you would carry out a controlled experiment to show that it is essential for the normal development of a green plant.   (6 marks)

(d) In what form and by what processes are mineral elements taken up by the roots of a plant?   (2 marks)

(e) Explain how the nitrogen of plant proteins is changed, after the death of the plant, into a form which other plants can use.   (5 marks)

(Joint Matriculation Board)

5 (a) What conditions are necessary for photosynthesis to occur in green plants?

(b) Describe an experiment to investigate the importance of one of these conditions.

(University of Cambridge Local Examinations)

6 (a) What substances are transported by:

    (i) the blood system of a mammal, and
    (ii) the vascular system of a flowering plant?

(b) **Briefly** explain how:
   (i) the flow of blood is maintained in a mammal, and
   (ii) the flow of water is maintained in a flowering plant.

(University of London)

7 (a) List the substances which a mammal may pass out of its body   (9 marks)
  (b) For each substance give **one** reason why it is released.   (9 marks)
  (c) Name the apertures by which these substances leave the body.
     You may tabulate your answer.   (7 marks)

(Oxford Local Examinations)

8 (a) Make a labelled diagram of a vertical section through the mammalian skin.
   (6 marks)

  (b) For a **named** mammal briefly describe how:
   (i) water is gained and lost   (7 marks)
   (ii) the temperature is raised and lowered   (5 marks)
  (c) How are these changes regulated by the animal?   (7 marks)

(Oxford Local Examinations)

9 The table below shows the effect of auxin concentration on the growth of the root and stem of a plant. A positive figure for growth response indicates stimulation, a negative figure indicates growth has been inhibited.

Auxin (IAA) Concentration parts per million	Growth Response Roots	Stems
1×10^{-5}	+ 15%	
1×10^{-4}	+ 35%	
1×10^{-3}	+ 20%	0%
1×10^{-2}	− 15%	+ 10%
1×10^{-1}	− 50%	+ 75%
1	− 85%	+ 160%
10		+ 150%
100		+ 10%
1000		− 90%

(a) Plot the data, graphically in a suitable manner, with both sets of data on the same graph.
(b) Which organ is the more sensitive to auxin?
(c) Describe, in words, the effect of auxin on the growth of the stem.
(d) Externally applied auxin is absorbed more readily by broad-leaved plants than by narrow-leaved plants. Suggest a use to which this property is put by the farmer and gardener.

(Southern Universities' Joint Board)

10 (a) What are the differences in (i) number (ii) structure and (iii) activity between the male and female gametes of animals?
  (b) What advantages does internal fertilisation possess over external fertilisation?
  (c) What are the advantages of the development of the embryo in the uterus of a mammal compared with the development of the embryo in the egg of a bird?

(University of Cambridge Local Examinations)

11 The diagram below shows a simple farm ecosystem—a cow grazing in a clover field:

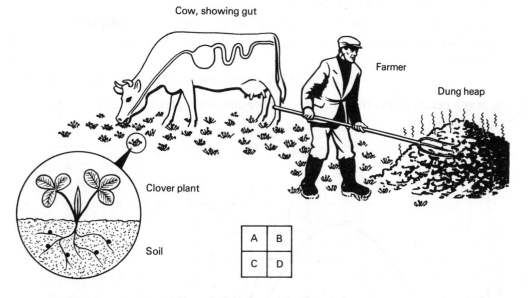

(a) Insert label lines from letters A–D to appropriate parts of the diagram (one from each letter) to show precisely the location of the processes stated below:

A   Proteins become amino acids
B   Proteins become ammonia
C   Organic matter becomes CO_2 and mineral salts
D   Non-symbiotic bacteria make nitrogen into nitrates

(b) Label the 'producer' organism in the ecosystem 'P'.

(c) State one way in which organic nitrogen compounds are lost in large quantities from this ecosystem.

(d) Indicate by an arrow and the label 'N' where, on one of the organisms shown, nitrogen is gained for the ecosystem.

(e) What process, common to **all** the organisms shown, causes a loss of organic carbon from the ecosystem?

(Oxford and Cambridge Schools Examination Board)

12 Four cylinders of potato were carefully dried on blotting paper and weighed. Each piece weighed 3 g. One was placed in each tube as shown in the drawing below.

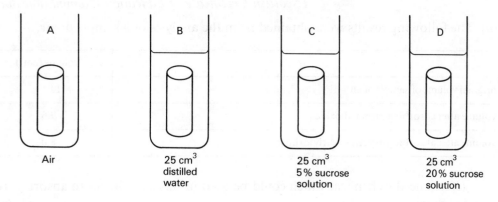

(a) After 48 hours, which potato cylinder would be the heaviest?   (1 mark)

(b) The movement of which substance was mainly responsible for the weight changes in the potato cylinders?   (1 mark)

(c) Name the process which was responsible for this movement in tubes B, C, and D.
                    (1 mark)

(*d*) A fifth potato cylinder, also weighing 3 g, was cut in half and both pieces were then treated in the same way as tube A.

After the same 48 hour period, how would the combined weight of the two halves compare with the weight of the single cylinder in tube A? Give a reason for your answer.   (2 marks)

(Scottish Certificate of Education Examination Board)

13 The graph below shows the rates of transpiration and water uptake by a sunflower on a bright summer day.

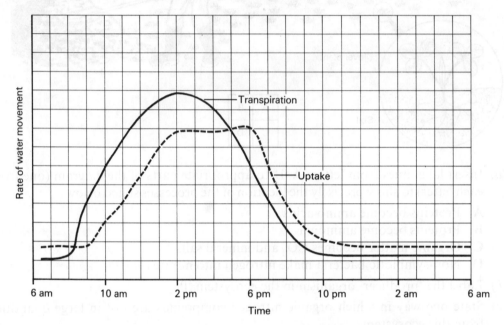

(*a*) Use the graph to find the time at which each of the following occurs:

  (*i*) the optimum rate of transpiration;   (1 mark)
  (*ii*) the rate of water uptake equals the rate of transpiration.   (1 mark)

(*b*) From the graph, explain why the water content of the plant increases during the time interval from 10 pm to 6 am.   (1 mark)

(*c*) When the lower surface of the leaves was coated with vaseline transpiration was greatly reduced. Coating the upper surface had very little effect.

Explain the difference.   (1 mark)

(Scottish Certificate of Education Examination Board)

14 (*a*) The following results were obtained from the analysis of a sample of air.

	volume (cm³)
original volume of sample of air	10
volume after absorbing carbon dioxide	9.6
volume after absorbing oxygen + carbon dioxide	8.0

  (*i*) Name the chemical which could be used in this experiment to absorb carbon dioxide.   (1 mark)
  (*ii*) Calculate the percentage of carbon dioxide and of oxygen in this sample of air.   (2 marks)

Space for calculation

(*iii*) Is this sample inhaled or exhaled air? Give a reason for your answer   (1 mark)

(*iv*) Explain why great care must be taken to avoid any change in **temperature** during the analysis of a sample of air.   (1 mark)

(*b*) (*i*) What type of respiration in human muscles leads to an accumulation of lactic acid?   (1 mark)

(*ii*) Why do cockroaches not require a respiratory pigment?   (1 mark)

(*c*) Name the specialised structures associated with gaseous exchange in:

(*i*) a green leaf;   (1 mark)

(*ii*) a recently hatched tadpole.   (1 mark)

(Scottish Certificate of Education Examination Board)

15 Underline the correct answer.

Which one of the following pathways best describe the route taken by air as it passes from the nasal cavity to the alveoli in the lungs?

trachea—larynx—bronchus—bronchiole

bronchus—larynx—trachea—bronchiole

larynx—trachea—bronchus—bronchiole

larynx—bronchiole—bronchus—trachea   (1 mark)

(Scottish Certificate of Education Examination Board)

16 In the study of gas exchange in a biological system, privet leaves and woodlice (slaters) were placed in test-tubes as shown below.

(Bicarbonate indicator becomes yellow when carbon dioxide levels are high and red when carbon dioxide levels are low.)

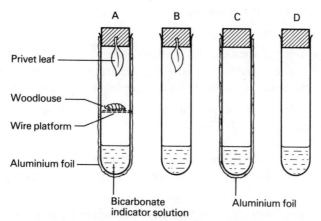

The test-tubes were left in light and the results obtained noted below:

	A	B	C	D
bicarbonate indicator	turned yellow quickly	turned deep red	no change	no change

(*a*) Give an explanation of the results in test-tubes A and B.   (2 marks)

(*b*) What is the purpose of including test-tubes C and D?   (1 mark)

(*c*) State **two** ways in which photosynthesis is important to animals.   (2 marks)

(Scottish Certificate of Education Examination Board)

17 (*a*) In an experiment, 50 cm³ of water was added to a measuring cylinder containing 50 cm³ of garden soil. The total volume of soil plus water was 80 cm³.

Why was the combined volume of soil and water not 100 cm³?   (1 mark)

(b) The table below shows comparisons between sandy and clay soils.

Sandy soil	Clay soil
1. Drains well but holds little water.	1. Drains badly but holds a lot of water.
2. Warms up rapidly and cools down quickly.	2. Warms up slowly and retains heat well.
3. Raises water well.	3. Does not raise water well.
4. Loses mineral salts by leaching.	4. Holds mineral salts well.

Which of the above comparisons is not correct? Give the number. (1 mark)

(c) Both sandy and clay soils are improved by the addition of lime (calcium hydroxide). State **two** ways in which lime improves a soil. (2 marks)

(Scottish Certificate of Education Examination Board)

Answers to GCE and SCE questions

The answers to the GCE and SCE questions given below are of about the right length. At the end of each answer there may be a 'Comments' paragraph. This includes possible alternative answers. If you do not fully understand the answers given here, refer back to the units on which the questions are based.

1 (a) (i) The shape of either a palisade or spongy mesophyll cell, Fig. 4.5, with the labelling from Fig. 2.2.

(ii) Fig. 17.5; don't omit the *name*.

(iii) Fig. 17.4; don't omit the *name*.

(iv) One of the four shapes on the bottom line of Fig. 17.2. The mark-scheme indicates that the detailed diagram of a generalised bacterium is unnecessary; don't omit the *name*. Label cell wall, cytoplasm, nuclear material.

(b) Select e.g. cell wall, chloroplast, nucleus, vacuole, contractile vacuole, pseudo-podium and consult units 2.2, 17.4

2 (a) Sunlight energy, trapped by chloroplasts, is used to combine water and carbon dioxide into glucose which contains the energy in its bonds. Oxygen is given off as a by-product. (Unit 4.6)

(b) (i) Moulds obtain from dead organisms (by saprophytic means—see unit 4.2) both materials for growth and energy (by respiring some of their food).

(ii) Caterpillars eat leaves, obtaining materials and energy thereby. (Unit 15.2)

(iii) Birds of prey eat prey to get their materials and energy. These have come from green plants fed on by the prey i.e. along a food chain. (Unit 15.2)

None of (i)—(iii) can trap sunlight energy or synthesise their own organic molecules in the way that green plants can.

COMMENTS: The answers are given in skeleton form and should be expanded.

3 (a) *Saprophytes* use dead organisms for food, digesting them with enzymes externally and absorbing the soluble products.

Parasites obtain food, often as juices, out of the bodies of much larger organisms (hosts) which are harmed but not killed. (Units 4.2 and 4.11)

(b) Malaria caused by *Plasmodium*. A mosquito injects the protozoan into a man in its saliva when it inserts its proboscis to suck blood. Mosquitoes become infected by sucking up blood from malaria patients. (Unit 17.4) (*c*) (*i*) Destroy the aquatic larval stage by 1. spraying *oils* on the water to suffocate them or 2. *insecticides* to poison them; 3. introducing *guppy fish* to eat them; 4. draining swamps to remove their habitat.

   (*ii*) Spray walls with persistent insecticides e.g. DDT to kill adults which land on them.

   (*iii*) Use *mosquito netting* around beds 1. to prevent infected mosquitoes infecting man 2. prevent malarial humans infecting new mosquitoes.

   (*iv*) Take *preventative medicines* e.g. chloroquin, daily, to kill any parasites injected into the blood. (Units 16.4, 16.10 and 17.4)

COMMENTS: The answers given are in skeleton form and should be expanded.

4 (*a*) Phosphorus, Calcium (Unit 4.3)

  (*b*) (*i*) P for making ATP; Ca for making the middle lamellae
     (*ii*) P for making ATP; Ca for bones and teeth (Unit 4.3)

  (*c*) *Method:* Place ten seedlings of cress on cotton wool wetted with distilled water. Repeat for a second batch of 10. Place one batch in the neck of a boiling tube filled with a complete nutrient solution and the other in a similar tube whose solution, however, lacks Calcium. Fit a bubbler to each tube to supply oxygen for roots when they grow down into the solution. Compare the growth of the two batches of cress after a week, keeping the tubes covered by a bell jar to avoid the addition of minerals to the cotton wool by dust. (Unit 4.10)

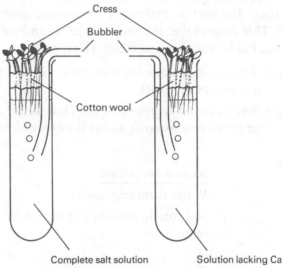

  (*d*) As ions, which enter partly by diffusion but mainly by active transport (which requires energy from respiration of the root cells). (Unit 5.2)

  (*e*) The proteins are turned into ammonia by decay (putrefaction) bacteria. Nitrifying bacteria turn ammonia into nitrates. Plants can absorb nitrate ions easily. (Unit 15.6)

5 (*a*) *Sunlight* shining on cells with *chloroplasts* which are supplied with *water* and *carbon dioxide*. (Unit 4.6)

  (*b*) *Aim:* to investigate the need for chloroplasts

     Method: Put a variegated plant in the dark for 48 hours to destarch its leaves.

     Test a leaf for starch with Iodine. This is done by boiling the leaf in water to kill it, then boiling in ethanol to decolourise it and finally dipping it in hot water before adding iodine to it in a petri dish. The whole leaf would go brown with iodine if it was destarched.

     The plant is now put in strong sunlight for four hours. Another leaf is detached and an outline of it and of the white area within it are drawn. The leaf is now tested with iodine, as above.

Result: The leaf goes blue black (signifying presence of starch) where it was green before and brown where it was white before.

Conclusion: The leaf can only make starch where chloroplasts are present— chlorophyll is necessary for photosynthesis. (Unit 4.6)

COMMENTS: Try to construct your own account along these lines for *sunlight* and *carbon dioxide* using Fig. 4.2 as guide.

6 (*a*) (*i*) Water, blood proteins, food (glucose, fats, amino acids, salts, vitamins), CO_2 (as bicarbonate ions), urea, hormones, O_2 (mainly in red blood corpuscles), haemoglobin (in corpuscles). (Unit 5.7)

(*ii*) In xylem: water, mineral salts e.g. nitrates. In phloem: water, sucrose, amino acids. (Unit 5.5)

(*b*) (*i*) Blood from the body passes into the right atrium (auricle) of the heart where it is pumped into the right ventricle. This pumps the blood to the lungs whence it returns to the left auricle, is pumped into the left ventricle and is then pumped into the dorsal aorta. Having gone via various arteries under pressure, the blood passes through capillaries into veins. Now under low pressure, the blood returns to the heart assisted by the non-return valves of the veins. (Unit 5.9)

(*ii*) Water evaporating from the leaf by transpiration causes leaf cells to osmose water from the xylem vessels. This causes a suction force that extends down into the root. The suction maintains an osmotic gradient across the cortex of the root. This ensures that the root hair cells can continue to osmose water out of the soil (so long as it is available). (Unit 5.3)

COMMENTS: (*a*) The question asks for *substances*; not, for example, the types of cell, nor energy (as heat).

(*b*) The question stresses *briefly*. Thus detail about how the heart pumps or about *how* osmosis works is not required.

7 Substances	Reason for release	Apertures
CO_2	Waste from respiration	
N_2	Not totally absorbed at alveoli in lungs	nostrils
O_2		
water	Osmoregulation	
urea	Waste from protein metabolism	end of urethra
salts	Excess from diet	
bile pigments	Waste from worn-out red blood cells	
cellulose	Indigestible cell walls	anus
oil	To waterproof skin	sebaceous gland
water	To lose heat by evaporation	sweat gland
water	To wash cornea	tear gland

(Units 6.6, 7.5, 4.12, 4.20, 7.7)

COMMENTS: Any *nine* substances would probably have been sufficient but a triple mention of water (thus excluding two of the other substances) may have been permissible to gain full marks.

8 (*a*) A diagram of the lower half of Fig. 7.5 (without the functions listed) would suffice.

(*b*) (*i*) Don't forget the *name*. Consult Fig. 5.7 showing a mouse, for answers.

(*ii*) Raised by: muscular exercise, shivering, liver metabolism. Lowered by: extra radiation using skin capillaries, evaporation of water in sweat. Consult units 7.4, 7.5. Conduction, convection are less important.

(*c*) Voluntary behaviour; e.g. swallowing water; involuntary (automatic) reactions: e.g. use of hair raising, sweat secretion, caused by nerve messages from the brain (hypothalamus); hormone secretion: thyroxin raising metabolic rate. Consult unit 7.5

COMMENTS: In (*a*) each label is probably worth about half a mark. Diagrams *without* any labels are simply designs: they have little significance. In (*b*) and (*c*) the marks correspond to the points being made (here only in skeleton form and not in full sentences, as they should be).

9 (*a*) See COMMENTS below

(*b*) Roots—they respond at a concentration that is extremely dilute. (Unit 9.12)

(*c*) At 1×10^{-3} p.p.m., auxin causes no more growth than is found in control plant stems. With solutions that are stronger there is progressively greater growth in length up till a strength of 1 p.p.m. auxin. Solutions stronger than this progressively decrease growth until at 1000 p.p.m. the auxin causes the stems to grow 90% less than untreated control stems i.e. it inhibits growth. (Units 9.12 and 11.1)

(*d*) The auxin may be used as a weed-killer causing broad-leaved plants to die of abnormal growth. This might be useful in a lawn or in a field of wheat where daises and poppies respectively, grow unwanted. (Unit 9.12)

COMMENTS:

(*a*) Note that you must have *both* sets of data plotted on the same graph paper, so use two colours. Include *units* (I.A.A.p.p.m., and % growth response) on the two axes. (Units 9.12 and 11.1)

(*c*) the question asks about the stem *alone*— do not waste time on the root.

10 (*a*) (*i*) ♂ (male): large numbers, ♀ (female): fewer
(*ii*) ♂ : minute, head and lashing tail ♀ : larger with much more cytoplasm (NB Draw diagrams).
(*iii*) ♂ motile ♀ : immotile (Unit 12.14)

(*b*) Fertilisation more certain; fewer gametes necessary; zygotes better protected; allows reproduction on land. (Unit 12.17)

(*c*) Better *protected, nourished* and supplied with *oxygen*; *wastes* more efficiently removed and *temperature* held constant. In the bird, the shell may crack or the temperature changes may kill; the CO_2 and O_2 move out and in by diffusion, inefficiently, and waste nitrogen is stored within the shell rather than being removed. (Units 12.15 and 12.33)

COMMENTS: This is a skeleton answer which should be put into proper sentences. Note that this is a 'contrast' type of question and the word 'whereas' should be used. (see Section IV, page 197).

11 (*a*), (*b*) and (*d*)

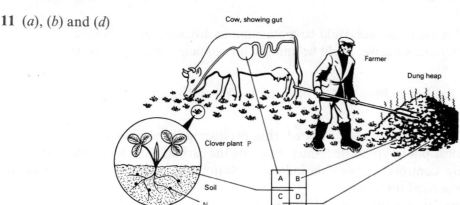

(c) Selling farm produce e.g. beef (or milk, or manure). (Unit 15.14).

(e) Respiration. (Unit 15.7)

COMMENTS: There are some alternative answers to the ones chosen.

Explanation of the answers chosen:

(a) A refers to digestion, B and C to decay; D to nitrogen fixation. Note the *non-symbiotic*

(b) A producer is a green plant, not the farmer.

(c) Note the word 'organic', referring to complex carbon-containing molecules. Loss of ammonia gas (NH_3) is therefore not correct as an answer here.

(d) Nitrogen-fixing bacteria in root nodules are indicated.

12 (a) B.
   (b) Water.
   (c) Osmosis.
   (d) The combined weight of the two halves would be less. The surface area for evaporation of water is greater, so water loss would be quicker. (Units 5.2 and 6.3)

COMMENTS: (a) B, because potato cells would take up water fastest and most easily from the weakest of the solutions.

13 (a) (i) 2 pm.
       (ii) 8.15 am or 5 pm.
   (b) More water is being taken up than is being lost, probably because stomata are closed during the night.
   (c) There are more stomata on the lower surface than the upper. Vaseline blocks them, so reducing transpiration. (Unit 5.4)

COMMENTS: Optimum means best.

14 (a) (i) Sodium hydroxide.
       (ii) The percentage of carbon dioxide is 4.0.
            The percentage of oxygen is 16.0.
            calculation $10 - 9.6 = 0.4$ in $10\,cm^3$ $\therefore$ 4 in $100\,cm^3$
            $9.6 - 8.0 = 1.6$ in $10\,cm^3$ $\therefore$ 16 in $100\,cm^3$
       (iii) Exhaled – inhaled air contains about 0.03% carbon dioxide.
       (iv) A gas expands when it is heated so the volumes would not be comparable.
   (b) (i) Anaerobic.
       (ii) Air goes direct to cells via the tracheal system—blood is not needed for this.
   (c) (i) Mesophyll cells.
       (ii) External gills. (Unit 6.6, Table 6.2; Units 6.3 and 6.4)

COMMENTS:

(a) (i) Alternative answer could be 'potassium hydroxide'; or 'soda lime'.
   (iii) Alternative answer could be 'inhaled air contains about 21% oxygen'.

15 Larynx – trachea – bronchus – bronchiole. (Fig. 6.14).

16 (a) A the woodlouse and leaf respired, thus producing carbon dioxide.
       B the leaf photosynthesised, thus removing the carbon dioxide from the tube.
   (b) They are 'controls'—to see if the indicator solution would change colour in any case.
   (c) Produces food for them.
       Produces oxygen for them. (Unit 6.2, Fig. 6.3)

17 (*a*) The water occupied the air spaces.
  (*b*) 3.
  (*c*) (*i*) Neutralises acidity.
     (*ii*) Flocculates clay particles. (Unit 15.5)

CSE QUESTIONS (ANSWERS ON PAGE 217)

1 The table below gives the energy content in Kcal/100 g of some common foods together with the percentages of fat, carbohydrate, protein and water in each.

Food	Kcal/100 g	%A	%B	%C	%D
Butter	745	0.7	16.8	–	82.5
Milk	68	3.3	88.3	4.4	3.6
Herring	168	16.0	72.0	–	12.0
Beef	318	23.5	55.0	–	20.5
Potatoes	88	1.9	81.0	15.1	–

(*a*) Which food has (*i*) the highest energy value and (*ii*) the lowest energy value?

(*b*) Study the figures in the columns and write in the space below, which of the following —proteins, carbohydrates, fats, water—corresponds with A, B, C and D.

(*c*) Give **two** kinds of food material which are essential for healthy life, but which are not shown in the table.

(*d*) How would you test a sample of milk for the presence of sugars and what result would you expect to see?

(*e*) Name **two** substances needed to ensure healthy growth of bones and teeth.

(Welsh Joint Education Committee)

2 The diagram below shows the blood supply through the liver.

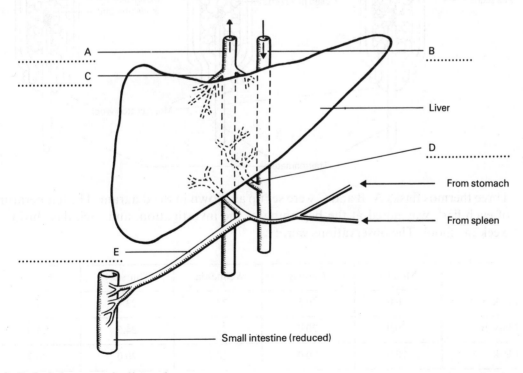

(*a*) Label the parts indicated.

(*b*) Which **two** substances would be present in greater concentration in vessel E after a meal?

(c) After a period of vigorous activity, there would be an increase in the concentration of a substance in vessel C. Name this substance.

(d) State **two** functions of the liver.

(e) Name a structure, other than blood vessels, associated with the liver and state its function.

(f) State **two** differences between the structure of blood vessels A and B

	Blood vessel A	Blood vessel B
Difference 1		
Difference 2		

(g) Many women have an iron deficiency.

  (i) What effect does this have on the amount of haemoglobin?

  (ii) How could they attempt to increase their body iron content other than by the use of iron pills?

  (iii) Why do women suffer from this deficiency to a greater degree than men?

  (iv) What effect would this deficiency have on a woman's athletic performance?

(Yorkshire Regional Examinations Board)

3

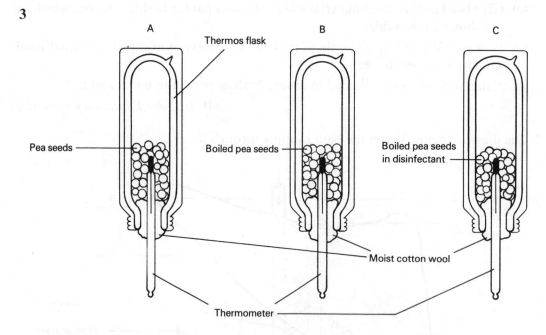

Three thermos flasks A, B and C were set up as shown in the diagram. The temperature of each flask was noted at the beginning of the investigation, and each day during a week in school. The observations were:

	Monday	Tuesday	Wednesday	Thursday	Friday
Flask A,°C	20.0	20.5	23.5	23.7	24.2
Flask B,°C	20.0	20.0	24.3	24.5	25.0
Flask C,°C	20.0	20.0	20.1	20.0	20.2

(a) What is the source of heat produced by the germinating peas?

(b) Why did the temperature in flask B rise towards the end of the week?

(*c*) Why is it important to use thermos flasks in this investigation and not ordinary glass bottles?

(*d*) What is the purpose of disinfectant in flask C?

(*e*) Why does the temperature in flask C change slightly during the week?

(*Welsh Joint Education Committee*)

4 The table below gives the names of certain structures which connect one organ of the human body with another. Complete the right hand column of the table to show **two** organs which are connected by each structure. One example of how to do this is given.

Structures	Organs connected by this structure
Bronchus	Trachea with lung
Bile duct	
Ureter	
Optic nerve	
Eustachian tube	

(*East Anglian Examinations Board*)

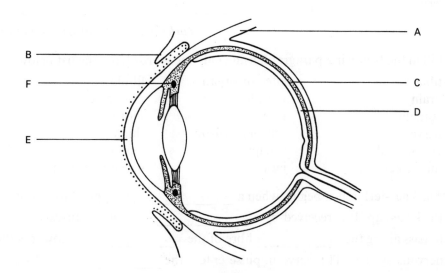

5 (*a*) Study the above diagram of a section of the human eye and then complete the table below which contains a list of functions of five of the parts shown in the diagram. For each function, fill in the letter and name of the correct part.

Function	Letter	Name
Prevents the reflection of light rays		
Sensitive to light		
Helps to bend rays of light		
Causes change of shape in the lens		
Moves the eyeball up and down		

(*b*) Describe clearly how you would show that you have a blind spot in your right eye by using a card with a cross and a spot marked on it.

(*c*) (*i*) Name **one** disadvantage of being blinded in one eye.
(*ii*) State **three** natural ways in which the eyes are protected.

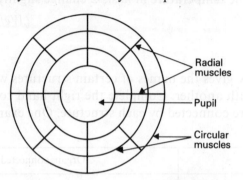

(*d*) The diagram above shows a front view of the iris and pupil of the eye. Complete the table below to show what happens to the structures named when the eye is in:
(*i*) bright light
(*ii*) darkness

Structure	Bright light	Darkness
circular muscles		
radial muscles		
size of pupil		

(Yorkshire Regional Examinations Board)

6 (*a*) Fill in the following paragraph using **only** the words from the list below:

tibia	effector organ	fibula
brain	receptor	motor nerve fibre
stimulus	nerve impulse	motor nerve ending
nerve	sensory neuron	thigh muscle
spinal cord	synapse	femur
motor neuron	jerk	nervous system

The knee-jerk reflex begins when a _____ is applied to a spot just below the knee-cap. It is received by a _____, and it causes a _____ to pass along the _____ fibre of the _____ towards the central nervous system. The nerve impulse enters the _____ and passes to the end of the sensory neuron. This does not connect with the _____ because there is a gap between them called a _____. The nerve impulse passes along the _____, passes out of the spinal cord, and towards the _____. The motor neuron ends in the thigh muscle as a _____, and the nerve impulse causes the _____ to contract. This causes the knee to _____.

(*b*) What is a reflex action?

(*c*) Which **four** structures are essential parts of this reflex?

(*d*) (*i*) What causes a reflex action to occur?
(*ii*) Give one **other** example of a reflex action.

(*e*) The result of the reflex action occurs in the effector. Name **two** different types of effectors.

(*f*) The knee-jerk occurs without the participation of the brain. How does the brain become informed of the knee-jerk reflex?

(*Associated Lancashire Schools Examining Board*)

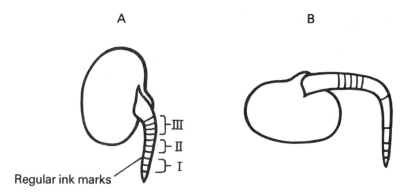

7 A young bean root was marked as shown in diagram A, then replanted horizontally and left in a plant pot for two days. It was then removed and observed to be in the condition shown in diagram B.

(*a*) What has happened after two days to the lines
    (*i*) in the region I and III?
    (*ii*) in the region II?

(*b*) What does this tell you about
    (*i*) the region of growth in the root?
    (*ii*) the influence of gravity on the root?

(*c*) What is this response called?

(*North West Regional Examinations Board*)

8 MOVEMENT AND GROWTH

(*a*) Label the **three** parts of the joint indicated.

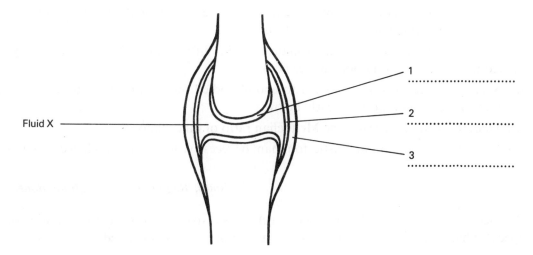

(*b*) What is fluid X and what is its function?

(*c*) Name **two** types of movable joint and say where each can be found in a mammal.

(*d*) Name the tissue which connects muscles to bones.

(*e*) Why are skeletal muscles always in opposing sets?

(*f*) Butterflies show distinct changes during their life cycle. Fill in the boxes to show the remaining three stages in the diagram of their life cycle.

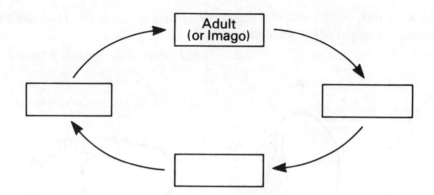

(g) (i) Name any vertebrate which shows distinct stages in its life cycle.
     (ii) What is the name given to the type of life cycle shown by the animal you have named and by butterflies?

(h) (i) When growing trees for sale nurseries price them according to their height. Give **one** reason why height is not always a suitable measurement for deciding the price of common plants.
     (ii) Dry weight is sometimes used to measure the growth of a plant crop. If you were given a large tray of freshly planted cress seeds, how would you measure their increase in dry weight over a two week period?

(Metropolitan Regional Examinations Board)

9 (a) State **two** advantages to a plant of wide dispersal of its seeds.

(b) (i) Name **one** wind-dispersed fruit. Make a labelled diagram of the fruit and explain how it is adapted to wind dispersal.
     (ii) Name **two** fruits having different methods of animal dispersal and explain how each is adapted to dispersal by animals.
     (iii) Make a labelled diagram of **one** of the fruits named in your answer to part (ii).

(c) State **two** dietary values obtained by man from fresh fruit.

(East Anglian Examinations Board)

10 Pure ebony-bodied male Drosophila (fruit flies) were crossed with grey-bodied virgin females. All offspring had grey bodies (F1).

This F1 generation was allowed to mate and the offspring consisted of 1310 grey-bodied flies and 430 ebony-bodied flies (F2).

(a) What is the ratio of grey-bodied to ebony-bodied flies in this generation? Show your working and answer clearly below.

(b) Does this ratio agree with the Mendelian ratio of inheritance?

(c) Is the ebony-body characteristic dominant or recessive to the grey-bodied characteristic?

(South Regional Examinations Board)

11 In mice the gene for black hair colour (a) is recessive to the gene for 'Agouti' or speckled hair colour (A) in which hair colour is not evenly distributed.

(a) Give the genotype of:
     (i) a pure breeding Agouti mouse;
     (ii) a hybrid Agouti mouse.

(b) (i) Give the genotype of a black mouse.
     (ii) Could a black mouse be produced by mating Agouti types?

(c) Write out the gene diagram for a cross between a black mouse (male) and a hybrid Agouti mouse (female).

(South Regional Examinations Board)

Answers to CSE questions

The answers to the CSE questions given below are about the right length for the examination. At the end of each answer there may be a 'Comments' paragraph. This includes possible alternative answers. If you do not fully understand the answers given here, refer back to the units on which the questions are based.

1 (*a*) (*i*) Butter. (*ii*) Milk.

   (*b*) A Protein, B Water, C Carbohydrate, D Fat.

   (*c*) (*i*) Vitamins. (*ii*) Salts.

   (*d*) Add Benedict's solution to an equal quantity of milk in a test tube and boil. It would go orange-yellow. (Fehlings test or Clinistix test are alternatives.)

   (*e*) (*i*) Calcium. (*ii*) Vitamin D. (Units 4.4 and 4.5)

COMMENTS: (*b*) Remember that water is the major constituent of any fresh food made of cells (which butter is not). The figures for milk confirm the 'water' column anyway. Butter gives the 'fat' column away. Potatoes are the give-away for 'carbohydrate'. (*c*) Alternative answer: roughage. (*d*) You must take care with questions on food to note whether 'what food' or 'what substance' or 'what kind of substance' is being asked for. [For example butter is a food; it contains vitamins (kind of substance) which happen to be vitamins A and D (substances)].

2 (*a*) A Vena Cava
       B Aorta
       C Hepatic vein
       D Hepatic artery
       E Hepatic portal vein. (Unit 4.20)

   (*b*) 1. Monosaccharides e.g. glucose.
       2. Amino acids. (Unit 4.20)

   (*c*) Glucose.

   (*d*) 1. Stores glycogen.
       2. Produces bile. (Unit 4.20)

   (*e*) Name of structure: Gall bladder.
       Function: Stores bile. (Unit 4.15)

   (*f*)

	Blood vessel A	Blood vessel B
Difference 1	Thin walled non-muscular	Thick walled muscular
Difference 2	Has non-return valves	Has no valves

(Unit 5.9)

   (*g*) (*i*) Reduced amount.
       (*ii*) Eating iron-rich foods, e.g. eggs.
       (*iii*) In pregnancy mothers provide iron for baby's blood and do not take in enough to replace it in their diet.
       (*iv*) Reduce it, because less oxygen can be carried owing to reduced haemoglobin circulating. (Unit 4.3)

3 (*a*) Respiration.

   (*b*) Bacteria had started to rot the peas and were respiring.

   (*c*) The amount of heat, generated by germinating peas, is small and it needs to be kept in by a thermos if it is to be demonstrated.

(d) It kills any bacteria that might enter the flask, so preventing their respiration.

(e) No thermos is perfectly insulating. Changing temperatures outside will affect the temperature inside slightly—particularly as a proper thermos stopper is not being used here. (Unit 6.2, Fig. 6.5)

4

Structures	Organs connected by this structure
Bronchus	Trachea with lung
Bile duct	Gall bladder with duodenum
Ureter	Kidney with bladder
Optic nerve	Eye with brain
Eustachian tube	Middle ear with upper throat

(Units 7.2, 4.15, 8.1 and 8.5)

5 (a)

Function	Letter	Name
Prevents the reflection of light rays	C	Choroid
Sensitive to light	D	Retina
Helps to bend rays of light	E	Cornea
Causes change of shape in the lens	F	Ciliary muscle
Moves the eyeball up and down	A	Eyeball muscle

(b) Cover over your left eye. Put the card 50 cm away from the head with the cross on the left and dot on the right. Look at the cross with the right eye while moving the card gradually towards the head. At one point the dot will disappear from view.

(c) (i) You lose your appreciation of distance
   (ii) 1. by the bony orbit of the skull
        2. by the eyelids—blinking reflex
        3. by the tears—washing away dust.

(d)

Structure	Bright light	Darkness
circular muscles	contract	relax
radial muscles	relax	contract
size of pupil	small	large

(Unit 8.3)

COMMENTS: (c) (i) Do not give examiners silly answers. 'You don't look so nice,' for example, is unlikely to gain a mark. Alternative answer: You collide with things more easily through having only half your field of vision. (d) In bright light the pupil becomes smaller, in the dark it becomes bigger.

6 (a) stimulus, receptor, nerve impulse, nerve, sensory neuron, spinal cord, motor neuron, synapse, motor nerve fibre, effector organ, motor nerve ending, thigh muscle, jerk.

(b) A rapid automatic unlearned response to a stimulus using a reflex arc.

(*c*)   (*i*)   Receptor.

     (*ii*)   Sensory neuron.

    (*iii*)   Motor neuron.

    (*iv*)   Effector.

(*d*)   (*i*)   A harmful stimulus.

     (*ii*)   Blinking reflex.

(*e*)   (*i*)   Muscles.

     (*ii*)   Glands.

(*f*)   Via a sensory relay neuron whose fibre ends in the brain. (Units 9.5 and 9.2)

7 (*a*)   (*i*)   Little or no change in distance between them.

       (*ii*)   Have become wider apart and root has curved downward.

   (*b*)   (*i*)   It is just behind the tip.

        (*ii*)   Causes root to grow downwards.

   (*c*)   Positive geotropism. (Unit 9.12)

8 (*a*)   1.   Cartilage

       2.   Synovial membrane

       3.   Synovial capsule.

   (*b*)   Synovial fluid for lubricating the joint.

   (*c*)

	Type	*Found in*
1.	Ball and socket	hip
2.	Hinge	elbow

   (*d*)   Tendon.

   (*e*)   Because muscles can only contract, not push. Once a muscle has contracted it can only be extended again when its antagonist contracts. (Units 10.8 and 10.4)

   (*f*)

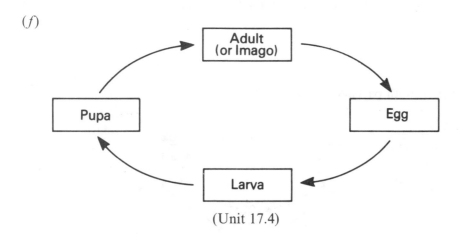

(Unit 17.4)

   (*g*)   (*i*)   Frog

       (*ii*)   Metamorphic. (Unit 17.22)

   (*h*)   (*i*)   A tall one may not be a strong plant. e.g. it may have been forced.

       (*ii*)   Take one half of the cress seeds, dry these in an oven at 110°C and weigh them. At the end of two weeks remove the cress seedlings carefully without damaging them as far as possible, dry in the oven at 110°C and weigh. Subtract weight 1 from weight 2. (Unit 11.17)

9 (*a*) 1. Avoids crowding—competition for light, mineral salts, water.
2. Promotes colonisation of new areas.

(*b*) (*i*) Dandelion. It is adapted by having a large surface area to catch the wind—pappus of hairs. NB. Add labelled diagram.

(*ii*) Cherry—swallowed whole by a bird. It flies away and the stone containing the seed is deposited in faeces. Cleavers—hooks catch on mammal fur and it gets brushed off later on

(*iii*) See COMMENTS below.

(*c*) Sugars, vitamin C. (Unit 12.13)

COMMENTS: This question does *not* ask for a section of the fruit—so Fig. 12.9, right-hand side, would *not* be required if a cherry were chosen. An external view is all that is required. For cleavers see Fig. 12.10.

10 (*a*) Let E represent 'grey' and e represent 'ebony':

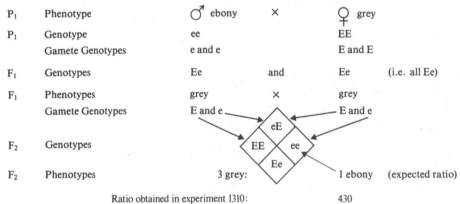

		$\male$ ebony	×	$\female$ grey
P_1	Phenotype			
P_1	Genotype	ee		EE
	Gamete Genotypes	e and e		E and E
F_1	Genotypes	Ee	and	Ee (i.e. all Ee)
F_1	Phenotypes	grey	×	grey
	Gamete Genotypes	E and e		E and e
F_2	Genotypes			
F_2	Phenotypes	3 grey:		1 ebony (expected ratio)

Ratio obtained in experiment 1310:   430

(*b*) Not exactly (3 × 430 = 1290); but it is close enough to 3:1

(*c*) Recessive. (Units 13.5 and 13.7)

COMMENTS: The fact that all offspring had grey bodies (F_1) shows that 'grey' is dominant to 'ebony'. If ebony had been dominant, the F_1 would all have been ebony and not grey.

11 (*a*) (*i*) AA
(*ii*) Aa
(*b*) (*i*) aa
(*ii*) Yes (if both parents are Aa)
(*c*)

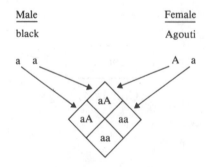

Male	Female
black	Agouti

(Units 13.5 and 13.7)

Index

Page numbers in bold type indicate the main references for those entries.